IMAGINING LANGUAGE IN AMERICA

IMAGINING LANGUAGE
IN AMERICA

FROM THE REVOLUTION
TO THE CIVIL WAR

Michael P. Kramer

PRINCETON UNIVERSITY PRESS   PRINCETON, NEW JERSEY

Library of Congress Cataloging-in-Publication Data
Kramer, Michael P., 1952–
Imagining language in America : from the Revolution to the
Civil War / Michael P. Kramer.
p.   cm.
Includes bibliographical references and index.
ISBN 0-691-06882-8
1. English language—Study and teaching—United States—
History—19th century.   2. American literature—19th century—
History and criticism.   3. English language—United States—
Historiography.   4. Language and languages in literature.
5. Linguistics—United States—History   6. Language and
languages—Philosophy.   7. Americanisms   I. Title.
PE2807.K73   1991
420′.7′073—dc20   91-16548

This book has been composed in Adobe Galliard

Princeton University Press books are printed
on acid-free paper, and meet the guidelines
for permanence and durability of the Committee
on Production Guidelines for Book Longevity
of the Council on Library Resources

Printed in the United States of America

1   3   5   7   9   10   8   6   4   2

To Jane

Contents

Preface   ix

Acknowledgments   xv

List of Abbreviations of Frequently Cited Works   xvii

Introduction: The Study of Language and the American
Renaissance   3

PART ONE: TEACHING LANGUAGE IN AMERICA   33

Chapter One
"*NOW* is the Time, and *This* is the Country": How Noah Webster
Invented American English   35

Chapter Two
"A Fine Ambiguity": Longfellow, Language, and Literary History   64

Chapter Three
"A Tongue According": Whitman and the Literature of
Language Study   90

PART TWO: THE PHILOSOPHY OF LANGUAGE
IN AMERICA   117

Chapter Four
Consensus through Ambiguity: Why Language Matters to
The Federalist   119

Chapter Five
Language in a "Christian Commonwealth": Horace Bushnell's
Cultural Criticism   137

Chapter Six
Beyond Symbolism: Philosophy of Language in *The Scarlet Letter*   162

Conclusion: From Logocracy to Renaissance   198

Notes   203

Index   235

MY SUBJECT is the different ways language was imagined in various American texts between the Revolution and the Civil War. I say *imagined* because my concern is not only with ideas about language but with the language that expresses those ideas—the literary forms in which they are presented and the cultural presuppositions that underlie them. Americans realized that their experiment in self-government put an extraordinary burden upon public opinion and, hence, upon the dissemination of information and political debate; and discourses on language—whose subject is, in these terms, the very foundation of the American polity—are rich repositories of nationalist hopes and fears. My contention is that to write about language during this critical period of corporate self-definition was thus to engage in a highly charged kind of fiction making. This book stands at the juncture of two contiguous but distinct fields of scholarly inquiry and their traditions of study and makes the relation between the two fields a question of theoretical importance.

The first field is familiar—the literature of the American Renaissance, defined nearly a half-century ago by F. O. Matthiessen as the writings of Emerson, Thoreau, Whitman, Hawthorne, and Melville. The field, so conceived and delimited, has come under increasing attack recently, and arguments have been made to reconstruct American literary history, in particular by revaluating writers of what has been termed the "other" American Renaissance, women and minority writers such as Frederick Douglass, Margaret Fuller, Harriet Jacobs, and Harriet Beecher Stowe.[1] For all this opposition, however, the canon continues for now to be the major factor in determining the content of Americanist literary scholarship and teaching of the antebellum period—for better or for worse. One of my purposes here is to join in the revisionist enterprise but from a wholly different point of attack.

The second field, the study of language in the United States during roughly the same period, has until recently remained an all-but-neglected area of intellectual history, stomping grounds for a few antiquarians, folklorists, and intellectual historians of language or education. Here we meet with no canon but find—along with several full-blown, sophisticated philosophies of language—obsolete textbooks, dated dictionaries, utopian schemes for standardizing the language or revolutionizing orthography, and self-righteous commentaries on the sad decline of public discourse.[2] Here the obscure and the celebrated stand side by side, presidents and preachers, philosophers and pedagogues:

John Adams, Charles Astor Bristed, Horace Bushnell, James Fenimore Cooper, Benjamin Franklin, Rowland Gibson Hazard, Thomas Jefferson, Alexander Bryan Johnson, Henry Wadsworth Longfellow, Elizabeth Peabody, William Thornton, and Noah Webster—to name just a few. With the growth of interest in these sorts of works and their writers over the last decade, it has become increasingly clear that interest in the study of language was pervasive during the period which produced the American Renaissance and, indeed, that language study constituted an essential part of intellectual discourse in the areas of politics, theology, pedagogy, and, not least of all, literature. I want to suggest that the recent emergence of the study of language as a serious field of inquiry gives us additional reason to rethink the disciplinary assumptions that have mediated our approach to the American Renaissance, not because we have heretofore been blind to issues of language but precisely because they have all along been central to the tradition Matthiessen bequeathed to us.

Since the word *language* has been conjured with in so many different theoretical ways in academic circles lately, let me say at the outset that I have no intention of arguing anything like a metacritical thesis about "linguistic moments" in the literature of the American Renaissance.[3] My argument here about the relation between literary texts and linguistic issues is more modest: I consider the contiguity of the two fields I have described to be concrete and historical, and I have tried to analyze the subject in those terms. Nor do I even mean to argue generally that a relationship should obtain between the writing of literature—any literature—and the study of language, though I think that a comparison of what a particular culture did with language and what it thought about language makes good scholarly sense. After all, we need not agree with all the details of Todorov's structuralist analysis to agree with him generally that "literature uses language both as point of departure and as point of arrival."[4] Writers, to risk a tautology, write with words; they take strength from the powers of language and are bound by its limitations. Particular writers may dazzle with their virtuosity, stretching their medium to its limits, forcing those limits to yield astonishing results, opening up new possibilities for expression. But as they strain, we understand, they are constrained: they must always work within the cultural confines of the language available to them. My argument concerns the perception prevalent among Americanist literary critics that the relationship of these American writers (and others) to their medium was *particularly* deliberate and self-conscious and for *particularly* "American" reasons. And I take up this critical perception precisely because it is not a new idea; some of the best scholars of the antebellum period have been saying it, in one way or another, for some time.

In other words, the linguistic turn of the critics of the American Renaissance needs to be distinguished from that of others. For all literary critics it is axiomatic (if often unstated) that literary performance is predicated upon linguistic competence. The proposition that the proper object of literary study is language rests necessarily upon this axiom and serves to distinguish the discipline of literary criticism from other sorts of textual study. To be sure, literary critics are not alone in viewing language as the central category in the study of human culture. Nor is the perception new: it can be traced at least as far back as Condillac and Vico (back, really, to the classical Greeks) and can be followed through the nineteenth century, on both sides of the Atlantic, emerging, mutatis mutandis, in Peirce and Nietzsche. We are aware of it now, perhaps, more than ever before. Indeed, Nietzsche's powerful trope has grown hackneyed: we believe almost without question that we all live within a prison house of language. Even though we have lately returned (again) to historicism, we nevertheless continue to read and write with an ever-present echo, words calling attention to themselves *as words*. As Terry Eagleton has observed, "Language, with its problems, mysteries and implications, has become both paradigm and obsession for twentieth-century intellectual life."[5] Still, literary criticism has always had a special stake in the study of language: a text that falls within the purview of a literary critic calls attention to itself in ways that it does not, generally speaking, when it is inspected by an intellectual historian, say, or a philosopher.[6] Many of us claim a special status for "literary" language, arguing (with Richards and the New Critics) that it is primarily emotive and nonreferential or (with Jakobson and the structuralists) that it "promot[es] the palpability of signs."[7] Or we can deny altogether (with Fish, for example, or the Derrideans) the distinction between "literary" and "nonliterary" and insist on the essential nonreferentiality of all texts. In either case, we agree that we must understand what language is before we understand what literature means, and for many of us in this new age of critical theory, language has for all intents and purposes replaced literature as the primary subject of inquiry. Given the character of literary criticism, then, it can hardly be considered unusual that critics of the American Renaissance would focus on issues of language. But if these critics share these assumptions, they also consistently insist that the justification for their focus lies not in a particular literary theory but in the material itself. They look to the literature—to the fourth chapter of Emerson's *Nature*, say, or Thoreau's puns, or Hawthorne's multivalent *A*, or Melville's doubloon, or Poe's mysterious hieroglyphics, or Whitman's "An American Primer," or to a variety of other stylistic and thematic elements—and claim that the American Renaissance is *about* language.

Imagining Language conceptually finds its genesis in this Americanist critical phenomenon, and it is for this reason that, in my introductory chapter, I offer a detailed historical and critical sketch both of Americanist literary historiography in the tradition of Matthiessen and Charles Feidelson and of Americanist linguistic historiography beginning with H. L. Mencken. The two discourses mirror each other, I suggest, in fundamental ways: while the literary critics tend to privilege those works whose stylistic self-reflexiveness indicates for them a philosophical (or, at least, quasi-philosophical) concern with language—I will call this textual characteristic *linguisticity*—the linguists see the growth and development of the English language in America as inseparable from the essentially literary history of its study. Both groups generally seem to acknowledge, furthermore, that their writers were deeply, imaginatively committed to America as an idea. So if we break down the disciplinary barriers that arbitrarily separate, say, Webster from Whitman or Bushnell from Hawthorne, we find a wide variety of writers who share a profound concern with the way Americans—*as Americans*—wrote and spoke. In this revisionary mode, the chapters that compose the bulk of this volume offer critical readings of individual works or series of works by writers from various walks of intellectual life (education, philosophy, theology, literature) whose ideas about the nature or use of language imaginatively merge with ideas about America so as to form cultural fictions, creative renderings of the nation—its meaning, its character, and how it works.

Thematically, I have arranged the chapters into two sections, each section treating a particular strain in the American study of language. The first, "Teaching Language in America," deals with the issues of linguistic and literary nationalism whose background I sketch briefly in the second half of the introduction. I consider three differently pedagogic figures who offer three different approaches to the issues (different ideas about language, about literature, about America) and who thus stand in three different relations to traditional literary history: Noah Webster, whose influential grammatical and lexicographic works occupy (at most) the margins of literary history, shares the critical stage equally with more conventionally (but differently) "literary" writers—Henry Wadsworth Longfellow, professor of modern languages and literatures at Bowdoin and Harvard, whose once-popular and respected poetry is rarely treated seriously in modern critical discourse, and Walt Whitman, champion of the American vernacular and "Wander-Teacher" manqué, generally considered to be the representative American poet. The second set of chapters is gathered under the rubric "The Philosophy of Language in America" and deals with ways language was conceived effectually to constitute American society and politics. An opening essay on *The Federalist* considers the language-related problems faced by the founding fathers in their debates about the Constitution and serves as a preface to two New England writers who, from different professional vantage points, fashioned critiques of American culture and society in the form of Romantic critiques of language: Horace Bushnell, the minister and theologian from Hartford, and Nathaniel Hawthorne, the romancer from Salem. Together the six essays represent an attempt to revise American literary history by turning the fundamental insight of linguisticity against itself—by placing each text in the context of the (primarily European) linguistic discourses from which it borrows and transforms ideas (Locke, Condillac, Rousseau, Schlegel, Humboldt, Coleridge, and so on) and by deferring conventional aesthetic and generic considerations and substituting as the sole criterion for analysis a strong linguistic imagination informed by a vision of America. What I hope will emerge from this shift in critical perspective—this merging of the methods and scopes of literary and intellectual history—is both a clearer sense of how the distinction we commonly make between imaginative and nonimaginative writing is of limited theoretical use and a broader perspective on the cultural significance of the phenomenon we call the American Renaissance.

Acknowledgments

To WRITE this book, I spent many excruciating hours alone—learning, as though I did not know it before, what a difficult and lonely thing it is to write a book. Still, I could not have completed it without the many friends, colleagues, and students who, over the years and in various ways, provided invaluable help, criticism, and encouragement and made this book substantially better than it would have been otherwise: Josephine Bloomfield, Adriana Craciun, Peter Dale, Margaret Davidson, Diana Dulaney, Emory Elliott, Eileen Elrod, Cristina Giorcelli, Thomas Gustafson, Biancamaria Tedeschini Lalli, Christopher Looby, Leslie Mitchner, Sean O'Grady, Werner Sollors, David Van Leer, Donald Weber, and above all, as always, Sacvan Bercovitch. Nor could I have completed it without the support of the University of California, Davis, through a Humanities Institute Fellowship, two Faculty Development Awards, and numerous Faculty and Junior Faculty Research Grants. And I could never have sustained myself without the extraordinary patience, kindness, and generosity of my family: my parents, Benjamin and Rose Kramer; my sisters, Joyce Friedman and Barbara Sabatino, and their families; my children, Nathaniel Stephen, Aryeh Chaim, and Elisa Rachel; and my wife, Jane Schindelheim Kramer, to whom I owe the greatest debt and to whom this book is dedicated.

Earlier versions of several chapters of this book have appeared elsewhere. Portions of the Preface and the Introduction were published as "The Study of Language and the American Renaissance: An Essay in Literary Historiography" in *ESQ: A Journal of the American Renaissance* 34 (1988): 207–227 and 282–307. Part of chapter 1 was delivered at the Biennial Conference of the European Association for American Studies in Budapest in 1986 and published as "Condillac to Michaelis to Tooke: How Noah Webster Invented a National Language; or, Was Tocqueville Wrong about American English?" in *The Early Republic: The Making of a Nation, the Making of a Culture*, ed. Steve Ickringill et al. (Amsterdam: Free University Press, 1988), pp. 212–227. Chapter 4 was delivered at an international conference on *The Federalist* held in Rome in 1987 and was published as "Perché la lingua è importante per il 'Federalits'?" in *Il Federalista: 200 anni dopo*, ed. Guglielmo Negri (Bologna: Società editrice il Mulino, 1988), pp. 369–392. Chapter 5 appeared as "Horace Bushnell's Philosophy of Language Considered as a Mode of Cultural Criticism" in *American Quarterly* 38 (1986): 573–590. I have included quotations from the following manuscript collections: Noah Webster Papers, Rare Books and Manuscripts Division, The New York Public Library, Astor, Lenox and Tilden Foundations; The Longfellow Papers, The Houghton Library, Harvard University. I would like to thank these libraries for their permission and assistance.

___ *Abbreviations of Frequently Cited Works* ___

AH   Irwin, John T. *American Hieroglyphics: The Symbol of the Hieroglyph in the American Renaissance*. New Haven: Yale University Press, 1980.

AL   Mencken, H. L. *The American Language: An Inquiry into the Development of English in the United States*. 4th ed. New York: Knopf, 1937.

AP   Bushnell, Horace. "American Politics." *The American National Preacher* 14 (1840): 189–204.

AR   Matthiessen, F. O. *American Renaissance: Art and Expression in the Age of Emerson and Whitman*. New York: Oxford University Press, 1941. Reprint. 1972.

AWE   Poirier, Richard. *A World Elsewhere: The Place of Style in American Literature*. New York: Oxford University Press, 1966.

BPW   Rousseau, Jean-Jacques. *Basic Political Writings*. Edited and translated by Donald A. Cress. Indianapolis: Hackett Publishing Company, 1987.

CE   Hawthorne, Nathaniel. *The Centenary Edition of the Works of Nathaniel Hawthorne*. Edited by Roy Harvey Pearce et al. 20 vols. to date. Columbus: Ohio State University Press, 1962–.

CHU   Locke, John. *An Essay concerning Human Understanding*. Edited by Alexander Campbell Fraser. 2 vols. New York: Dover, 1959. Vol. 2.

DAR   Bell, Michael Davitt. *The Development of American Romance: The Sacrifice of Relation*. Chicago: University of Chicago Press, 1981.

DEL   Webster, Noah. *Dissertation on the English Language*. Boston, 1789. Reprint. Menston, England: The Scolar Press, 1967.

DIA   Tocqueville, Alexis de. *Democracy in America*. Translated by Henry Reeve. Revised by Francis Bowen. Edited by Phillips Bradley. 2 vols. New York: Vintage Books, 1945.

D&N   Whitman, Walt. *Daybooks and Notebooks*. Edited by William White. 3 vols. New York: New York University Press, 1978.

DOP   Longfellow, Henry Wadsworth. "Defence of Poetry." *The North American Review* 34 (1832): 56–78.

DSQ   Bushnell, Horace. *A Discourse on the Slavery Question*. Hartford, 1839.

ELA   Krapp, George Philip. *The English Language in America*. 2 vols. New York: Ungar, 1925.

FNE   Bushnell, Horace. *The Fathers of New England*. New York, 1850.

GC   Bushnell, Horace. *God in Christ*. Hartford, 1849.

GGT   Baron, Dennis E. *Grammar and Good Taste: Reforming the American Language*. New Haven: Yale University Press, 1982.

GI   Webster, Noah. *A Grammatical Institute of the English Language, Part One*. Hartford, 1783.

KAT   Longfellow, Henry Wadsworth. *Kavanagh, a Tale*. Edited by Jean Downey. New Haven: College and University Press, 1965.

LAC   Cameron, Kenneth Walter, ed. *Longfellow among His Contemporaries*. Hartford: Transcendental Books, 1978.

LHWL   Longfellow, Henry Wadsworth. *The Letters of Henry Wadsworth Longfellow*. Edited by Andrew Hilen. 4 vols. Cambridge: Harvard University Press, 1966.

LNW   Webster, Noah. *Letters of Noah Webster*. Edited by Harry Warfel. New York: Library Publishers, 1953.

LOG   Whitman, Walt. *Leaves of Grass: The First (1855) Edition*. Edited by Malcolm Cowley. New York: Viking Press, 1959.

LSE   Sismondi, J.C.L. Simonde de. *Historical View of the Literature of the South of Europe*. Translated by Thomas Roscoe. 2 vols. London, 1846.

NG   Dilworth, Thomas. *A New Guide to the English Tongue*. 13th ed. London, 1751. Reprint. Leeds, England: The Scolar Press, 1967.

NUM   Whitman, Walt. *Notebooks and Unpublished Prose Manuscripts*. Edited by Edward F. Grier. 6 vols. New York: New York University Press, 1984.

NYD   Whitman, Walt. *New York Dissected: A Sheaf of Recently Discovered Newspaper Articles by the Author of Leaves of Grass*. Edited by Emory Holloway and Ralph Adimari. New York: Rufus Rockwell Wilson, 1936.

OGL   Longfellow, Henry Wadsworth. *Origin and Growth of the Languages of Southern Europe and of Their Literature*. Edited by George T. Littel. Brunswick, Maine: Bowdoin College Library, 1907.

ONW   Longfellow, Henry Wadsworth. "Our Native Writers." In *The Native Muse: Theories of American Literature*, edited by Richard Ruland. New York: Dutton, 1972.

PAE   Simpson, David. *The Politics of American English, 1776–1850*. New York: Oxford University Press, 1986.

PLG   Bushnell, Horace. *Politics under the Law of God*. Hartford, 1844.

PSR   Newman, Samuel P. *A Practical System of Rhetoric*. 10th ed. New York, 1842.

RAR   Carton, Evan. *The Rhetoric of American Romance: Dialect and Identity in Emerson, Dickinson, Poe, and Hawthorne*. Baltimore: Johns Hopkins University Press, 1985.

SAL   Feidelson, Charles, Jr. *Symbolism and American Literature*. Chicago: University of Chicago Press, 1953.

SIM   Bushnell, Horace. *The Spirit in Man: Sermons and Selections*. New York: Scribners, 1903.

T&S   Hawthorne, Nathaniel. *Tales and Sketches*. Edited by Roy Harvey Pearce. New York: The Library of America, 1982.

TWW   Bushnell, Horace. "The True Wealth or Weal of Nations." In *Representative Phi Beta Kappa Orations*, edited by Clark Sutherland Northrup et al., pp. 1–23. Boston: Houghton Mifflin, 1915.

UI   Bushnell, Horace. "Unconscious Influence." *The American Pulpit* 2 (1847): 230–241.

WOW   Gura, Philip F. *The Wisdom of Words: Language, Theology, and Literature in the New England Renaissance*. Middleton, Conn.: Wesleyan University Press, 1981.

WP   Bushnell, Horace. *Work and Play; or, Literary Varieties*. New York, 1864.

WTP   Paine, Thomas. *The Writings of Thomas Paine*. Edited by Moncure Daniel Conway. 4 vols. New York, 1894.

IMAGINING LANGUAGE IN AMERICA

The Study of Language and the American Renaissance

THE AMERICAN RENAISSANCE AS THE STUDY OF LANGUAGE

The rebirth of American literary studies that begins with *American Renaissance* is based upon the disciplinary assumption that the proper study of the literary critic is words and not ideas.[1] Matthiessen set out to convince us, first of all, that we ought to take antebellum literature seriously as *literature*, not as documentary sources for intellectual or social history. Under the aegis of Eliot, Richards, and the New Critics, he rescued antebellum literature from writers like V. L. Parrington and V. F. Calverton, underscoring the critic's "obligation . . . to examine an author's resources of language and of genres, in a word, to be preoccupied with form."[2] With the critical focus shifted from "what our fathers thought" (Parrington's phrase) to "*what* these books were as works of art" (Matthiessen's phrase), antebellum writing emerged from *American Renaissance* born again, newly justified in terms of what Matthiessen confidently referred to as "the enduring requirements" of great literature (*AR*, ix, vii, xi). We could now speak with impunity of the literature's diction and rhetoric, of its symbolism, allegory, paradox, ambiguity, organicism. Matthiessen showed us that in that "extraordinarily concentrated moment of expression" of the 1850s, America came into its "first maturity" and claimed "its rightful heritage in the whole expanse of art and culture" (*AR*, vii).

But it was not only a change in scholarly perspective that Matthiessen offered: he did more than apply New Critical principles to the well-wrought writings of Emerson, Thoreau, Hawthorne, Melville, and Whitman. The literature of the American Renaissance was shown not merely to be susceptible to formal analysis but to invite it by exhibiting a heightened sensitivity to the "poetics of language," adumbrating, if not exemplifying, the very principles that sustained Matthiessen's analysis.[3] Moreover, *American Renaissance* presents not only a creative literature of extraordinary "imaginative vitality" but also—and I would argue more importantly—a critical literature of remarkable theoretical sophistication, one that spoke directly to literary sensibilities formed by Eliot and Richards. "Emerson, Thoreau, and Whitman all commented very explicitly on language as well as expression," Matthiessen explained, "and the creative intentions of Hawthorne and Melville [though they wrote little of a theoretical nature] can be readily discerned through scrutiny of their chief works" (*AR*, vii). Matthiessen's identification of the age, in his subtitle, with Emerson and Whitman speaks directly to this aspect of his work: their theories of language literally bracket *American Renaissance* and provide the conceptual parameters for the work. Emerson in particular, who "wrote no masterpiece," still deserved titular status ("the Age of Emerson") because of his enormously influential "theory of expression" (*AR*, xii). In fact, Matthiessen at one point in his introduction clearly defined his "main subject" as "the *conceptions* held by five of our major writers concerning the function and nature of literature" and theoretically restricted the significance of his literary analyses to "the degree to which their practice bore out their theories" (*AR*, vii; italics mine).[4] So although *American Renaissance* conceptually begins with the several masterpieces produced during the 1850s, that "one extraordinarily concentrated moment of expression," Matthiessen quickly and subtly shifts his focus to the ideas which the forms of these works expressed, "to the writers' use of their own tools, their diction and rhetoric, and to what they could make with them." He is interested in the works themselves only insofar as they inevitably give way to "the total pattern of [the writers'] achievement" (*AR*, xv). In other words, *American Renaissance* is about the study of language in America before the Civil War, at least among the five writers he canonizes. The significance of the works lies in the fact that they embody a particular—and, he believed, a particularly *American*—mode and theory of expression.

Over the three decades that followed the publication of *American Renaissance*—i.e., until New Criticism was challenged and uprooted by the various theoretical approaches that have redesigned today's academic landscape—the linguisticity that Matthiessen discovered in antebellum texts was transformed, in books and articles and university classrooms, into a critical commonplace. Most often, Matthiessen's discovery remained implicit, informing countless exercises in practical criticism. But in 1953, in *Symbolism and American Literature*, Charles Feidelson confronted the linguisticity of the American Renaissance, distilled it, and located it within an intellectual-historical continuum that provided the study of the "unified phase of American literature" with a conceptual framework which has remained influential even after the wane of the New Criticism whose theoretical assumptions Feidelson shared.[5] Unlike Matthiessen, Feidelson did not blur the distinction between his own critical enterprise and the aesthetic concerns of his subjects by conjuring with "the enduring requirements for great art." The American Renaissance did not represent for him an extraordinary, timeless aesthetic achievement but the emergence of a particular mode of perception and a concomitant literary practice that were "precipitated by the continued pressure of intellectual conditions" (*SAL*, 74). To be sure, by rejecting "the whole expanse of art and culture" for "intellectual conditions," Feidelson did not intend to subsume the literary beneath the intellectual. He implicitly argued, rather, that we cannot ultimately separate the two. The methodological chasm separating Parrington's "what our fathers thought" and Matthiessen's "what these books were as works of art" is bridged, in *Symbolism and American Literature*, by new considerations: *how* our fathers thought and *how* the literature manifested that thought.

Feidelson represents the *literature* of the American Renaissance as the outgrowth of two clearly discernible *intellectual* traditions. One is European, "the whole seesaw movement from Descartes through the English empiricists to Kant, issuing in the nineteenth-century split between materialism and idealism" (*SAL*, 70). The other tradition is indigenously American, "one continuous movement from the Puritan era through the new learning of Locke [embodied in the American Enlightenment] to the new philosophy of Emerson" (*SAL*, 108). Both traditions issue similarly in theories of language. The European tradition, continually struggling with the consequences of Cartesian dualism, eventually produces the symbolist, who turns to language in order to solve the problem of mediation: he conceives of words not as arbitrary signs but as constituting (in Wilhelm von Humboldt's formulation) "a sort of middle ground between man and the external . . . [which] not only represents objects to the mind's eye but . . . also gives us the impression produced by them, thus blending and uniting our receptivity with the self-determining, active energy of our being" (*SAL*, 75). The American tradition was from the beginning "harassed by a problem of expression" (*SAL*, 76): combining "a kind of symbolic perception" that was fundamentally alogical (seeing the course of human events in terms of biblical history) with strict Ramist logic, the Puritans bequeathed to their descendants a philosophical method that "was actually at odds with itself" (*SAL*, 77, 91). Over time, and with the importation of Lockean and Baconian empiricism, the gap between vision and explanation widened, "language was tortured" in the attempt to reconcile them, and a new, less-fettered rationalism, which rejected the symbolist half of the Puritan bequest, came to dominate the intellectual scene (*SAL*, 96). The American Renaissance stands historically at the juncture of the European and American traditions: post-Kantian philosophy gives terminology and authority to the indigenous American predilection for symbolism, and a new organic approach to language emerges to define the period. Symbolism is thus for Feidelson "a governing principle: not [simply] a stylistic device, but a point of view; not a casual subject, but a pervasive presence in the intellectual landscape" (*SAL*, 43). The linguisticity of antebellum literature—the fact that its "technique" was also its "theme"—is seen to be at bottom an attempt to reimagine philosophical method. Literary and intellectual history merge in the language of Emerson, Thoreau, Poe, Hawthorne, Whitman, and Melville.

In short, Feidelson accepts Matthiessen's fundamental insight—that our classic writers seem to be preoccupied with the problem of language—but he rejects, at least in part, his predecessor's "method and scope." Symbolism and the theory of language that it presupposes are Feidelson's subjects from the very beginning. As a consequence, the scope of his study widens. Matthiessen's canonical five (plus Poe) remain center stage, but they are surrounded by a diverse group of players—mostly churchmen and philosophers, not artists—who are not simply foils for the stars, contexts for major texts, but who play significant roles in the unfolding of Feidelson's intellectual drama. Their writings matter, too, if not quite as much. The inclusion of Horace Bushnell as a "version of Emerson" is of tremendous significance, for in the few pages devoted to the Hartford theologian, the disciplinary barriers separating literary from nonliterary writing are breached. Bushnell, who sought to resolve the Trinitarian-Unitarian controversy with a theory of symbolic language, stands shoulder to shoulder with Thoreau: together they look backward to Winthrop, Willard, Mather, and Moody and forward to Richards, Empson, Cassirer, and Langer. Bushnell's presence indicates—or at least implies—that symbolism was not only the concern of literary figures. And with the broadening of scope comes a diversification of method. Theoretical analysis and "practical criticism" share explicatory duties—whatever is needed to get at the "pervasive presence" of symbolism. To be sure, some writers are more important for what they say about language than for how they say it in language: this is what finally distinguishes, for example, Thoreau from Bushnell. And those whose contribution resides in how they say it are, by the force of disciplinary logic, ultimately more important. But all are crucial to Feidelson's design—to understand the linguisticity of the American Renaissance as part of a broadly based cultural and historical phenomenon.

Feidelson's enduring reputation can be attributed not only (perhaps not even predominantly) to a residual New Critical bias in the hinterlands of academe but, ironically, to those who most vociferously attack the assumptions upon which New Criticism rests. Postmodernist critics identify their critical program as a deliberate rejection of the logocentrism of critics like Matthiessen and Feidelson, critics who found in the language of literature a plenitude of meaning that seemed to be lost in society itself. To the postmodernists, the valorization of the literary word—of the symbol, of organic form—is seen as a sort of fetishism; they insist that the relation between word and meaning is always already contingent, that meaning cannot be spoken of as inhering in words. Nevertheless, Feidelson is considered today by them as a significant critical precursor. In effect, *Symbolism and American Literature* authorizes its own revisionary studies: as its notion of symbolism is rejected, its fundamental premise concerning the linguisticity of the American Renaissance is reaffirmed. The issue is not *that* the literature is about language but *how* it is about language. As Feidelson argued for the modernity of the American Renaissance, so recent critics argue for its postmodernity. In other words, antebellum writing should not only be deconstructed (they say) but should be seen as a foreshadowing of deconstruction.

Let me give two prominent examples. The first is John Irwin's highly acclaimed study, *American Hieroglyphics*, a formidable book that deliberately revises both Matthiessen and Feidelson.[6] Like Matthiessen, Irwin relies heavily on the idea of an American canon—but with one significant difference: Poe not only joins Matthiessen's canon but obtrudes himself, as it were, at the very center of Irwin's book, dominating in terms of sheer bulk and critical complexity and substituting for the reassuring organicism of Emerson and Whitman a more profoundly disquieting poetics. Like Feidelson, Irwin grounds his study in intellectual history—not the prevalent history of Western philosophy (from Descartes to Kant) or the dominant American tradition (from Puritan to Yankee) but the more obscure episode that begins with Champollion's decipherment of the Rosetta stone in the 1820s and the subsequent rise of Egyptology and historical anthropology. Crucial as well, for Poe in particular, is the debate over the origin of language, something like an intellectual obsession in eighteenth-century Europe (soliciting contributions from, among a host of forgotten others, Locke, Condillac, Rousseau, and Herder) that fell into disrepute with the rise of historical linguistics in the nineteenth century. In this decentering of intellectual history, Feidelson's modernist symbol is discarded in favor of the ancient Egyptian hieroglyph, a move that leads Irwin to reconsider not only "the various ways in which a sign can be linked to its referent" but also "the larger reciprocal questions of the origin and limits of symbolization and the symbolization of origins and ends" (*AH*, 6, xi).

The critical revisionism of *American Hieroglyphics* significantly expands our sense of the relation between the study of language and the American Renaissance. First, and most simply, contemporaneous interest in language is shown to be still more extensive than even Feidelson allowed. By documenting the widespread fascination with Champollion and hieroglyphic writing among intellectuals of all sorts (as well as among the general public), Irwin opens up a new area of the intellectual history of language study and adds another (more exotic) dimension of cultural rootedness to the "pervasive presence" of symbolism in the period. Moreover, the notion that the American Renaissance represents the cultivation of an alogical, organic language, of form fused with content, words with things, of symbols generating an "inconclusive luxuriance of meaning" (SAL, 15)—this notion, common to both Matthiessen and Feidelson, is challenged: rather than seeing the more problematic works of Poe, Hawthorne, and Melville as failures or aberrations, Irwin sees them as accurate renderings of minds that have come to recognize the abyss at the end of the search for language and meaning. If nothing else, Irwin leaves us with a sense that the ways in which our "major" writers thought about language were more varied, more profound, and more problematic than had previously been assumed.

My second example is Evan Carton's The Rhetoric of American Romance, a significant addition to the tradition I have been sketching because it offers itself as an explicitly revisionary critique, not of Matthiessen and Feidelson, but of Lionel Trilling and Richard Chase on the nature of American fiction.[7] Trilling and Chase had, following Henry James, recast Hawthorne's well-known generic distinction between the romance and the novel in sociocultural terms, arguing that because the fabric of American society was too thin to sustain the realistic novel, American writers turned away from society and looked to the sea, to the forest, to the heart and mind of man, in a word, to the romance. Carton seems to find this thesis—lately attacked along several fronts though still highly influential—a useful but limited way of characterizing the peculiar nature of mid-nineteenth-century American literature and "seeks to revitalize our understanding of American romance" by removing both the generic and, for all practical purposes, the cultural specificity of the term. He redefines romance as "a specific and urgent kind of rhetorical performance," a mode of expression—indeed, a kind of philosophical discourse—that "explores and exploits the structural properties of language itself" (RAR, 1, 4–5). Romance is no longer to be characterized by the marked discontinuity between American fiction and American society but by the unbridgeable gap between word and thing. Hawthorne and Poe part company with Cooper and Simms and are joined by Emerson and Dickinson: "The questions that [these four writers] raise about language's mediation between reality and the imagination—questions of its authority, its method, its effectiveness, its morality—constitute," Carton argues, "the common bond among them, the heart of romance" (RAR, 247).

In effect, Carton collapses one critical tradition into another: Trilling and Chase are recast in the image of Matthiessen and, in particular, Feidelson. Indeed, following Feidelson, Carton places the "cultural epoch" represented by his four American writers at the historical juncture of "a pungent [post-Cartesian] philosophical milieu" and "an indigenous Puritan sensibility," a time when "the tensions that generate romance were particularly high" (*RAR*, 2). Literary history merges here with the history of philosophy: Emerson, Dickinson, Poe, and Hawthorne stand shoulder to shoulder with Kant and Hegel; and what the Germans could not accomplish "discursively," the Americans accomplish "performatively and imagistically" (*RAR*, 2). Disciplinary distinctions are reduced to *mere* methodology. To be sure, Carton has his own version of the contemporaneous European philosophical context: rather than calling upon Humboldt to introduce the notion of symbolic mediation, he uses Kant and Hegel to define the milieu in terms of two opposing needs, one "to distinguish the immanent, empirical, or lawful use of reason from the transcendent and illusive judgments of pure reason" and another "to overcome this static and self-alienating distinction through dynamic synthesis, through a phenomenology of spirit" (*RAR*, 2). And Carton's "romance," like Irwin's "hieroglyph," significantly refashions Feidelson's "symbol": unlike the symbol that conceptually resolves post-Cartesian dualism, romance sustains the Kant/Hegel opposition in the form of a dialectic. Nevertheless, both concepts represent a critical turning in upon language as the medium of philosophical discourse, and both stand upon the same fundamental assumption, that the literature of the American Renaissance forms a chapter in the intellectual history of language study.

Unlike Feidelson, or Irwin for that matter, Carton does not describe at any length the contemporaneous intellectual environment that supported his four romancers. No Bushnells here. Still, though he chooses to define the philosophical milieu exclusively in terms of two major European thinkers, even Carton hints that something about the post-Revolutionary period must have generated the rhetorical performances he labels "romance" and distinguishes with the adjective "American." But he only hints, and only in passing. Indeed, even Feidelson and Irwin, though they ground their studies more centrally in American intellectual history, assert the Americanness of the literary/intellectual phenomenon they delineate without speculating in more than an offhand manner on the cultural meaning of their writers' profound interest in language. In failing to do so, they have chosen to reject (in Feidelson's case) or to ignore (in Carton's and Irwin's) an essential aspect of Matthiessen's understanding of the American Renaissance. For Matthiessen understood the unprecedented concentration of creative energies in America—and the linguisticity that characterized them—in strikingly cultural and ideological terms. The five writers, he explains, were united in "their devotion to the possibilities of democracy" (*AR*, ix). They "felt it was incumbent upon their generation to give fulfilment to the potentialities freed by the Revolution, to provide a culture commensurate with America's political opportunity" (*AR*, xv). This was the impetus behind Emerson's "probing to the origins of speech in order to find out the sources of its mysterious powers" (*AR*, 30). His discovery was twofold: first, that language was "fossil poetry," that it was "material only on one side," and that in its true, undefiled state, it formed "the bridge that enabled man to pass from concrete appearance to spiritual reality"; second, that it retained its unfossilized state only among the common people, in "the language of the street" (Emerson, quoted in *AR*, 33, 32, 35). This discovery exploded the Tocquevillean assumption that democratic culture was inherently unpoetic. American language, the language of the people, was poetry: the cultivation of this organic, democratic language is, for Matthiessen, what defined the age of Emerson and Whitman and constituted "America's way of producing a renaissance." "Never does one come closer to the age's sense of the enormous fertility of life," Matthiessen writes, "than when these men are discovering the fresh resources of words" (*AR*, 30).

For Matthiessen, the discourse on language, as manifested at least in the works of his five writers, represented the mind of America more than all the discourses on politics or economics. This, finally, is what underlay his revisionary method and scope. Matthiessen's ultimate goal was not simply literary criticism but "cultural history": "An artist's use of language is the most sensitive index to cultural history," he reasoned, "since a man can articulate only what he is, and what he has been made by the society of which he is a willing or unwilling part" (*AR*, xv). There is a curious tension between the subjects of the first and second clauses of this methodologically crucial sentence, between "artist" and "man." Clearly Matthiessen was not equating the two; he was not interested in analyzing the speech of common (or other) men, Emerson's linguistic discovery notwithstanding. In fact, the first clause effectually negates the second: if an artist's language is historiographically more important, more "sensitive," it must be because it articulates more than ordinary language. Nor, for that matter, was Emerson simply an artist. He was *the* artist whose thought and expression created the conditions for a literature that could become an "index" of American culture. "No American writer before Emerson had devoted such searching attention to his medium"; no writer had heretofore expressed America (*AR*, 30). Matthiessen's five writers had, in effect, to reject much of American culture in order to write American literature. "Artist" and "man" meet and become one only in the rarefied domain of ideology. For Matthiessen, his writers' uses and theories of language—the conceptual core of *American Renaissance*—are less reflections of the America they inhabited than projections of their myths of America.

Which is to say that, for Matthiessen (so construed), the self-conscious search for language and form in antebellum America was overtly ideological, issuing from the perceived gulf—and a desired link—between what America meant and what it was. And if this thesis is more implied than asserted in *American Renaissance*, it becomes clearer in later works that understand the linguisticity of the American Renaissance in terms of what is seen as the peculiar position of the American writer in American society. I refer in particular to Richard's Poirier's *A World Elsewhere* and Michael Bell's *The Development of American Romance*.[8] Like Carton's *Rhetoric of American Romance*, these post-Matthiessen studies take their place in the history of American literary scholarship alongside both the tradition of Feidelson and the tradition of Trilling and Chase, but in markedly different ways.

Consider first Poirier's classic *A World Elsewhere*. Like the other critics I have touched upon here, Poirier grounds his study in the empirical observation that something is unusual and obtrusive about style in American literature.[9] Indeed, he claims, obtrusive style identifies and defines American writing: the various, remarkable ways in which American writers use language "demand our attention altogether more than do ideas or themes" (*AWE*, 36). We might also think of Poirier as a twofold inversion of Trilling and Chase: first, the generic distinction between romance and novel is translated into a stylistic distinction "between works that create through language an essentially imaginative environment for the hero and works that mirror an environment already accredited by history and society" (*AWE*, 7); second, the putative thinness of the American social fabric is replaced by the oppressive nature of its social system. He explains: "American literature is a struggle with already existing literary, social, and historical organizations for power over environment and over language itself," and that struggle—to follow the Emersonian injunction to build one's own world—is manifest in "extravagances of language," as if only in and through a linguistic environment "that thwarts any attempts to translate [it] . . . into the terms of conventional environments" can freedom be achieved (*AWE*, ix, 7). To be sure, Poirier admits, the struggles are inevitably lost because the "pressures of time, biology, economics, and . . . social forces . . . are ultimately the undoing of American heroes and quite often of their creators" and because, after all, language can never really be free from history and society (*AWE*, 5). And because—Poirier seems not to have caught this irony—for all its subversiveness, the creation of a literary world elsewhere re-creates, in imaginative terms, "the creation of America out of a continental vastness" that it opposes (*AWE*, 4). Nevertheless, it is the struggle itself which concerns Poirier, the repeated attempts to liberate language that marks the literature as American.

Poirier, it should be made clear, does not purport to be writing a variety of intellectual history. Like Matthiessen, he declares his focus to be style; unlike Matthiessen, he rigorously maintains his course. His writers, from Emerson and Cooper on, are not philosophers in disguise. Their involvement with language was "unprogrammatic": artistic, not intellectual; performative, not reflective. Nor does he recruit thinkers like Hegel or Bushnell to help translate performance into concept. Still, he cannot conceive of American literature apart from American culture. His attempt to make sense of American literature on its own terms—to define its very literariness, its linguisticity—cannot be separated from his understanding of the "historical forces" that shape American culture. If the history Poirier finds "lurking in . . . stylistic and formal characteristics" is not a history of ideas, it is, however, an ideological history, an account of the effect of political situations (broadly construed) on literary style (*AWE*, ix). Each stylistic extravagance is an ideological gesture, representatively American because it reflects as it deflects the historical forces that have shaped it. Like Matthiessen, Poirier sees the linguisticity of American literature to represent the always unbridged distance between the delimited world of political liberties and the never-never land of unlimited imaginative freedom. In short, for Poirier, the historical forces that shape American culture also make writers treat language differently, make them fight against the conventionality of language, make them see the words *as* words, as "the sounds, identities, and presences shaped by [the] technical aspects of expression" (*AWE*, viii). To be sure, Poirier only assumes those historical forces are there: he does not locate them outside the language of the works he studies. But this failure makes the assertion all the more significant: it indicates how self-evident he considered it.

In marked contrast to Poirier, Michael Bell takes great pains to locate the historical forces that fostered the linguisticity of American romance outside the texts themselves.[10] He finds it in a cultural atmosphere he labels "orthodox American opinion," a clear "consensus of American ministers, moralists, and critics that the writing or reading of imaginative fiction was at best frivolous and usually dangerous" (*DAR*, 12, 11). Joining a deeply felt Puritan aversion to nonpractical literature with Scottish Commonsense psychology, orthodox opinion believed that "imagination, if not strictly controlled, posed a threat both to individual happiness and to social cohesion" because it severed the link between the mind and reality (*DAR*, 12). Societies, especially an experimental, democratic society whose future was uncertain, had to rely on reason for order and stability. An unfettered imagination led to passion and insanity, and Americans, beset by fears of anarchy and the destruction of their still experimental society, were encouraged to banish the products of the imagination from their midst. For Brown, Irving, Poe, Hawthorne, and Melville to choose to write romances, especially American romances, in the face of such hostility was, Bell argues, consciously to embrace the roles of deviants but also to harbor a profound ambivalence about their "sacrifice of relation" to American society.

It was out of this ambivalence that the linguisticity of the American romance emerged. The condemnation of romance accentuated its fictionality—the disjunction between the words on the page and the world outside—and threw the writers back upon their medium to mediate between them and the country that denigrated them, to discover a way to sustain and express their ambivalence. Neurosis became art. The defining characteristics of their romances—their penchants for ambiguous situations, affective language, symbolic descriptions, unreliable narrators, and so on—are seen by Bell to be explorations, in stylistically experimental terms, of the gap between statement and intention, language and meaning, words and things. This gap, which so frightened their Commonsense critics, seemed to them (most explicitly to Hawthorne and Melville) to manifest, as analogy and embodiment, America's sacrifice of relation to its Revolutionary ideals, the chasm between its promise of liberation and the exigencies of social stability. The romancers' heightened sensitivity to the powers and limitations of language is seen, in other words, as both the symptom of their psychological dislocation and the subject of their political reflections. Bell explains the linguisticity of American romance as an element of a complex cultural process by which the new republic was trying to define its corporate identity and to come to terms with its Revolutionary heritage.

Literary, intellectual, psycho-, and social history are conjoined in *The Development of American Romance*. The foregrounding of linguistic issues in the works of Brown, Irving, Poe, Hawthorne, and Melville is approached as a cultural phenomenon that cannot be explained apart from what Bell understands as the concrete (biographical and historical) circumstances of its production. Bell tries to avoid having ideology stand in for history. When he employs the adjective "American," he does not mean to distill myth from fact: the linguisticity of American romance is not an assertion of true Americanness over and against orthodox American opinion but an example of the ways ideas about America and the actuality of its history are both factors in American cultural production.

My point so far is this. From Matthiessen to Bell and Carton, Americanist literary historiography has considered linguisticity to be a defining feature of the American Renaissance. The looseness of my terminology is intentional. I have deliberately expanded the term *American Renaissance* to refer to a period ranging from soon after the Revolution to beyond the Civil War and to an array of authors from Brown to Dickinson, for each of the critics I have surveyed has built upon Matthiessen's foundation—upon the idea that certain authors and not others sufficiently represent a unique American tradition—no matter what authors he has chosen to include or exclude, or what time period is covered, or what he believes constituted American culture. And I have used *linguisticity* to refer to the variety of stylistic and thematic phenomena described by these critics: symbolism, ambiguity, hieroglyphics, romance, verbal extravagance, wordplay, narrative unreliability—anything that would indicate a more than ordinary consciousness of how to do things with words. The lack of agreement among the critics as to details makes their general concurrence, I think, all the more suggestive.

Between Feidelson's philosophers and Bell's neurotics lies a broad expanse of scholarly ground, crowded with questions, still largely unanswered, about the study of language and the American Renaissance. One in particular: if we are ultimately interested in notions of language, why not make that the primary area of study? One answer is, of course, that putative literary worth defines the critic's field of study—both limits it and authorizes it—prior to the asking of any broader intellectual questions that may arise. The idea of a literary canon (however constituted) allows a scholar to avoid addressing these larger, interdisciplinary questions and, as a consequence, to make sometimes unjustified assumptions about the relation between literature and culture. The originative questions of the critics I have surveyed are restrictively literary—how to make sense of certain characteristics of particular works—but their answers strain at the disciplinary restrictions that bind them. Ironically, the same critical impulse that cultivates sensitivity to language hinders the critic from following through on his discoveries. But my purpose is not to denigrate any of these formidable critical achievements because of what they failed to do but to point out what, it seems to me, they have done. Taken singly, each of these studies either demonstrates or implies that literary linguisticity must be culturally contextualized, whether as part of a pervasive intellectual presence or as the product of other cultural forces. Taken together, these studies repudiate the narrowness of scope of any individual study and imply a more broadly cultural and philosophically diverse interest in language. They propose that the study of language and its relation to antebellum American culture ought to come to the fore and assume its rightful place in the whole expanse of American literary and intellectual history.

THE STUDY OF LANGUAGE AS
LITERARY HISTORY

Literary scholars began in earnest to explore the study of language in antebellum America in the early seventies, not as a field in its own right but as a source for clarifying certain aspects of their understanding of the

American Renaissance, in particular the extensive and sometimes peculiar wordplay in Thoreau's *Walden.* In a series of path-breaking articles,
Michael West and others revealed, first of all, that Thoreau's knowledge
of contemporary philology and rhetoric was quite considerable—he had
studied Charles Kraitsir, Walter Whiter, Richard Trench, George
Campbell, and Dugald Stewart, among others.[11] To modern sensibilities, some of these works may have seemed eccentric, even ridiculous,
especially those like Kraitsir's *Glossology* and Trench's *On the Study of
Words* which were grounded in a speculative etymology that, like the
debates over the origin of language, was discredited with the concurrent
rise of linguistic science in Europe. But we learned that Thoreau (along
with other respectable intellectuals) evidently took them seriously and,
moreover, that the linguisticity we so admired in his work was of a piece
with, and in some ways a product of, his interest in the study of language. Broadly construed, the Thoreauvian revelations exemplified what
could be gained by bringing the study of language to bear upon the
writings of the American Renaissance. Before Thoreau's readings sur-
faced in these articles, critics (as opposed to linguistic historians and a
very few others) were generally unaware of the very existence, let alone
the prevalence, of such a discourse: Feidelson's few pages on Horace
Bushnell remained the only treatment of nonliterary manifestations of
the study of language in Americanist literary criticism.[12] Now it seemed
possible that the linguisticity of the American Renaissance could be contextualized within a nonliterary discourse that was more historically and
culturally immediate than Feidelson's two broadly conceived intellectual
traditions. Still, a question remained unasked: could it be that Bushnell
was less a version of Emerson than, along with Emerson, Thoreau, and
others, a participant in a larger intellectual discussion, one which was
not restricted by the disciplinary prejudices that tell us what is literature
and what is not?

The first scholarly work to make use of these revelations and to ex-
pand their scope was Philip Gura's *The Wisdom of Words.*[13] Gura felt that
the linguisticity of the American Renaissance had become so widely accepted over the years that the overused terms *language* and *symbol* had
become nearly emptied of meaning. The stated purpose of *The Wisdom
of Words* was to "resurrect" the subject of linguisticity, not by shifting
critical perspective and substituting new or retooled terms (e.g., *hieroglyphics, romance*) for the well-worn *language* and *symbol,* but by "establish[ing] the [immediate historical] context from which discussions
of language and symbol originated among certain American romantics"
(*WOW,* 3, 6). Gura was not out to offer a radically revisionary account
of symbolism in American literature: he was satisfied that Feidelson was
right, both about the nature and importance of symbolism and about its
source in the Puritan theological tradition. *The Wisdom of Words* opens

up the study of language in antebellum America to further view by translating Feidelson's "pervasive presence" of symbolism into a concrete cultural phenomenon.

Gura finds the seedbed of American symbolism in the denominational debates between Trinitarians and Unitarians that raged in New England in the decades before the Civil War. Specifically, the controversy over the relation of biblical language to theological truth—questions of whether biblical language should be taken literally or figuratively, whether paradoxical expressions like "Logos made flesh" should be subjected to the judgment of reason or accepted on faith—this controversy, grounded in the Lockean and Commonsense critiques of language and the Higher Criticism of the Bible, "contributed to an environment in which one's whole manner of expressing 'truth' had to be renovated, even if one were not affiliated strongly with any particular religious group" (WOW, 7). A resolution to the controversy, in theoretical terms at least, was achieved by Romantic theologians such as James Marsh, whose edition of Coleridge's Aids to Reflection (1829) in large part introduced European Romantic thought, especially the distinction between Reason and Imagination, to New England. The most significant figure was Feidelson's Bushnell, whose Coleridge-influenced God in Christ advanced a controversial theory of poetic or symbolic hermeneutics. "Logos made flesh" need not be accepted literally or explained figuratively but was to be apprehended symbolically, Bushnell explained. For, given the materialist base of all words, complex spiritual truths cannot be expressed in language except through paradox and ambiguity. Both the Unitarians and Trinitarians were wrong, Bushnell argued, because they did not understand how language worked.

Gura is less concerned with the theological resolution of the controversy than with its literary ramifications. Indeed, as Gura sees it, Marsh and Bushnell must be understood primarily as "transitional figures": the theological context in which their ideas of symbolism were conceived seriously limited the uses to which they could put them but "proved immensely liberating to men whose respect for a strict theological consistency was not as great as theirs"—men, Gura argues, like Emerson, Thoreau, Hawthorne, and Melville, who were able to transform narrowly conceived ideas into "innovative and fruitful forms" (WOW, 71, 5–6). In short, theological debate "cleared the way for" the flowering of symbolism and ambiguity in the American Renaissance. Or, alternately, Marsh, Bushnell, and their fellows were "harbingers" of Emerson, Thoreau, Hawthorne, and Melville. Whatever the trope, Matthiessen's valorization of his five writers clearly informs Gura's recontextualization of their writings. To be sure, Gura's four are less sons of the Revolution than "heirs to an age characterized by an increasing skepticism regarding man's ability to decipher, let alone justify, the ways of God to men."

And they are less intent on creating a literature "commensurate with America's political opportunity" than with finding "a prose style commensurate to the complexity of the 1850s" (*WOW*, 7). Like Irwin, Carton, and Bell, Gura is inclined to see the antebellum period more as the age of Hawthorne and Melville (and Poe) than as the age of Emerson and Thoreau (and Whitman). And he is more inclined to describe the American Renaissance as an essentially religious movement (à la Feidelson) than as a politically driven phenomenon (à la Matthiessen).[14] These are significant differences. But given the fundamentally literary-historical nature of Gura's approach—the privileging of literary texts that he shares with Matthiessen—the differences must be seen less as wholesale revisions than as shifts in perspective. Ironically, although *The Wisdom of Words* may actually be seen more as a work of intellectual and cultural history than as an exercise in practical criticism—Emerson and company are just as often "thinkers" as they are "writers"—Gura's purview is defined by the prepossessions of the literary critic.

This is not, strictly speaking, to repudiate Gura's conclusions so much as to indicate the issues that form the horizon of his work and to prepare the way conceptually for the emergence of the study of language as a field in its own right. To accomplish this, I would suggest, Gura's summary assertion that "the study of language in early nineteenth-century America . . . must be viewed as an inextricable part of the cultural matrix from which our classic American writers emerged" ought to be reformulated (*WOW*, 5). First of all, the literature of the American Renaissance should be seen as part of, not the issue of, the study of language in early nineteenth-century America. To relegate religious discourse to the status of "matrix" for a more prestigious literary discourse is potentially to deny the historical integrity of each. Literature emerges from its context, or flowers from it, only in the eyes of literary historians; religious historians can just as easily depict theology flowering from literary soil. Emerson is as much a "harbinger" of Bushnell as Bushnell is a "version" of Emerson. Bushnell does not need Hawthorne to redeem his importance for the history of American symbolism, nor does Hawthorne need Bushnell to type him forth.[15] Each writer produced texts "about" language, certainly not in a vacuum or free of the sorts of intangible influences that are generally designated "intellectual climates" or "cultural milieus," but equivalent in all but disciplinary terms. And if, as I have been suggesting, our true subject has always been the study of language, then each text ought to be given its due: *Nature, God in Christ*, and *The Scarlet Letter* each deserves serious critical attention on its own terms.

Second, the scope of the study of language needs to be widened beyond speculative etymologists and philological theologians. In choosing with Feidelson to bracket the political side of Matthiessen and to focus on the religious and philosophical, Gura illuminates one or two aspects of a broad, multifaceted cultural phenomenon, convincingly arguing that Marsh, Bushnell, Emerson, Thoreau, Hawthorne, and Melville studied language as a way of maintaining faith in a complex world. But much of the complexity of pre–Civil War America was political, and much of the writing about language was, too, from Madison's appropriation of the Lockean critique of language in *Federalist* 37 to the Webster/Worcester dictionary wars that heated up in the 1860s. At stake is not the nature of truth but the success of the American experiment in self-government: implementing the democratic political process, neutralizing sectional hostilities, absorbing a polyglot immigrant population, defining relations with Great Britain, abolishing (or maintaining) the institution of slavery. One can hardly contemplate the complexity of the antebellum decades without due consideration of these sorts of issues. Nor, moreover, can discussions of antebellum religion be depoliticized: to speak of a search for spiritual "truth" apart from the battles for political power is to ignore one of the great truths of American history, that the separation of church and state did not lead to the divorce of religion and politics. Indeed, the interconnectedness of religion and politics contributes much to our sense of the period's complexity. Ideally, when it is told, the history of the study of language—including the linguisticity of the American Renaissance—should reflect this.

The study of language in America has been construed politically in various ways, most obviously, perhaps, in the linguistic patriotism that emerged after the Revolution and continued through the Jacksonian period and beyond: in John Adams's calls for an American language academy, in Thomas Jefferson's defense of neology, in the mixed diction of Joel Barlow's poetry, in Noah Webster's efforts to standardize spelling and pronunciation, in James Fenimore Cooper's and Edward Everett's defenses of American speech. The argument that ran through these suggestions—if a summary argument may be gleaned from the many and various pronouncements—was similar to the well-known arguments for literary independence, that the language spoken by Americans should reflect the new political reality of nationhood: no longer should American English conform to British (aristocratic) standards.

No great distance needs to be traveled from post-Revolutionary linguistic patriotism to "art and expression in the age of Emerson and Whitman." Matthiessen, we recall, understood the linguisticity of the American Renaissance to be an aesthetic correlate of American democracy. Emerson discovered the poetry in language not only by reading Schlegel and Coleridge (and Reed and Oegger) but by "turning his ear to the strong accents of daily talk" (*AR*, 35). Not only did he transform Locke's argument for the source of all words in sensible ideas (*spirit* originally meant "breath") into an affirmation of the symbolic nature of the universe, but he also joined the chorus in overturning the related eighteenth-century notion that educated, refined speech was more "proper" and "pure" than common speech. ("What can describe the folly and emptiness of scolding," Emerson asked, "like the word *jawing*?" [quoted in *AR*, 35].) Matthiessen admits that the democratic aspect of Emerson's theory of language—the deliberate attempt to recapture American speech—was widespread at the time, pointing briefly to Theodore Parker, Bronson Alcott, Sylvester Judd, and James Russell Lowell. But these writers remain on the periphery of Matthiessen's "cultural history," for they were unable to follow Emerson in transforming the patriotic impulse into American art. And virtually no mention is made at all of the political champions of American English.[16] The exemplar of the true "rediscovery" of American speech in *American Renaissance* is Whitman, who not only believed that "the fresh opportunities for the English tongue in America were immense, offering themselves in the whole range of American facts" but trumpeted his belief theoretically in *An American Primer* (1855), and, much later, in "Slang in America" (1885) and poetically in the colloquialisms, neologisms, and even the foreign idioms of *Leaves of Grass* (*AR*, 517). But we would seriously distort the historical and cultural significance of his various attempts to reproduce and to create an identifiably American language if we ignored the fact that Whitman was in effect echoing, and playing upon, the ideas of the many language-conscious Americans who preceded him, ideas which differed from his only in degree. Noah Webster's campaign for what he termed "Federal English"—his calls for a vocabulary drawn from American experience, a standard pronunciation that reflected American speech, a grammar grounded in common American usage, and a national language academy to oversee it all—this campaign, which boasted the great publishing successes of Webster's own *American Spelling Book* and the monumental *American Dictionary of the English Language*, also paved the way for Whitman's observation toward the end of his life that *Leaves of Grass* was "only a language experiment—that it is an attempt to give the spirit, the body, the man, new words, new potentialities of speech—an American . . . range of self-expression."[17] That we may appreciate the breadth and variety of the study of language, as well as understand the cultural significance of the linguisticity of the American Renaissance, this thread of American intellectual history—and the historiography that charts it—needs to be followed, too.

The first historians of the study of language in America—in particular of linguistic patriotism—were historians of American English, a fact that goes to the heart of this introductory essay and speaks to the close, if always tenuous, relationship between rhetoric and reality in American culture studies. I refer specifically to the works of H. L. Mencken and George Philip Krapp. Mencken's *The American Language*, first published in 1919, is the earliest and best-known of modern studies of the subject.[18] According to Mencken, the history of the language spoken in the United States begins innocently enough with the arrival of the very first settlers who "had perforce to invent Americanisms"—words like *maize, canoe,* and *bluff*—"if only to describe the unfamiliar landscape and weather, flora and fauna confronting them" (*AL*, 3). The language continued to grow in this way, of course, accruing words not only from Native Americans but from the many ethnic groups that emigrated to the New World over the next three centuries. Americans also changed the language by coining new terms with combinations of common words (*bullfrog, popcorn, backlog*), by changing the meanings of English words (*store, rock, lumber*), and by preserving Anglo-Saxon archaisms (*sick, hustle, chore*). Mencken tells this part of the story—a tale of energy, ingenuity, invention, and national pride—with characteristic verve and relish. "America began to stand for something quite new in the world— in government, in law, in public and private morals, in customs and habits of mind, in the minutiæ of social intercourse," he writes. "And simultaneously the voice of America began to take on its characteristic tone-colors, and the speech of America began to differentiate itself unmistakably from the speech of England" (*AL*, 133). But this, for Mencken, is only part of the story. The full drama of American English is not to be found solely in the record of the unself-conscious development of the language itself but in the history of attitudes about the language, a history of cultural power struggles, of attacks and counterattacks, played out not in some Jacksonian backwoods but in schoolrooms, in legislatures, and, most importantly, on the printed page.

The American Language may thus be said to comprise two interwoven narratives: on one hand, a linguistic melodrama, in which the "loutish ingenuity" of ordinary speakers overcomes the aristocratic pomposity of schoolmarms and aesthetes through the sheer force of American exuberance; on the other hand, an updated and Americanized version of the battle of the books, pitting (in the roles of moderns and ancients) the brave and defiant champions of "American as the living language of a numerous and puissant people" against the English and the (even worse) Anglomaniacal defenders of an effete British standard (*AL*, 52). The dual nature of the story is crucial. *The American Language* is as much an intellectual history as it is a linguistic history: language is considered not only as a natural and spontaneous reflection or expression of "the American mind" but also as a pervasive subject of discussion and debate. To the extent that philological activity actually does influence linguistic development, its inclusion in a history of that development is certainly reasonable: the wide dissemination of Webster's spelling books and dictionaries is a good, if not a scientifically measurable, example. But Mencken's account of the discourse on American English goes far beyond this sort of connection. The idea of an American language is as important to Mencken as the language itself, its literary avatars as important as its speakers, the conception of Webster's dictionary as important as its influence. In large part, the reason lies in Mencken's own authorial circumstances: doing battle himself with the "gogues" and pedagogues of his day—and with the genteel tradition as a whole—he conceived of his own philological project as part of the continuing linguistic history he was charting. The contentiousness of Webster, Cooper, Everett, and the many others he conscripts mirrored his own. As a result, the story of the language draws meaning from the ideological battles that accompanied it. Each utterance—each *hellroaring*, *highfalutin*, *rambunctious*, and *scalawag*—becomes a highly charged speech act because of the literary context in which Mencken presents it. To be sure, this sort of historiography leads inevitably to the confusion of history and ideology, of fact and rhetoric, of observation and projection, as Mencken's critics would point out.[19] But his depiction of the ways in which, and the extent to which, Americans had invested imaginative energy in the discourse on language cannot be so easily dismissed.

For the notion of imaginative investment appears again, in somewhat different form and with different ideological overtones, in George Philip Krapp's *The English Language in America*. When Krapp published his two volumes in 1925, he intended to avoid the "impressionistic" and "polemic" pitfalls of works like Mencken's *American Language*, works that "have usually been more significant as inquiries into social prejudices than into linguistic history."[20] Krapp presents himself as a "disinterested student of American English" and goes to great length to separate Mencken's two narratives, arguing that in the main, despite all the "heated sentiment" imbuing the discourse on American language, the English spoken in America remains very much like the English spoken in Britain. Nevertheless, he too tells a double story, admitting that American linguistic history is different from others, because "in America, speech has not been taken for granted quite so easily" (*ELA*, 1:3). "Though the English language in America did not experience a new birth with the separation of the colonies from Great Britain," Krapp explains, Americans nevertheless began to look at their language "from a new angle" after the Revolution. "The special history of American English" began in a moment of national self-consciousness, when linguistic difference was more a matter of opinion than a matter of fact. Therefore, Krapp argues, "the changing opinions which [Americans] held with respect to [language] must be counted as a part of its essential character" and recorded as part of its history (*ELA*, 1:5).

Krapp agrees with Mencken that language in democratic America shares in the "exuberant development" of the country as a whole, that it has been treated "playfully, sportingly, violently," free from "the restraining sense of conventional propriety to the extent that [it] may have been in eighteenth and nineteenth century England, where the conventions of speech were established by a respected and obeyed upper class" (*ELA*, 1:52). But he insists that the development of American English has nevertheless been mediated, especially in "its more serious uses" (i.e., the written language and educated speech), by a "strong sense of authority" (*ELA*, 1:52). The story Krapp tells in *The English Language in America* is significantly different from Mencken's in that it focuses heavily on the deliberate cultivation and resultant emergence of a standard American English as a national language. Between the ideal American speaker and his speech lies a chasm, as it were, bridged by reflection and design. Although "a nation as a whole rarely gives thought to the trend of development of its speech," he explains, Americans gave serious thought to "the *formation* of a native American speech which should not only be distinctive for American life but should also help the new nation to a realization of those inner purposes and aspirations which were still engaged in the struggle for existence" (*ELA*, 1:6; italics mine). It is as a consciously political instrument of linguistic development that the discourse on language—every textbook written, every appeal to Congress, every spelling and elocution lesson—played its primary, defining role within American linguistic history.

The English Language in America is thus a history of imaginative, and by and large literary, achievement. Because a necessary part of that achievement is self-awareness, Krapp includes certain men of letters in his history not because they contributed to the development of American English but because they either projected the development or captured it in process—because, in effect, their writings adumbrate *The English Language in America*. Noah Webster, for instance, is clearly an important instrumental figure, but Krapp finds his ideas about linguistic uniformity and the creation of a national language of equal, if not greater importance than his pedagogic and lexicographic efforts. Although Webster believed hypothetically that linguistics should be descriptive not prescriptive, Krapp explains, he "did not really conceive the possibility of resting contentedly on the practices of popular speech," whether the local custom of New England or any other region (*ELA*, 1:42). He believed, rather, that in the post-Revolutionary situation the principles of descriptive linguistics (Horace's *usus est jus et norma loquendi*) needed to be compromised in favor of "a certain amount of artificial manipulation" (*ELA*, 1:11). In other words, American English "must be to some extent theoretical and unreal," a fiction, a generalization "based upon the speech of educated speakers" but ultimately "the speech of no community at all" (*ELA*, 1:11, 12, 11). Krapp not only approves of Webster's "compromise" but sees it as prophetic of American linguistic history: standard American English was, in fact, invented, if not solely through the efforts of an individual like Webster, then through the collective efforts of an expanding nation bent on unity. Similarly, Cooper is used to explain and defend—and to give historical and literary authority to—Krapp's conceptualization of the invention of American English. Cooper understood the state of the English language in America, Krapp writes, in paradoxical terms. In *Notions of the Americans* he describes a vast and various nation that spoke an amazingly uniform and universally intelligible language but possessed no official standard—no court, no single cultural center, no elite caste—to determine uniformity. What they did possess, however, was a "*conception* of a national speech," which provided "a guide to conduct as effectual as any recognized or formal rule could be" (*ELA*, 1:15; italics mine). Cooper theorized that Americans spoke "'*reasonable* English,'" a term which served, Krapp explains, "to distinguish between an instinctive social and traditional attitude towards speech, and one in which habits are determined to a greater extent by choice and intention" (*ELA*, 1:15).

In short, just as the critics of the American Renaissance were convinced of the linguisticity of antebellum literature, so the early modern historians of the English language in America were convinced of the language's essential literariness. And just as Mencken's history of the study of language justifies his own linguistic project, so does Krapp's. Consider, for example, the vicissitudes of Walt Whitman's linguistic reputation. In *The American Language* Whitman is an authentic hero, "the first [serious American writer] to explore the literary possibilities of the national language," a man who "ranged himself squarely against the pedagogues who, then as now, were trying to police American English, and bring it into accord with literary English" (*AL*, 73, 74). Mencken refers to *An American Primer* as "an eloquent plea for national independence in language, and in particular for the development of an American style, firmly grounded upon the speech of everyday" and quotes approvingly the following line: "I see that the time is nigh when the etiquette of salo[o]ns is to be discharged from that great thing, the renovated English speech in America" (*AL*, 73).[21] Krapp quotes the same line but to belittle Whitman as a writer who, like others who agreed with him, "did scarcely more than express this desire" and who, "when it came to the actual use of the language for literary purposes . . . could not forget 'the etiquette of saloons,' the cultivated tradition of the past" (*ELA*, 1:21). I am less concerned here with the accuracy or inaccuracy of the two evaluations than with the ground upon which the two histories diverge, i.e., the relation of the study of language to actual language use. Mencken was more apt to celebrate each patriotic polemic, each democratic reform—whether ultimately accepted or rejected—as an expression of American linguistic character, and he would hold in contempt the maligners of "loutish ingenuity" and imaginative power; Krapp was quick to reject the more outlandish demands and suggestions of the linguistic patriots, and he honored only those whose writings supported the hypothesis that Americans were eminently *reasonable* (both sensible and deliberate) in their linguistic choices. Each narrative is informed by a different ideological stance, but neither man could conceive of the history of the language as a thing apart from the history of its study.

More recently, the history of American English has lost its hybrid nature.[22] With the growth of academic specialization, linguists like Albert H. Marckwardt, Charlton Laird, and J. L. Dillard have taken over writing the history of language in America and, with the understanding that the actual development of American English was due less to philological planning and polemic than to more complex (and less rational) sociocultural causes, have all but expunged the history of the study of language from their pages.[23] And the study of language, freed from its positivist attachment to American English, has been taken up by literary critics and intellectual historians, who not only acknowledge the gap between the language(s) Americans used and the languages some imagined but regard the difference between the two as the subject of their discourse.[24]

Dennis Baron's *Grammar and Good Taste*, for instance, is the first scholarly work dedicated solely to the "history of language planning and reform in America."[25] Although his overall scope is broad—pre-Revolutionary times to the present—Baron confines himself primarily to the century following the Revolution, "a period in which the major patterns of American language reform crystallized," and, with minimal reference to actual usage, he surveys the various and manifold efforts of professional and (very frequently) amateur linguists to fiddle with the way their countrymen spoke and wrote (*GGT*, 3). Webster's Federal English is given extensive consideration in a chapter of its own. Franklin, Cooper, and Whitman are discussed as well, along with other figures mentioned by Mencken and Krapp: John Witherspoon, John Pickering, Charles Astor Bristed, Edward Everett. But Baron goes well beyond his predecessors in his encyclopedic presentation of now-obscure works relating to language: tracts on orthographic reform, like William Thornton's *Cadmus; or, A Treatise of the Elements of Written Language* (1793) and James Ewing's *The Columbia Alphabet, Being an Attempt to New Model the English Alphabet* (1798); calls for an academy to regulate language, like Joel Barlow's *Prospectus of a National Institution to Be Established in the United States* (1806) and William Cardell's "Circular

Letter from the Secretary of the American Academy of Language and Belles Lettres" (1821); popular grammar texts like Lindley Murray's *English Grammar Adapted to Different Classes of Learners* (1795), Samuel Kirkham's *Grammar in Familiar Lectures* (1825), and Goold Brown's *Institutes of English Grammar* (1825); and commentaries on proper usage, like Matthew Harrison's *Rise, Progress, and Present Structure of the English Language* (1848) and Edward S. Gould's *Good English; or, Popular Errors in Language* (1867). The very plethora of these works alone justifies their separate treatment. But Baron is not simply elaborating upon the scraps from Mencken's and Krapp's tables. By removing the history of language from the history of its study and by greatly enlarging his scope, Baron signals a significant revision of the historical understandings that inform *The American Language* and *The English Language in America*. He accords linguistic reform a history of its own because, by and large, it existed in a world far removed from the language it sought to reform. Difference is a precondition for Baron's analysis, just as interconnectedness was for Mencken's and Krapp's.

We might say that Baron understands language reform as a kind of literary genre (a species of the jeremiad), complete with its own history, its own conventions, its own recurring themes and tropes.[26] The collective story line: the American language is corrupt and threatens the well-being of the nation; it needs to be purged of (variously) unphonetic spellings, improper grammar, foreign idioms, Americanisms, regional dialects, the name "English." The ending is routinely patriotic and apocalyptic: "The *American Language* will thus be as distinct as the government," as William Thornton wrote in *Cadmus*, "free from all the follies of unphilosophical fashion, and resting upon truth as its only regulator" (*GGT*, 75). And as with other literary genres, the relationship of language reform to American culture is often complex and unclear. Baron thus pointedly introduces his survey as the "history of the *failure* of language reform in America" (*GGT*, 6; italics mine). *Failure* is a critical word, indicating at once the presence and absence of relation: Baron clearly understands the efforts at reform as exercises in futility, but he does not see them as empty gestures. While recognizing that "the schemes to direct, reverse, or otherwise alter the course of the language have always fizzled out," he stresses the fact that, nevertheless, the attempts have persisted and that "American language reformers have been able to arouse the linguistic consciousness, or at least the linguistic insecurity, of the nation" (*GGT*, 2, 5–6). His closing critique of such recent best-selling examples of the genre as Edwin Newman's *Strictly Speaking* (1974), John Simon's *Paradigms Lost* (1980), and William Safire's *On Language* (1980) not only testifies to the truth of Baron's conclusion but ironically undercuts his caveat to "those who would modify the language of [America's] people" that all such attempts at reform "are doomed to fail" (*GGT*, 6). In other words, what emerges from Baron's study is not simply the uselessness or foolhardiness of the attempts at language reform but also the profound ambivalence Americans feel toward the language they speak and write, an ambivalence that sustains the ample literature of language reform as it rejects its prescriptions.

The distance between American linguistic thought and practice in the crucial post-Revolutionary and pre–Civil War years is also the subject of David Simpson's *The Politics of American English, 1776–1850*. But Simpson measures it differently from Baron, taking as his subject not reform and its failure (which foregrounds the rupture between the discourse and the subject it addresses) but the interactive connections between, on one hand, "the development of American English between the Declaration of Independence and the middle of the nineteenth century" and, on the other, the "range of arguments that surrounded [the language's] coming into being."[27] For Simpson, the history of language in America is not easily narrated, for the language itself is not easily delimited. He would argue that it cannot be defined adequately either by Krapp's reasonable uniformity or even Mencken's exuberant fecundity because both deny the historical and political complexity of language use and choice. American English needs to be conceived, rather, as a complex phenomenon, reflecting and affecting the different peoples and the different tensions and anxieties that characterized American culture at the time. The connections between this language and the writings about it are suitably manifold and diverse: some of the works within the "range of arguments" (from tracts and manifestos to poems and novels) succeed in reflecting the language in all its complexity, others in distorting it, still others in masking it. Simpson even allows that "two generations of linguistic pioneers," Webster in the forefront, were to an extent responsible for the way the language developed. But in each case, Simpson makes clear, the work offers only an image of the language, not the language itself. Linguistic literature is thus presented as a type of fiction, its fictionality lying not (as it did for Baron) in its total divorce from linguistic reality but in its engagement with it, for better or worse. Simpson conceives of the history of language study as a series of imaginative renderings, politically motivated and ideologically charged, of the American linguistic situation before the American Renaissance. More deliberately than Mencken, Krapp, or Baron, Simpson fashions his history as a work of literary criticism: although he declares his aim to be in part a demonstration that an English "significantly, if not substantially" different from that used in England had developed by the end of the period he documents—which coincides by design with the beginning of Matthiessen's "extraordinarily concentrated moment of expression"—the documentary and descriptive aspects of Simpson's historiographical project are clearly subsumed by the interpretive and critical (*PAE*, 3). The material he examines is predominantly either scholarly or belletristic: the works of literary figures like Hugh Henry Brackenridge, James Kirk Paulding, James Fenimore Cooper, and Ralph Waldo Emerson are scrutinized for the "image[s] of the language" they project, and linguists like Noah Webster are valued for "the trends and tensions that show up in [their] writings" (*PAE*, 129, 56). The existence of the complex world of linguistic phenomena outside of and prior to the examples he examines is for the most part assumed in *The Politics of American English*, an assumption largely and solidly based on the early archival scholarship of Mencken and Allen Walker Read (more than on Krapp, whose emphasis on, and valorization of, standard English strikes no responsive chords in Simpson) and informed by the conviction shared with contemporary sociolinguists like J. L. Dillard that American English is continually in flux, that at any point it is various rather than unified, and that linguistic purity is a myth. Still, the "mere existence" of this "language still becoming" (the title of the introductory chapter) is absolutely crucial to Simpson's argument (*PAE*, 3). Indeed, the existence of this linguistic *Ding an sich* is the touchstone of the fictionality of language study: Simpson analyzes the literature primarily in terms of its willingness to confront, or its desire to deny, the multiplicity of language in America—regional, class, and ethnic dialects, neologisms and Americanisms, orthographic reforms—and the complex social relations that such a language reflects.

To understand American literature and culture this way is to offer a pointed, revisionary critique of Matthiessen's *American Renaissance*. Like Matthiessen, Simpson insists on looking at his writers "from the specific point of view of language and diction" (*PAE*, 15). Like Matthiessen, too, he sees language as the key to cultural history: "This importance [of language] is experienced individually, in the life of every speaker," Simpson writes, "and also collectively, as a historical constituent in our wider cultural situation" (*PAE*, 5). But he does not understand an artist's "resources of language" in the same way as does Matthiessen. In a self-proclaimed "tendentious" closing chapter on the Transcendentalists, Simpson argues that Emerson's view of language was profoundly reactionary. His "speculation about language *itself*, as a whole," his emphasis on symbolism and organicism, his blurring of the distinction between individual utterance and universal being, and his failure to discuss actual linguistic tensions and divisions—all these together indict Transcendentalism as "the literary and philosophical correlative of the mythology of manifest destiny" (*PAE*, 231). Even Emerson's occasional poetic embracing of American English—of "the language of the street"—is maligned: rather than representing the artistic fulfillment of the Revolution, his "sporadic" use of colloquialisms depends for its effect "precisely on the hegemony of the norms of syntax and vocabulary they pretend to subvert" (*PAE*, 244). If the "age of Emerson and Whitman" is wedded to this theory of language, Simpson argues, then our valorization of the American Renaissance needs to be revaluated.

As Irwin turns to the uncanonized Poe to revise Matthiessen's understanding of the linguisticity of the American Renaissance, so Simpson turns to Cooper. In two long chapters, Simpson carefully and thoroughly examines the ideas Cooper expressed about American English in *Notions of the Americans* and *The American Democrat*, his actual usage of American spellings and locutions in his letters, and, in particular, the social world of language that is imagined in the Leatherstocking tales. If Cooper applauds American linguistic uniformity in his cultural criticism, he nevertheless fills his novels with "the unassimilated languages of America," assiduously, if not always accurately, reproducing the peculiarities of regional dialects, ethnic accents, and the varieties of Native American speech (*PAE*, 229). This "babel of voices," combined with the characteristically unlettered speech of Natty Bumppo himself and other linguistic phenomena, articulate a theme of "linguistic tension" that "remains an important part of [Cooper's] analysis of the wider strains emerging within the republic" (*PAE*, 159, 185). What Simpson finds in Cooper's novels is a world "dominated by strife and division" and in Cooper himself "a consciousness divided by precisely the tension that informed much of the theory and experience of the Jacksonian period" (*PAE*, 231, 154). As a result, he writes, Cooper's art is characterized less by organicism—Matthiessen's yardstick—than by conflict and irresolution, and he privileges this sort of art precisely for being "as ungainly as the historical conditions it represents" (*PAE*, 231). *The Politics of American English* may be seen, in fact, as a version of Lukács's *The Historical Novel*, with Cooper playing the role of his model, Walter Scott, the writer whose fiction embodies the ideal of literary art—fidelity to world historical forces. So construed, Simpson not only critiques Matthiessen but inverts (or, perhaps, subverts) him: meeting him on his own ground—that of language—he retraces Matthiessen's removal of his five writers from the domain of social history to that of literary criticism. The Progressive Parrington is not rehabilitated, to be sure, but in *The Politics of American English* literature becomes once more documentary—if not the source of social-historical knowledge, then a confirmation of it. Language remains the focus of the literary critic's inquiry, but Simpson no longer perceives it as a timeless aesthetic entity so much as a concrete historical fact. And the study of language blurs the disciplinary boundaries separating literary, intellectual, and political history.

I do not mean to offer Simpson as a model for a new post-Revolutionary and pre–Civil War literary history grounded in the contemporaneous study of language. Like the other works I have surveyed in the second half of this Introduction, *The Politics of American English* is partial, in both senses of the term. Still, Simpson's tendentious inversion/subversion of Matthiessen offers a convenient point of departure for some summary and concluding remarks. First of all, and ironically, Simpson reaffirms, even as he seeks to redefine, the fundamental notion of the linguisticity of the American Renaissance. He has less overturned Matthiessen's literary analysis of Emerson than adopted an accusatory stance toward it: they both see the same Emerson, but they value him differently. Indeed, by detailing the considerable interest in language among American men of letters between the Revolution and the Civil War, the historians of the study of language in general establish the essential historicity of the findings of Matthiessen, Feidelson, and the literary critics who followed them: despite their various critical stances and, in some cases, their eschewing of historical referentiality, we can confirm with some degree of assurance that they were indeed responding to manifest characteristics of the texts themselves.

But what Simpson has done directly—and what Baron and the others have done indirectly—is challenge the particular way linguisticity is approached and contextualized. The resurrection of Webster, Cooper, and the other students and observers of language (belletristic and non-belletristic, well known and obscure) disputes the assertion that Emerson was the first American writer to think profoundly about language or even that he was the first to think about language in a Coleridgean way. He was only the first American writer *whom we value for particular aesthetic and ideological reasons* to have done so. Furthermore, the pervasive presence of a Humboldtian symbolism in American Renaissance writers cannot be taken to be indicative of its pervasiveness in the culture at large: symbolist discourse can be seen to have been only one of many subdiscourses generated by a larger intellectual and cultural concern with language—a subdiscourse that, again, *we value for particular aesthetic and ideological reasons*. Nor can we any longer see philosophical symbolism as the only, or even the primary, subdiscourse of which the American Renaissance is the literary expression: we must now take into account at least linguistic patriotism and biblical hermeneutics, if not Egyptology as well. In short, language was clearly a subject that fired the minds and imaginations of diverse thinkers and writers in diverse ways in

America from the Revolution to the Civil War, and the scope of the Matthiessen-Feidelson thesis needs to be significantly revised to account for this.

This is not to suggest that intellectual history ought to replace literary history and certainly not that content analysis is more evidentially sound than stylistic analysis. But literary critics who have pretensions toward cultural and intellectual history cannot sit comfortably within the confines of the protective walls formed by the canon. And intellectual historians cannot be satisfied with a purely documentary understanding of the broader range of texts they study. I have been trying to argue throughout that literary critics who have focused upon the linguisticity of American texts have generally tended to write forms of intellectual history and that intellectual historians who have taken the study of language for their subject have inevitably written forms of literary history. The logic of my history dictates that some interdisciplinary methodology needs to be adopted. If, for instance, both Webster and Whitman thought imaginatively about language and produced texts in order to reflect that thought, then some common ground needs to be established upon which a comparative textual analysis of their writings can begin.

Some such ground has already been suggested by the majority of the writers I have treated, both literary critics and linguistic historians. As I have pointed out, Matthiessen, Poirier, Bell, Mencken, Krapp, Baron, and Simpson each believed that ideas about language were inextricably intertwined in the minds of Americans with ideas about America. That is to say—if I may offer a composite argument—that public discourse on language, in its various manifestations, was grounded in the ideology and rhetoric of American exceptionalism, that however Americans thought about language—profoundly or superficially, abstractly or concretely, poetically or prosaically—they very often thought about it in terms of its actual or potential use in an *American* (i.e., democratic, privileged, blessed) society or its status as *American* (patriotic, pure, prophetic) expression. Literary analysis of these writings can and should proceed from the imaginative interplay of these two sets of ideas.

Let me offer an early, brief, and explicit example as a coda to this Introduction. Even before the Revolutionary War had ended, indeed, in the wake of a series of military defeats at the hands of Clinton and Cornwallis, John Adams sent a letter from Amsterdam, urging Congress to establish an "American Academy for the refining, improving, and ascertaining the English Language."[28] In a few fecund paragraphs, Adams offers numerous disparate and fragmentary arguments (he calls them "hints") to support his recommendation, bolstering them with assertions of their indisputability and self-evidence, linking them so as to make them appear mutually supportive by virtue of their contiguity, and muting contradiction by accentuating the positive and forgoing elaboration. Each and all of these hints suggest that the nascent United States had—or ought to have—a special relationship to language: Adams determines from their recurrent concurrence in history that republics, eloquence, and linguistic purity are causally related; he posits the Condillacian principle that form of government, language, and national character are reciprocally influential; he notes that the classical republics have provided models of eloquence which continue to form "an essential part of the education of mankind" and links this fact (through sheer syntactic force) to the "liberty, prosperity, and glory" of the United States; he remarks that France, Spain, and Italy (not a republic among them) have already established greatly successful language academies but that England has failed to do so, leaving the honor and opportunity to Congress; he predicts that linguistic uniformity will cultivate political unity; he expects "that eloquence will become the instrument for recommending men to their fellow citizens, and the principal means of advancement" in America's democratic polity; and he foresees that, with America's continued growth and expanded international connections, English is "destined" to replace French, as French had replaced Latin, as "the language of the world."[29] Informed by an inclusive and expanding vision of America, Adams's letter moves with seeming effortlessness from ancient history to rising glory, from Old World to New World, from colony to world power, each time reiterating a trope of progress that elides the current critical state of the war: substituting speech acts for military acts, Adams asserts the power of language by using a language of American power.[30]

Adams's call for a language academy went unheeded, but his list of "the motives which the people of America have to turn their thoughts early to this subject" can yet serve as an introduction to the manifold literature on language produced in the decades that followed. In its rhetorical complexity, Adams's letter stands at the threshold of, and clearly anticipates, a period during which language was "loaded"—not only in the sense of ethnic and class multivocality that Simpson elaborates, but in the sense that language was widely perceived to be the very lifeblood of the new nation (*PAE*, 7). Adams's prose looks forward both to his son's sanguine description of the republic as a "dominion of the voice . . . where every citizen . . . has the means and opportunity of delivering his opinions, and of communicating his sentiments by speech" and to the satiric portrait in *Salmagundi* of the young United States as "a pure unadulterated LOGOCRACY or *government of words*," where everything is done "*viva voce*, or by word of mouth," and power is measured by "the *gift of the gab*" and by "*force of tongues*."[31] In the historical narrative that, as I see it, the efforts of scholars over many decades combine to tell, Adams's brief letter foreshadows a multifarious series of works: among others, Webster's *Dissertations on the English Language*; Hamilton, Madison, and Jay's *The Federalist*; Longfellow's "Defence of Poetry"; Bushnell's *God in Christ*; Hawthorne's *The Scarlet Letter*; Whitman's *An American Primer*. But to read the narrative we will have to hold our disciplinary creeds in abeyance and contend with the linguists.

Part One

TEACHING LANGUAGE IN
AMERICA

"*NOW* is the Time, and *This* is the Country": How Noah Webster Invented American English

STRICTLY SPEAKING, Noah Webster did *not* invent American English. The language spoken in the United States, shaped by the host of diverse factors that constitute American culture in a complex and ongoing process of change and development—this language cannot in good conscience be joined syntactically to the subject *Noah Webster*, nor to the verb *invent*.[1] To be sure, Webster did try to have an impact upon the development of American English—and to an extent he did succeed: the enormous popularity and influence of the *Blue-Back Speller* (originally published as the first part of *A Grammatical Institute of the English Language* in 1783) and of the *American Dictionary* of 1828 can hardly be denied or even measured.[2] But not even Webster himself, little known for his humility, would ever have made my title's extravagant claim. His declared goal, however grandly he or his hagiographers proclaimed it, was standardization and (less successfully) reform. He appealed repeatedly for a national language, in print and at the podium, but he did not, by any stretch of the imagination or looseness of definition, invent American English. However, we are still faced with what may be rhetorically termed the *inventio* in Webster's philological writings: although he may not be said to have actually invented the language—perhaps because he did not—he did work hard to fictionalize it, to take hold of the unruly creation brought forth by the culture upon the continent and, by transcribing its words and formulating its rules in his various texts, to re-create it in the image of the America he imagined. To read Webster on language is to read American literature.

This is not how Webster's writing has traditionally been perceived. In *The Quest for Nationality* (1957), for instance, Benjamin Spencer could remark that no one in the post-Revolutionary period more "unremittingly insisted that 'America must be as independent in *literature* as she is in *politics*'" than Noah Webster. But Spencer was led to infer that, despite the memorable battle cries, "belletristic authors could find among his exhortations disappointingly few hints as to how such independence might be achieved." He painted Webster approvingly as an indefatigable linguist, "toil[ing] at *lexicography* in order to free America from a reliance on English opinions and English books" but falling short of the politico-aesthetic goal of a truly American literature, a goal not achieved until (following Matthiessen) the middle of the nineteenth century. For Spencer, Webster was only a type, as it were, of the fully realized American writer, adumbrating the coming of Whitman (Spencer's example), but caught in the progressive design of American literary history as a lesser, partial precursor.[3]

Spencer's brief account of Webster is significant for several reasons. First of all, it exemplifies the sort of problematic disciplinarity I have tried to outline in my Introduction, a disciplinarity that at once valorizes literary works because they articulate theories of language and discounts linguistic works because they are not literary. Spencer includes Webster in *The Quest for Nationality* precisely because he is a lexicographer and then limits his importance through a categorical distinction between lexicography and literature: both critical acts are authorized—just as his history of ideas is emplotted—by the historical and aesthetic assumptions that sustain Matthiessen's canon. Second, Spencer's account embodies clearly what I take to be the central problematic of Webster scholarship in general: the need to make sense of apparently conflicting tendencies in Webster's writings, to reconcile, most significantly, Webster's strident nationalistic rhetoric with the seemingly tamer substance of his major work. Earlier scholars, intent on building Webster's reputation, tended to obscure the problem, celebrating Webster's rhetoric, while either ignoring, denying, glossing over, or apologizing for the derivative, "un-American" aspects of his texts.[4] More recently, scholars have looked squarely at Webster's inconsistencies, placing them at the center of what has become a significant reappraisal of Webster's life and work. The new interest in the study of language in America—in its political, social, philosophical, and aesthetic implications—and a more profound understanding of the conflicts and anxieties that characterized American life during the period of the early republic have transformed Webster from a previous generation's "schoolmaster to America" into, as one writer has recently summarized it, "a man of many parts—complex, full of intellectual tensions and paradoxes . . . often confused."[5] Spencer's particular resolution of the problem falls between these two approaches and is of a piece with his disciplinary assumptions. By fixing him at a particular point within the progressive continuum of American literary history defined by Matthiessen, he is able (tacitly) to reconcile Webster's persistent calls for literary independence and his inability either to produce or suggest suitable models: like all the other writers who lived before "the Age of Emerson and Whitman," Webster lived too soon and his efforts were bound to be partial. But to achieve this narrative resolution, Spencer must necessarily suppress Webster's own eighteenth-century understanding of the quest for a national literature and the role of his own writing in that quest. More generally, he must ignore the literary sophistication of the post-Revolutionary generation.[6]

Three decades after its publication, *The Quest for Nationality* remains the most comprehensive survey we have of the campaign for a uniquely American literature, and if it distorts the nature of Webster's philological efforts, it also reminds us at the same time that Webster may be considered in terms of a *literary* tradition—both American and (as a revolutionary tradition has to revolt against something) European. And it is precisely in this respect—as a literary problem—that the question of Webster's contradictory tendencies has yet to be addressed.[7] After all, what gives coherence to Webster's long, prolific, and fascinatingly variegated career is the fact that he was, above all, a man of letters: over the course of sixty years he wrote or compiled dozens of books, pamphlets, and articles on everything from politics and religion to natural history and epidemiology, not to mention the primary focuses of his career, language and education. Though much scholarly attention has been given to Webster as a linguistic and educational reformer, and though we now understand better the importance of politics and religion in his evolving intellectual makeup, we still do not appreciate Webster as a writer, as a determined, self-conscious practitioner of (as he understood it) a distinctly American discourse. Yet, from the very beginning, when he first "look[ed] into our language and the methods of instruction practiced in this country" and became "convinced of the necessity of improving the one and correcting the other," he thought of his efforts at reform in literary terms, that, as he put it, "a person of [his] youth may have some influence in exciting [in America] a spirit of *literary* industry" (*LNW*, 3–4; italics mine).[8] This is not to suggest that Webster was literary in the same way Whitman (or Longfellow) was to be literary. To the contrary (and most simply, for there are other important distinctions), Webster and his contemporaries included in the category of literature much writing—scientific, political, theological—that Whitman (and we latter-day Romantics) would pointedly exclude, and vice versa.[9] What I want to suggest is that, in general, we can learn much about Webster by taking his writing seriously in the ways we take more conventionally literary writing seriously and that, in particular, Webster's early writings on language—*A Grammatical Institute of the English Language* and *Dissertations on the English Language*—need to be considered, not as the harbingers of literary nationality, but as significant and rhetorically complex early attempts to imagine both an American language and linguistics and, thereby, to define and exemplify American literary independence.

THOMAS DILWORTH AND THOMAS PAINE

Noah Webster compiled the initial two parts of his first work, *A Grammatical Institute of the English Language*, in 1782, while he was teaching school in Goshen, New York, and "the American army was lying [nearby] on the bank of the Hudson." He published the first part of it—the elementary speller that would become one of the three best-selling books in American history—"at the close of the revolution," only months after the Treaty of Paris formally put an end to the hostilities.[10] The timing was of great significance to Webster: even late in his career, well after his youthful enthusiasm for revolutionary principles had subsided, Webster would continue to recall the coincidence of events. It is no wonder, then, that the original title of the *Institute* was *The American Instructor* or that the slim, otherwise unpretentious volume was couched in a rhetoric of revolution. Forcefully attacking his British predecessors, Webster's now oft-quoted introduction sought to establish fundamental connections between the political transformations of the previous eight years and the pedagogic and linguistic reforms he envisioned for the new republic. "Europe is grown old in folly, corruption and tyranny," Webster wrote. Now that the war was over, it was imperative that Americans carry the revolution into the world of letters, for, he felt, "an attention to literature must be the principal bulwark against the encroachments of civil and ecclesiastical tyrants, and American Liberty can die only with her *Maecenases*."[11]

But in many ways Webster's book was neither revolutionary nor particularly American. For the most part, *A Grammatical Institute of the English Language* constituted a modest revised version of Thomas Dilworth's popular *New Guide to the English Tongue* (1740) and, as such, a minor variation on a well-known British theme.[12] Webster argued that "the *standard* of pronunciation"—perhaps his major concern in *Part I*—should be neither radically democratic nor particularly American "but the customary pronunciation of the most accurate scholars and literary Gentlemen," and he readily deferred to Johnson's dictionary on matters of "spelling and accenting . . . as in point of orthography this seems to be the most approved authority in the language" (*GI*, 6, 11).[13] Indeed, the major contemporaneous criticism leveled against his *Institute*—by, among others, a pseudonymous "Dilworth's Ghost"—was plagiarism.[14] And in fact, Webster did little to deny the derivativeness of his text. In applying to the Connecticut legislature for copyright, he described his speller in terms of its "amendments" to Dilworth and his proposed grammar (the second part of the *Grammatical Institute*) as "an abridgment . . . extracted from the most approved modern writers upon the subject, with his own observations and some notes pointing out the most common and flagrant errors in speaking and writing, the whole being reduced to the capacity of children" (*LNW*, 1–2). After publication, when answering the accusation that he had been guilty of merely "compiling and transcribing" his *Institute*, he remarked only "that every grammar that was ever written is a compilation," reasoning that the "man who arranges the principles of the languages in the best form and reduces the ideas to the easiest method compiles the *best* Grammar" (*LNW*, 13).

To be sure, some of Webster's pedagogic reforms were substantial—his revision of Dilworth's method of syllabic division, for example.[15] And his substitution of "the names of the United States, the counties in each, &c." for Dilworth's "twelve or fifteen pages devoted to names of English, Scotch, and Irish towns and boroughs" was certainly, and appropriately, American (*GI*, 11, 10). Moreover, Webster was not alone in feeling acutely the need for change: others readily concurred and greeted Webster's revisions as welcome innovations. "Dilworth's grammatical plan is much worse than nothing," Joel Barlow wrote to him. "It holds up a scarecrow in the English language, and lads once lugged into it when young are afraid of all kinds of grammar all their days after." Upon reading the *Institute*, Timothy Pickering acclaimed it as "the very thing I have so long wished for, being much dissatisfied with any spelling book I had seen before." Elizur Goodrich agreed that it was "not only ingenious, but a real improvement upon former treatises of this kind" and even cautioned the fledgling author that his "zeal" to reform Dilworth's method of syllabification was "rather intemperate."[16] Still, Webster's claim that "one half of [Dilworth's] work is totally useless and the other half defective and erroneous" was certainly exaggerated (*GI*, 10).[17] Webster's former teacher Joseph Buckminster, who observed in support of his student that "no person that has paid any attention to the State of our language or the manner in which children are led to an acquaintance with it but have been sensible that there was room for improvement," chided Webster for the shrillness of his criticisms of Dilworth and wondered, rather pointedly, "if an ill natured world does not ascribe some of [Webster's critical] observations not so much to [Dilworth's] deficiencies as to [Webster's] desire to give currency to [his] Institute."[18]

We see the sort of interpretive quandary Webster presents to the historian. On one hand, he labors to secure a place within the current discourse on linguistic pedagogy, to be perceived as someone who has mastered a tradition (a primarily conservative tradition at that) and has preserved its best features. On the other hand, his stance is rejectionist and he presents the changes he introduces as revolutionary in nature. Given

Webster's strident personality, Buckminster's evaluation of his student's self-promotional motives offers a cogent biographical explanation. And certainly other equally compelling psychobiographical interpretations may be found of the young American's verbal tar-and-feathering of the author—by then an institution—whom Barlow called "the nurse of us all." But to resort to these or other sorts of extratextual explanations (like Spencer's historical antecedence) is not so much to explain Webster's rhetoric as to explain it away. It does not change the fact that Webster's revolution against Dilworth (such as it was) is inscribed in the text itself—in the rhetoric of its preface, in the contiguity of its preface and the body of the text—and announces itself as a set of intertextual responses, both to the *Institute*'s generic British predecessors (particularly the *New Guide*) and to the radical political writing that flourished in America during the war years (particularly the works of Thomas Paine). Webster may seem to say one thing and mean another, but the paradoxical nature of Webster's revolution is manifestly a literary problem, not an ethical one, and deserves to be understood as such.

We can best begin to appreciate the literariness of Webster's hostility toward Dilworth by looking closely at the *New Guide*, not primarily to elucidate its substantive methodology but to uncover its imaginative underpinnings—to fill in the cultural spaces (as it were) between the columns of spelling words and lists of grammar rules and to bring to the surface the ideological assumptions that underlie the text and inform, most explicitly, the narrative, figurative, and even compositorial structure of its preface. To understand how Webster invented *American* English, in other words, we will first have to explain how Dilworth invented English.

To some extent, all attempts to standardize language bespeak an imagined world of stability, stratification, and deference—as well as an actual world somewhat more volatile—and the *New Guide* plainly exemplifies this. It was specifically intended as a primer for use in "the several *Charity-Schools* in *Great-Britain* and *Ireland*" and was tellingly dedicated to the benefactors of these schools, men characterized by "Zeal for the Glory of GOD, and the *Public Good* of these Nations," to whom "the poorer Sort of People owe their *Obedience*."[19] The theme of obedience announced immediately after the title page is elaborated throughout the volume, most thoroughly in the reading exercises presented in part 4. Here Dilworth gathers together, in prose and poetry, "several divine, moral, and historical Sentences," which he feels "may not only serve the *Master* to exercise his *Scholars* . . . but may render the Business of *Reading* as *useful* and *pleasant* as possible to the *Learner*" (*NG*, ix). Although the pleasantness of the readings may not be immediately apparent to us, the usefulness of these maxims for the overt dissemination of hegemonic values may be seen even at a brief perusal. The exercises encourage expanded literacy as they staunchly defend the legitimacy of the House of Hanover and the existing class structure of British society: work hard, love God, fear sin, be loyal to the King, be content with your lot, stay out of prison, respect your elders and betters, learn how to read.[20] These values, so clearly articulated in part 4, are variously inscribed throughout the volume. They may be found underlying a note on usage—as when Dilworth remarks that "it argues . . . a Disrespect and Slighting to use *Contractions* to our *Betters*, and is often puzzling to others" (*NG*, 126)—and may even be said to be implied in the catechistic presentation of grammar rules.[21] And they are neatly summed up in the prayers "for the Use of Schools" that close the volume: "And because Thou hast made no Man for himself only, but all of us for the mutual Help of each other, grant that we may so diligently apply ourselves to our Studies, that increasing every Day in Piety and good Literature, we may at length become not only useful to ourselves, but ornamental also, both to the State we live in, and to the true holy catholic Church" (*NG*, 151). Weaving together the laws of God, Nation, and language, the *New Guide* serves up the elementary study of language as a tool for the socialization of (most directly) lower-class boys in mid-eighteenth-century Britain.[22]

Dilworth's preface justifies the *New Guide*—its pedagogy and its politics—by identifying it as an integral aspect of English Reformation history. During the Middle Ages—Dilworth calls them "the Days of Darkness and implicit Zeal"—men "grop'd their Way to Virtue and Knowledge" because they "were taught little more than to mumble over a few Prayers by Heart, and never called upon to read, much less permitted to enquire into the Truth of what they professed." However, "since the Sunshine of the *Gospel* of *Jesus Christ* has risen amongst us," "Improvements in Learning" have been encouraged, and "*Ignorance* has gradually vanished" (*NG*, iv).[23] *Gradually*—this key word collapses within itself the two centuries of British history prior to the publication of the *New Guide* and conceals the political upheavals and religious conflicts—including most prominently the two seventeenth-century revolutions—that followed upon the heels of the Reformation, indeed may be said to have been a result of it. This suppression is crucial to the design of the preface. Having metaphorically represented the Reformation as a slow and gradual natural process, Dilworth then transplaces the word "gradually" to spin a web of mutually reinforcing analogies that join nature, history, and psychology to the pedagogic method of the *New Guide*: as the rising sun gradually banishes darkness, so the Reformation has gradually spread true religion, so learning and literacy have gradually increased, so "all Learning gradually ascends from the first Knowledge and use of *Letters*, *Syllables* and *Words*," and so (leaping nimbly from *is* to *ought*) language "should be taught in the same order, proceeding gradually from Words of *two Letters*, to words of *three*, *four*, *five*, &c. *Letters*" (*NG*, iv, vi). The typographic composition of the preface seems to underscore this theme: the argument unfolds gradually, smoothed by the placement of key transitional words syntactically belonging to the opening of a paragraph—"Thus," "But," "Therefore," "And," etc.—at the conclusion of the paragraph preceding it.[24] And so, through an intricate rhetoric of gradualism, "the Knowledge of the Will of Him our Creator" (ironically shown in the very texture of the text to be revealed in nature and history as well as in Scripture) is linked logically/analogically to "a true Knowledge" of spelling.

Essentially, Dilworth's argument is drawn from the same Protestant well that sustained the Puritan defense of plain style a century earlier: precision in language use is "of so great Consequence to human Creatures," because through "the Use of *Letters*, *Syllables* and *Words* . . . Man may . . . arrive to the Knowledge of the Will of Him our *Creator*, revealed in the sacred Oracles of his Divine Word" (*NG*, v). But while the Puritans' reformist approach to language reflected the fundamental and widespread changes (social and economic, as well as religious) that overwhelmed British society in the sixteenth and seventeenth centuries and helped fuel a revolution, Dilworth's preface makes clear that his pedagogic reforms were conceived to be fundamentally conservative.[25] Much was morally at stake, to be sure, and the preface paints the alternatives in starkly oppositional terms, offering what amounts to a moral economy of spelling: incorrect spelling is "wrong," "depraved," "unfortunate," "barbarous," "cruel"—in short, "an Evil"; whereas correct spelling is "true," "proper," "right," "natural," "just"—in short, "Order" and "Perfection" (*NG*, iv–vi). And not any method would do: "It is as bad to learn the *first Rudiments of Literature* under wrong and depraved Habits, as not to learn them at all" (*NG*, iv). But the rhetoric of gradualism—the location of the primer within an inclusive and highly integrated gradualist framework of sacred, secular, and natural history, the manner in which the *New Guide*'s substantive methodology reflects that framework, and the spatial arrangement of the preface to underscore both—this rhetoric harnesses the force of the moral imperative at the very moment it is unleashed. The very fact that Englishmen may "boast of greater Advantages than our Forefathers" mutes the warning, "let us take care, lest we frustrate that great Work begun amongst us, by a negligent Prosecution of our Duty" (*NG*, iv). Zeal, not zealotry, was required for spreading literacy. The *New Guide* was meant to be new but not—emphatically not—revolutionary.

So considered, the popularity of the *New Guide* represented more to Webster at the close of the Revolution than the prevalence of an outdated method of teaching children how to read. It signaled, rather, the embeddedness of profoundly counterrevolutionary literary tendencies, and Webster may be seen to have composed the *Institute* with the general aim of contesting Dilworth by incorporating the fact of the Revolution into his text, from the title page—which advertises the primer "for the Use of *English* Schools in AMERICA"—on through the preface, the various syllable and word lists, and the reading exercises. Many of his nonsubstantive revisions of Dilworth simply and frankly proclaim the new political reality: the much-remarked lists of American toponyms that replace Dilworth's lists of British toponyms, and, perhaps most notably, "A Chronological Account of [forty] remarkable Events in America" (events which, except for the first half-dozen, chronicle the Revolution) that closes the volume (*GI*, 118–119). Other revisions seek to implement Revolutionary literary change: Webster eschews the conventional (and conventionally obsequious) dedicatory preface, for instance, preferring to let the book "make its own way in the world"—literary practice here reflecting the democratic-capitalist ideology of self-making (*GI*, 14). Others are more subtly Revolutionary: the model conversations Webster presents in the section "Familiar Phrases, and easy Dialogues, for young beginners" suggest the intercourse of equals—each interlocutor self-assertive yet respectful of the integrity of the other—without calling attention to themselves as such.[26] Similarly, "deviations from propriety and the standard of elegant pronunciation" are presented as "provincial and local distinctions," not as matters of class (*GI*, 7n). Although the moralistic tone (and some of the language) of many of Dilworth's preliminary reading exercises remains, the imagined world of the *Institute* is clearly not the stratified, antirevolutionary world of the *New Guide*.

If the *New Guide* buries the English revolutions of 1640 and 1689 beneath the rhetoric of gradualism, the *Grammatical Institute* places the Revolution of 1776 at its conceptual core. Webster wants not only to make the Revolution present in the text but to *revolutionize* the text itself, and what marks this is not simply the imagined world in which the text is couched but the *Grammatical Institute*'s insistence that it is different from Dilworth. The *Grammatical Institute* presents itself not simply as a version of the *New Guide* but as a self-conscious enactment of a revisionary process, noting where, how, and to what extent Dilworth's method and text (as well as those of other grammarians, like Daniel Fenning) have been emended. Several revisions are noted in the text itself, but they are most extensively and emphatically presented in the introduction. Here the Revolution enters the text not only as a fact, not only as a political presence, but as a rhetorical structure: revisions are introduced, as it were, under the auspices of the Revolution and take on its character. Just as Dilworth turns in his preface to the Reformation for ideological justification, so Webster turns in his introduction to the Revolution. Just as the *New Guide* is presented as an extension of the Reformation, so the *Grammatical Institute* is offered as an extension of the Revolution. Indeed, Webster seems to be working here with an open copy of Dilworth's preface in front of him, closely following his rhetorical strategy. But the Revolution does not simply stand in as an American Reformation: the distinction in content between the two authorizing events undercuts and overturns the structural similarities. "Previously to the late war," Webster writes, "America preserved the most unshaken attachment to Great-Britain," politically and intellectually. "But by a concurrence of those powerful causes that effect *almost instantaneous revolutions* in states, the political views of America have suffered *a total change*" (*GI*, 3; italics mine). In substituting "instantaneous" and "total" for "gradual," Webster presents the Revolution as the overthrow of the ideological stance inscribed in Dilworth's Reformation. Hence the attack on Dilworth's defenders: "Those who rail so much at *new things* ought to consider, that every improvement in life was once *new*; the reformation by Luther was once *new*; the Christian religion was once *new*; nay their favourite Dilworth was once a *new thing*" (*GI*, 13). Innovation is here valorized as revolutionary (not gradual) change and Dilworth's now ironical title is made to bear the full weight of the primer's obsolescence. *Once* new, now superseded: "As Mr. Dilworth's New Guide (which by the way, is the *oldest* and most imperfect guide we use in schools) is commonly used and his authority become as sacred as the traditions of the Jews, or the Mahometan bible, I shall take the liberty to make some remarks upon it, with that plainness that is due to truth" (*GI*, 8). In short, the *Grammatical Institute* is an American book because it stages a literary revolution in its pages.

Let me underscore at this point that I am not trying to make a case for including the *Grammatical Institute* in an American literary tradition that is, in essence, revolutionary. Nor am I suggesting that the *Grammatical Institute* is *in fact* revolutionary. My point is, rather, that Webster imagined that, in order to "give fulfilment to the potentialities freed by the Revolution," his primer would have not only to amend Dilworth and to reflect the new political realities but also to engage Dilworth and the British grammatical tradition in rhetorical battle. And in adopting this approach, he was influenced heavily by the Revolutionary writings of Thomas Paine. In the early 1780s, under the tutelage of the Genevan Huguenot minister John Peter Tetard, Webster began an intensive reading of Paine's works (as well as the writings of Montesquieu, Rousseau, and the Abbé Raynal), and the echoes of his rhetoric in the introduction to the *Institute* are unmistakable.[27]

Paine is generally recognized to have changed the nature of the debate between Great Britain and the American colonies, to have (in a word) revolutionized Revolutionary writing. Whether or not this is precisely true, it can be accurately noted that a deliberate disruption of conventional political discourse is the foundation of his literary strategy. "Volumes have been written on the subject of the struggle between England and America," he wrote in *Common Sense*. Prior to the battle of Lexington and Concord, arguments "advanced by the advocates on either side of the question . . . terminated in one and the same point, viz., a union with Great Britain." Now that the battle had commenced, "the period of debate is closed," and all those "plans, proposals, &c . . . are like the almanacks of the last year; which tho' proper then, are superceded and useless now." In short, "a new æra for politics is struck—a new method for thinking hath arisen."[28] The key to Paine's literary enterprise lies in the dash that conjoins these two balanced clauses, that posits typographically an ambiguous, reciprocal relation between politics and thought and between cause and effect. The purpose of *Common Sense*, indeed of all Paine's works, was to effect political change through intellectual change—to construct/discover the link between the political situation and its sustaining ideologies, to sever the link, and to substitute new modes of thought that would lead to further political action—to move, as it were, from one clause to the other. It follows that, although Paine's target is ultimately the king and the British Constitution, he takes direct aim at other political writers, those who have "so confounded society with government, as to leave little or no distinction between them," those who have failed to see that "the phrase *parent* or *mother country* hath been jesuitically adopted by the King and his parasites, with a low papistical design of gaining an unfair bias on the credulous weakness of our minds," those whose writings consist of anything less than "simple facts, plain arguments, and common sense" (*WTP*, 1:69, 86–87, 84). Writing itself (rightly understood) is defined as a process of rational deconstruction and offered as a mode of revolution. "The Republic of Letters is more ancient than monarchy, and of far higher character in the world than the vassal court of Britain," he wrote in *The American Crisis*; "he that rebels against reason is a real rebel, but he that in defence of reason rebels against tyranny, has a better title to '*Defender of the Faith*,' than George the third" (*WTP*, 1:179). Political designations are here exploded through literary trope: the king is dethroned and the author is crowned king.

Moreover, and most significantly for Webster, the American situation is the focal point of Paine's literary-political revisionism. "It was the cause of America that made me an author," Paine wrote in 1783, "and if, in the course of more than seven years, I have rendered [America] any service, I have likewise added something to the reputation of literature, by freely and disinterestedly employing it in the great cause of mankind, and showing that there may be genius without prostitution" (*WTP*, 1:375–76). To be sure, Paine did not intend to write American literature per se. He considered what he wrote "pure nature" and did not hesitate to bid farewell to the United States at the end of *The American Crisis* and look forward to "whatever country I may hereafter be in" (*WTP*, 1:196, 376). Because "the cause of America [was] in a great measure the cause of all mankind," the cause of literature transcended any particularist designations of place (*WTP*, 1:68). "Universal empire is the prerogative of a writer," he explained. "His concerns are with all mankind, and though he cannot command their obedience, he can assign them their duty" (*WTP*, 1:179). Still, the American political situation is presented in Paine's writings as an exemplary literary situation. America, he wrote in *The Forester's Letters*, "hath a blank sheet to write upon" (*WTP*, 1:154). And at the close of *A Dialogue* he predicted "that America is the theatre where human nature will *soon* receive its greatest military, civil, and literary honours" (*WTP*, 1:167). For the young Webster, the suggestion of the convergence of American history with universalist literary purpose must have been extraordinarily resonant.

For when he turned in 1783 to the pursuit of literature, Webster brought with him a Painean model for revolutionary writing. For Webster, as for Paine, revolution was first and foremost a battle against the intellectual inertia that impels social bodies to resist change. Like the author of *Common Sense*, who observed that "a long Habit of not thinking a Thing *wrong*, gives it a superficial appearance of being *right*," Webster understood that "Mankind . . . believe a thing *right* and *best*, because they have never suspected otherwise, or because it is the general opinion" (*WTP*, 1:67; *GI*, 13). Like Paine, too, he believed that the success of the American Revolution was due to the ability of Americans to overcome that inertia. In April 1783, Paine issued the closing number of *The Crisis*, remarking that "there is no instance in the world, where a people so extended, and wedded to former habits of thinking . . . were so instantly and effectually pervaded by a turn in politics, as in the case of independence; and who supported their opinion, undiminished, through such a succession of good and ill fortune, till they crowned it with success" (*WTP*, 1:376). A few months later, Webster similarly announced in the *Institute* that "greater changes have been wrought, in the minds of men, in the short compass of eight years past, than are commonly effected in a century" (*GI*, 3). But Webster felt that the intellectual revolution which had supported political independence had not spilled over into cultural attitudes. "Popular prejudice is in favor of Dilworth," he wrote to John Canfield, "and because he was universally esteemed in Great Britain half a century ago, people are apt to slumber in the opinion that he is incapable of improvement" (*LNW*, 4). Americans had remained intellectually enthralled by the British, and Webster cautioned that it had become "their duty to attend to the *arts of peace*, and particularly to the interests of *literature*; to see if there be not some errours to be corrected, some defects to be supplied, and some improvements to be introduced into our systems of education as well as into those of civil policy" (*GI*, 4). For Webster, the literary scenario after the war replayed the political scenario before the war.

So, blithely leaping from politics to pronunciation, Webster composed his introduction as a postwar gloss on, or sequel to, Paine's Revolutionary writings. Thomas Dilworth plays the villain for Webster, just as King George III played it for Paine, though clearly the true antagonist for both is the loyalist state of the American mind. As political independence was effected through a desacralizing of British political discourse, so literary independence could only be effected through a frank recognition that "their methods of education [exemplified by Dilworth] are equally erroneous and defective." And as desacralization for Paine entailed a radical rewriting of political history, so for Webster it entailed a rewriting of linguistic history. According to Webster, intellectual discourse on the English language had altogether but a brief and disreputable history because the British had "attended more to the study of ancient and foreign languages, than to the improvement of their own." Like political ideas before the war, "this ridiculous practice had found its way to America" and had become so ingrained in the American schools "that the whispers of *common sense*, in favour of our native tongue, have been silenced amidst the clamour of pedantry in favor of Greek and Latin" (*GI*, 4; italics mine). True, some efforts had been made "to reduce our language to rules, and expunge the corruptions that ignorance and caprice, unguided by any standard, must necessarily introduce," but for the most part British grammarians "study the language enough to find the difficulties of it—they tell us that it is impossible to reduce it to order—that it is to be learnt only by the ear—they lament the disorder and dismiss it without a remedy" (*GI*, 4–5).[29] Given this history of failure and corruption, Webster had to admit that Dilworth's *New Guide* "was a great improvement upon former methods of education" but could still argue that "almost every part of it was originally defective" and that "the late revolution had rendered it *still more improper* in America" (*GI*, 10; italics mine).

Still more improper: were it not for the Revolution, Dilworth would still be improper, still in need of basic revision. (Indeed, many of Web-

ster's complaints are articulated in the works of British grammarians.)
But the Revolution had made the question of the *New Guide*'s propriety
an American issue—and in a rather complex way. For Webster's sense of
propriety involves a fundamental ambiguity that goes to the heart of his
Painean Americanization of Dilworth.[30] On one hand, Webster uses
"proper" to mean "one's own," "particularly suited to," implying a fundamental relativism: what is "proper" to one individual, nation, or situation is not necessarily "proper" to another. In this sense, the impropri-
ety of Dilworth lies in the various un-American characteristics I have
noted above, most simply in the "twelve or fifteen pages devoted to
names of English, Scotch and Irish towns and boroughs," for which
Webster substituted "the names of the United States, the counties in
each, &c." Dilworth's lists were not *properly* American; they neither belonged to the nation nor were particularly suited to its new independent
state. On the other hand, Webster was not a thoroughgoing relativist,
and he also uses the word to mean "just," "correct," "true"—denoting
an absolute relation to an unimpeachable, universal standard. "Let
words be divided as they *ought* to be pronounced . . . and the smallest
child cannot mistake a *just* pronunciation," he writes. "The only reason
why we divide syllables for children, is to lead them to the *proper* pronunciation of words" (*GI*, 9; italics mine). Clearly, Webster is not concerned here with a uniquely American articulation but with the correct
articulation, with being different from England by being better. Moreover, he is explicitly concerned more with this absolute sense of
"proper" than with the relativistic one, more with the "defective and
erroneous" half of the *New Guide* than with the "totally useless." The
Grammatical Institute was not supposed to invent a new language or to
privilege American usage simply because it was American but "to diffuse
an uniformity and purity of *language*" in America. By their very contra-
dictions, the two meanings of "proper" are made to correspond: Webster wanted to make proper English properly American.

The literariness of the *Grammatical Institute*—the way it imagines
American language and American linguistics—is rooted in the ambiguity of "proper." Webster's incorporation of Dilworth into his American
text establishes the continuity of grammatical discourse at the very moment that it proposes change: the ambiguity of American propriety embraces both. His appropriation of Paine at once presumes an America
whose difference from England is already defined geographically (hence
his lists of toponyms) and politically (hence his Revolutionary chronology) and projects an America culturally undefined, a "blank page" (to
use Paine's words) waiting to be written upon: again, the ambiguity of
American propriety embraces both. The peroration to Webster's introduction embodies this strategic doubleness by offering a series of

rhetorically discrete attempts to express America's relationship to Old World culture. (In the expansive rhetoric of the closing paragraph, Webster—again perhaps following Paine—substitutes Europe for Great Britain.) One attempt presents a Europe "grown old in folly, corruption and tyranny," where "laws are perverted, manners are licentious, literature is declining and human nature debased." America, in contrast, is still "in her infancy," and for her "to adopt the present maxims of the old world, would be to stamp the wrinkles of decrepid age upon the bloom of youth and to plant the seeds of decay in a vigourous constitution" (*GI*, 14). The biological absurdity of the trope affirms rejection, separation, and (organic) independence. Another attempt depicts Americans standing with "the experience of the whole world before our eyes," and it insists, "It is the business of *Americans* to select the wisdom of all nations," while rejecting the folly. As they had done with Europe's "maxims of government," so they should do with its "manners" and "literary taste." American difference is here defined not so much by rupture as by a process of selection, purification, improvement, whose object, still unfulfilled, is (echoing Paine) "to add superiour dignity to this infant Empire and to human nature" (*GI*, 14–15). What made Webster's speller American for him was not its organic originality but the yoking together of these two disparate rhetorics of difference, its declaration of intellectual independence and its ability to discriminate between the good and the bad in Dilworth (and other writers) and to make changes where needed. What had been perceived by Spencer as a failure of American literary will—the inability to give substance to his strident rhetoric—can in this way be seen as a manifestation of a self-consciously American and essentially literary imagining.

CONDILLAC TO MICHAELIS TO TOOKE

I have been arguing that the invention of American English in Webster's *Grammatical Institute* is, on its own terms, both literary and American—indeed, that its literariness issues from its self-conscious Americanness and that we can learn much about American linguistic imagining by discussing the text in relation to other literary texts, styles, and traditions, and by analyzing its use of tropes, narrative strategies, and its resulting ambiguities. In this section I will further clarify the literary way in which Noah Webster invented American English by turning to *Dissertations on the English Language* (1789), Webster's attempt to elucidate the theoretical underpinnings of the *Grammatical Institute* and, in so doing, to locate himself *as an American* within the current European discourse on language.

But as a way of preparing the conceptual ground for my analysis, let me first introduce in some detail a markedly different understanding of American English, Alexis de Tocqueville's account in the second volume of his classic study of Jacksonian America. While Webster spoke of the prospect of American English in the absolute terms of propriety, purity, and correctness, Tocqueville believed that language was fundamentally ideological, that (in other words) as "the chief instrument of thought," it assumed the character of those who spoke it.[31] Accordingly, the "language of a democracy" he described was as protean as the culture he observed (*DIA*, 2:68). In "the general stir and competition of minds," Americans created countless neologisms and transformed old terminology by developing "new acceptations" (*DIA*, 2:68, 69). As quickly as linguistic innovations became current, they were rendered obsolete and replaced by fresh phraseology. Rules of linguistic decorum were ignored. Exact meanings became lost in a haze of abstract terminology and indiscriminate usage. And in this atmosphere, Tocqueville surmised, no Americans could be "permanently disposed . . . to study the natural laws of language" (*DIA*, 2:73).

Webster launched his language crusade, convinced that "American glory [was] begin[ning] to dawn at a favourable period, and under flattering circumstances" (*GI*, 14). Written a half-century later, the European's account could not contrast more sharply with the American's projection. In part, the striking differences between the two versions can be explained if we acknowledge, with Dennis Baron, the inevitable failure of programmatic language reform. But only in part. For, besides the fact that Webster's speller and, later, his dictionary were enormously popular, this explanation can account neither for the persistent counter-claims throughout this period (in Cooper's *Notions* and elsewhere) that Americans indeed spoke better English than the British nor for alternative evaluative judgments of similar phenomena, like Jefferson's defense of neology. In other words, the differences between Webster and Tocqueville can be accounted for less empirically than conceptually: Tocqueville and Webster imagined both language and America differently. The basic question Tocqueville asked did not leave room for the American's sense of incompleteness, of tenuousness, of promise. "How has the American Democracy modified the English language?": Tocqueville's assumption was that language, like other cultural phenomena, was fundamentally related to political condition, and his most important conceptual forebear here was certainly Condillac.[32] Accepting Locke's position on the arbitrariness of language—that words bore no necessary relation to ideas—Condillac argued that language was arbitrary only in a theoretical or originary sense but was otherwise subject to certain conditions which made its character necessary, and, in the sense that it bears a relationship to ideas, necessarily ideological. "Signs are arbitrary the first time they are employed," he wrote. "But I would fain know whether it be not natural for every nation to combine their ideas according to their own peculiar genius." Language stands, theoretically, as the final variable in a cultural equation: "As government influences the character of a people, so the character of a people influences that of language."[33] For Tocqueville, the American democracy provided the perfect test case for this theory of linguistic relativity. After all, in America the English language had been transplanted from an aristocratic society to a democratic one: the changes should have been clear and recognizable.

And so, Tocqueville found, they were. He noted three categories or modes of linguistic change engendered by the American mind, which was, in turn, engendered by the equality of condition—each involving the creation of ambiguity, but of a sort different from that which I have attributed to Webster's *Grammatical Institute*, or, for that matter, from that which we generally attribute to the writers of the American Renaissance. First, *neology*. (These rubrics are my own.) In aristocracies, society is in a state of repose, so language is basically static. Words are introduced into the language slowly and, for the most part, by scholars who need new terms for intellectual or scientific advances. But "the constant agitation that prevails in a democratic community tends unceasingly . . . to change the character of the language, as it does the aspect of affairs" (*DIA*, 2:69). Because most Americans are involved in the areas of business and politics—and in democratic America the majority determines the character of the language—new words bear the impress of those mundane, unrefined activities. Because few Americans occupy themselves with the more elevated fields of metaphysics and theology, the language will "gradually lose ground" in those fields (*DIA*, 2:70). Americans will use classical roots inappropriately, adopt regional or technical terms, retool common terminology—in short, they will give various new meanings to words already defined, thus introducing and perpetuating ambiguity. "This is a deplorable consequence of democracy," Tocqueville wrote, since "without clear phraseology there is no good language" (*DIA*, 2:71). Second, *stratification*. In aristocracies, class distinctions lead to a differentiation of dialects: "a language of the poor and a language of the rich, a language of the commoner and a language of the nobility, a learned language and a colloquial one" (*DIA*, 2:71–71). The process of differentiation then serves to compound social stratification. In America, on one hand, because no class distinctions structure society, no dialects exist. On the other hand, discriminations within language disappear, too. "The rules which style had set up are almost abolished," Tocqueville wrote; "the line ceases to be drawn between expressions which seem by their very nature vulgar and others which appear to be refined." The result: "as much confusion in language as there is in society" (*DIA*, 2:72). Third, *abstraction*. The democratic predilection for general ideas (reported by Tocqueville several chapters earlier) finds expression in the passion for generic or abstract terms. As before, something is lost and something gained. Abstract terms allow speakers and writers to "enlarge thought and assist the operations of the mind by enabling it to include many objects in a small compass," but they also "obscure the thoughts they are intended to convey" (*DIA*, 2:73). Tocqueville explained: "An abstract term is like a box with a false bottom; you may put in it what ideas you please, and take them out again without being observed." In democratic America, men "are apt to entertain unsettled ideas, and they require loose expressions to convey them" (*DIA*, 2:74).

Such is the substance of Tocqueville's cogent analysis of American English. But the accuracy of his conclusions are less at issue here than the validity of his methodology. Because he lacked sufficient fluency in English, Tocqueville accepted the testimony of "Englishmen of education" as to the peculiarities of the American idiom (*DIA*, 2:68). Prejudicial witnesses certainly, but who else (he might have reasoned) would recognize the nature and significance of the differences? Anyway, many American commentators were saying much the same thing regarding their countrymen's linguistic practices: Witherspoon in *The Druid*, Brackenridge in *Modern Chivalry*, Irving in *Salmagundi*, and so on. Moreover, Tocqueville was not really relying (he said) on their observations (he called them "complaints") but was offering them as the empirical justification of his abstract theorizing. Their remarks, he wrote, "led me to reflect upon the subject; and my reflections brought me, by *theoretical reasoning*, to the same point at which my informants had arrived by practical observation" (*DIA*, 2:69; italics mine). In other words, empirical research recapitulated abstract theorizing. The circularity of this procedure did not occur to him. Or rather, the necessary validity of his methodology rested upon the belief that societies—or, better, political cultures—develop in remarkably logical ways. The sociologist need only understand the political institutions of a society and the social conditions that they sustain in order to "know" its cultural characteristics. Indeed, he readily admitted that "in America [he] saw more than America; [he] sought there the image of democracy itself, with its inclinations, its character, its prejudices, and its passions, in order to learn what [Frenchmen] have to fear or to hope from its progress" (*DIA*, 1:15).[34] And so, each chapter of volume 2 of *Democracy in America* is a corollary of its title: American literature as democratic literature; American philosophy as democratic philosophy; American religion as democratic religion; American language as democratic langauge. Which makes for some rather predictable reading.

It also makes for a distorted picture of American linguistic thought and practice. For example, Tocqueville chose to privilege speech over writing in his analysis of democratic language, because "American authors may be said to live rather in England than in their own country, since they constantly study the English writers and take them every day for their models." American authors—among them, I suppose, Noah Webster—are then not "immediately subjected to the peculiar causes acting upon the United States" (*DIA*, 2:68). They are not yet *truly* American. Yet he was quite willing to accept aristocratic English as the standard that was modified by American democracy, even while admitting further on in the chapter that different classes in aristocratic societies develop substantially different dialects, each in accord with the "habits of the mind" peculiar to its class. In short, Tocqueville's remarks on American language were generated by his preconceptions of difference between aristocratic and democratic societies. Still—and as such— they clearly represent an attempt to demonstrate the manifest presence of an *American* language, socially, politically, and ideologically defined. Each of his categories issued from what he saw as the American national character: the impulse to neologize, the resistance to a fixed language, the desire to mix high and low, the passion for general terms. "How American Democracy Has Modified the English Language" thus exemplifies Condillac's theory of linguistic relativity: "As government influences the character of a people, so the character of a people influences that of language."

When Noah Webster began to read Condillac's *Essay on the Origin of Human Knowledge*—on 10 August 1786, by his own account—he was touring the states, promoting his *Grammatical Institute*, campaigning for copyright legislation, crusading for a national language, and, to support himself, reading the lectures that would eventually become *Dissertations on the English Language*. He studied Condillac, along with such other writers as James Beattie, Hugh Blair, Joseph Priestley, and, most significant here, Johann David Michaelis and John Horne Tooke, as part of a program to collect "everything from books and men which will confirm my principles or improve the work."[35] Although some substantial aspects of his linguistic program do change during this period—his championship of orthographic reform, for instance, and his adoption of Tookean grammar—he read by and large purposively, searching for passages to substantiate the rudimentary fiction of American English he began to invent in the *Grammatical Institute*. What I want to present here is a map of his misreadings, a hypothetical (and partial) reconstruction of the imaginative process that informed Webster's philosophical borrowings. Let me emphasize that my reconstruction is hypothetical. *Dissertations* is a confusing, inconsistent work, a mélange of linguistic rules, philological theories, literary criticism, and cultural polemic held together more by the intensity of its rhetoric than by the coherence of its argument, by myth more than logic. My purpose in situating Webster within a particular discourse of ideas is not to dispel the confusion, neither to impose order nor to suggest actual intellectual growth, but to make literary sense of Webster's first theoretical work. As a critic might systematically analyze a symbol's multiple levels of meaning in order to appreciate its aesthetic complexity, so I will consider several "sources" of thought in the *Dissertations* (Condillac, Michaelis, Tooke) in order to evoke the ideological—and hence literary—complexity of Webster's invention of American English.

To begin with Condillac: "As government influences the character of a people, so the character of a people influences that of language." Americans and Britons now had different governments; they were (nominally, if not otherwise) separate peoples; their languages had to reflect that difference. This is, more or less, what Tocqueville would argue a half-century later. But Condillac's equation must have posed fundamental problems for Webster, for though he appropriates its terms, he never fully adopts its logic. To begin with, the preconditions for linguistic difference were not yet extant in America. "Our constitutions of civil government are not yet firmly established," he noted repeatedly during this period; "our national character is not yet formed."[36] Condillac's equation bespeaks a prior history of political, cultural, and linguistic development. A strict application of Condillac could have meant only one thing to Webster: no national government, no national character, no national language. Condillac allowed that when a language (perhaps like American English) is "not formed upon the ruin of others," its "progress must be a great deal more rapid" because it already possesses "a character from its original." He understood, too, that great men could play a role in linguistic history, indeed, that language "is not perfected without the assistance of eminent writers" who enrich it "with a multitude of new turns of expressions, which from the relation they bear to its character, enlarge it more and more." But neither of these correlatives is taken up in any significant way by Webster. Moreover, Condillac insisted that "the character of languages is formed insensibly," that linguistic formation and linguistic change are the necessary and inevitable products of complex historical processes and not of conscious fabrication or programmatic reform.[37] But Webster was impatient, and his sense of crisis inclined him to cast historical necessity in the form of patriotic imperative. "*NOW* is the time, and *this* is the country,"

Webster wrote. "LET us then seize the present moment, and establish a *national language* [and a national character] as well as a national government."[38] Each of the three variables in the American cultural equation is independent, subject to manipulation: the relation among them is not causal, as it is in Condillac, but conjunctive. And so, in the *Dissertations*, speculation stands in for analysis, prescription for description, prophecy for history. And so, beginning in this very fundamental way, Webster's national language must be seen as an invention and the text of the *Dissertations* itself as a sort of American fiction.

The content of the fiction—its plots and characters, heroes and villains—needs to be outlined. For both Webster and Tocqueville, American English was an imaginative construct, but Webster imagined the transformation of English in America in a manner significantly different from Tocqueville's. The Frenchman found (and assumed) that perceptible changes in established meaning and in recognized style manifested themselves through the ideological changes which resulted from changes in social condition. The American, for the most part, did not. All living languages do change, he believed, but in different ways and for different reasons. Over the course of time, American English would be "as different from the future language of England, as the modern Dutch, Danish and Swedish are from the German, or from one another," but only partly and not even primarily because of *democracy* in America. "The vicinity of the European nations, with the uninterrupted communication in peace, and the changes of dominion in war," he wrote, "are gradually assimilating their respective languages." America, on the other hand, "placed at a distance from those nations, will feel, in a much less degree, the influence of the assimilating causes" (*DEL*, 22). Ethnic diversity did not seem to trouble Webster because, he believed, "intercourse among the learned of the different States which the revolution has begun, and an American Court will perpetuate, must gradually destroy the differences of dialect which our ancestors brought from their native countries" (*DEL*, 19). Americanization will be determined by "numerous local causes, such as a new country, new associations of people, new combinations of ideas in arts and science, and some intercourse with tribes wholly unknown in Europe, [which] will introduce new words into the American tongue." All these changes—essentially limited to additions to the American lexicon—are "necessary and unavoidable," but Webster made no attempt to understand them ideologically: they emerged not so much from the character of the people as from their situation (*DEL*, 22–23).[39] In fact, after mentioning lexical change briefly in the first dissertation, he ignored it completely, shifting attention away from those elements of language which would accurately register the social changes he envisions. The plot changes. In the bulk of the text, linguistic nationality pertains exclusively to the areas of pronunciation, grammar, and (in an appendix) orthography—i.e., to the mechanics of language rather than the substance—and, as in the *Grammatical Institute*, Webster's concern was more that American English be correct than that it issue from a peculiarly American character. Indeed, Webster's use of the word "character" in the *Dissertations* and other writings of the period—and his understanding of the concept of national character—involves a fundamental ambiguity similar to that of "proper." On one hand, "character" refers to the "peculiar qualities, impressed by nature or habit on a person, which distinguish him from others": so defined, a person—or a nation—may possess a good character or a bad character. On the other hand, it can also denote only "distinguished or good qualities; those which are esteemed and respected," as when we "enquire whether a stranger is a man of *character*." Condillac's relativism necessarily required the first definition. Webster's Americanism would not allow for that sort of contingency: it could countenance only national character as *the* national character.[40]

It is rather in Condillac's remarks about the growth and decline of languages—as opposed to their ideological origins—that Webster seems to have found most support—and an alternative plot—from the *Essay*. Indeed, the paradigm of linguistic history that Webster drew from the *Essay* confirmed him in a decidedly nonideological view of language. According to Condillac, languages originate in social intercourse and, with "the assistance of eminent writers" and the principle of "analogy," move toward perfection, a historical stage measured by such criteria as clarity, precision, elegance, and comprehensiveness.[41] The more a language is structured by analogy (a term never strictly defined by Condillac) the more perfect it is.[42] When a language reaches this stage, the nation's arts and sciences enter their golden age, a period that in English history, Webster (like others) believed, began during the reign of Elizabeth and culminated during the reign of Queen Anne. But nothing corrupts like success. Literary competition leads to stylistic experimentation, and "as every style analogous to the character of the language . . . hath been already used by preceding writers, he has nothing left but to deviate from analogy." The language is plagued by the influx "of strained and subtle conceits, of affected antitheses, of specious paradoxes, of frivolous and far-fetched expressions, of new-fangled words, and in short, of the jargon of persons, whose understandings have been debauched by bad metaphysics."[43] "One would think," Webster commented, "that Condillac had designed here to give a description of the present [i.e., during the reign of George III] taste of the English writers, and a state of their literature" (*DEL*, 31). Americans should no longer follow British standards of grammar and pronunciation primarily because the English no longer spoke or wrote good English: "the taste of her writers is already corrupted, and her language on the decline" (*DEL*, 20).

The overtly ideological aspects of Condillac's philosophy of language are largely suppressed in *Dissertations on the English Language*. When Webster asked Americans to establish a national language, he was not asking for a new language to emerge from the new republic but for pre-Revolutionary English to reassert itself. It seems not to have occurred to him (or not to have mattered) that the language spoken in the United States would then still reflect (following Condillac) the English, not the new American character he wanted to establish. To be sure, Webster couched his nonideological linguistic ideas in a history of the English language that was modeled on the Whig justifications of the American Revolution: just as British politics had become corrupt during the reign of George III, so had its language; just as America had become (in the words of Thomas Paine) an asylum for mankind, so it would become the asylum for perfect, analogical English. *Translatio imperii, translatio linguae*. But linguistic purity, not linguistic relativity, was clearly the central issue for Webster. It should not be surprising, then, that linguistic nationality entailed not only resistance to British dominance but a rejection of local dialects—even though, like the lazy Southern drawl or the nasal New England whine, they issued from the established character of the region. Ironically, it is in the matter of provincial dialects that Webster does apply a version of Condillac's equation, arguing that "the drawling, nasal manner of speaking in New England," which "proceeds immediately from not opening the mouth sufficiently," is due "almost solely" to "the nature of their government and a distribution of their property." Here, Webster writes, among a provincial people living in "a state of equality" and "not possessing that pride and consciousness of superiority which attend birth and fortune," may be found "the peculiar traits of national character." But though he clearly finds their psychological qualities—their character, in both senses—admirable, he finds their pronunciation "so disagreeable" that "too much pains cannot be taken to reform the practice" (*DEL*, 106–108). The exception proves the rule: though Webster held that "national" character does influence the way people speak, he did not conclude that the "national" language should be formed on that basis.

But if Webster made little effort to make his national language peculiarly American in a way Tocqueville would have recognized, he did strive in various ways to present his own scholarly endeavors as ideologically appropriate for the new republic and, in so striving, Webster assumes a central role in his own narrative. His dedication to Benjamin Franklin, a paean to the Puritan ethic, provided the model for a new American Scholar. "In his philosophical researches," Webster wrote,

Franklin "has been guided by experiment, and sought for *practical truths*," applying the "*facts* (which compose all our knowledge)" that he collects "to the most useful purposes of government, agriculture, commerce, manufactures, rural, domestic and moral economy." Moreover, "in communicating his ideas he does not sacrifice truth to embellishment." On the contrary, "his stile is plain and elegantly neat," leading "the reader, without study, into the same train of thinking." Webster concludes that Franklin "writes for the child as well as the philosopher, and always writes well, because he never takes pains to write" (*DEL*, v). Here is pragmatism and plain style, in stark contrast to contemporary British pedantry and pretentiousness, in which "simplicity of stile is neglected for ornament, and sense is sacrificed to sound" (*DEL*, 34). In the same spirit, and as in the *Grammatical Institute*, Webster transforms the dedication itself into a mode of literary revolution. "Dedications are usually designed to flatter the Great, to acknowledge their services, or court their favor and influence," he wrote. "But very different motives have led me to prefix the venerable name of FRANKLIN to this publication" (*DEL*, iii). To be sure, Webster was deceiving his readers (and himself, perhaps) by denying his own rather obvious design to flatter. But this revisionary opening nevertheless foreshadows his presentation of what he conceived to be a properly American linguistic methodology.

Repeatedly throughout the *Dissertations*, Webster pledged his allegiance to democratic philology. "I have no system of my own," he insisted. "The business of a grammarian is not to examin [*sic*] whether or not national practice is founded on philosophical principles; but to *ascertain* the national practice" (*DEL*, 37, 204). "The *general practice* of a nation is the rule of propriety," which should "be consulted in so important a matter, as that of making laws for speaking" (*DEL*, 24). Linguistics, in other words, should be at bottom descriptive. In America, Webster implies, the people decide. He enlists support for this methodology and for his accompanying attack against the linguistic power brokers in England, from Bishop Lowth to Samuel Johnson (one of the heroes of the *Grammatical Institute* is now a villain), from a passage in Johann David Michaelis's *A Dissertation on the Influence of Opinions on Language and of Language on Opinions*. "It is not for a scholar to give laws nor proscribe established expressions," Webster quotes; "if he takes so much on himself he is ridiculed, and deservedly; it is no more than a just mortification to his ambition, and the penalty of his usurping on the rights of the people." To explain his position, Michaelis offers a political trope, which Webster must have found particularly compelling: "Language is a democratical state, where all the learning in the world does not warrant a citizen to supersede a received custom, till he has convinced the whole nation that this custom is a mistake." Even were this not so, "scholars are not so infallible that every thing is to be referred to them," and "were they allowed a decisory power, the errors of language," Michaelis sarcastically suggests, "instead of diminishing, would be continually increasing." It is "imperious" for them to suggest that people "be compelled to defer to their innovations, and implicitly to receive every false opinion of theirs."[44] Webster expands upon Michaelis's central metaphor to describe the current situation in Great Britain: where "a Johnson, a Garrick, or a Sheridan" can "dictate to a nation the rules of speaking" just "as a tyrant gives laws to his vassals"; where "even well bred people and scholars, often surrender their right of private judgement to these literary governors"; where their pronouncements have "the force of law; and to contradict it, is rebellion" (*DEL*, 167–168). He thus clears the ground upon which a national language, conceived in liberty, may be brought forth. His fiction can be read as a romance of American English, with himself (by implication) as an American hero, defender of "the rights of the people" from the usurpations of linguistic pretenders.

With the help of Michaelis, Webster can argue that the Americanness of American English is defined by its reliance on common usage and is sustained by the enabling gesture of the democratic linguist—but only by distorting Michaelis's basic intentions, transforming what is essentially a descriptive account of "the influence of a people's opinions on the languages" into a prescriptive attack against his linguistic competitors. According to Michaelis (whose focus is on the meaning of words, not pronunciation or grammar), each different nation forms its language consensually, according to its particular "way of thinking." For instance, the Germans attribute goodness to their deity and call him *Gott*; the Jews, beneficence, and call him *El*. As society grows more complex, certain classes of people may exert a disproportionate amount of influence in the coining of new expressions: women, for instance, with "those pretty mouths, which the graces seem to animate, and whose every word meets with ecchos [*sic*], delighting to repeat it"; and "classical authors, [whom] every body is eager to read." But ultimately, even in this later stage, the people "are indeed the supreme legislators." The influence of the linguist in forming or reforming language is not so much pernicious (as Webster would have it) as it is negligible: he "may be [intimately] convinced of the truth of his doctrines[, h]e may make a clamour about the justness of expressions, he may protest against vulgar errors," but "no body minds him." "For instance," wrote Michaelis, "should a stickler for Copernicus and the true system of the world, carry his zeal so far as to say *the city of Berlin sets at such and such an hour*, instead of making use of the common expression, *the sun sets at Berlin at such an hour*, he speaks the truth to be sure; but his manner of speaking is pedantry."[45]

Michaelis presented the rule of common usage as a description of the way things necessarily are, always and everywhere; Webster, as an assertion of how they should be in America and are not elsewhere.

Let me summarize briefly at this point: Webster offered two standards for his national language, analogy and common usage, one sustained by a selective reading of Condillac, the other by a distortion of Michaelis. Both are couched in the popular rhetoric of the American Revolution, but one seeks to maintain the preestablished purity of the English language, the other to discover American preferences. For my purposes here, I have separated these strands; in the *Dissertations*, Webster presented them as the woof and warp of a single conceptual fabric: "The *rules of the language itself*, and the *general practice of the nation*, constitute propriety in speaking" (*DEL*, 27). Which leads, as it emerges from Webster's text, to a considerably complicated relation between common usage and analogy. Consider, for instance, that the argument from usage proceeds in two distinct directions. When Webster referred to "the *general practice* of a nation" (*DEL*, 24), he was asserting a federalist principle to discourage regional dialects and to promote standardization. "A sameness of pronunciation is of considerable consequence in a political view," Webster wrote, "for provincial accents are disagreeable to strangers and sometimes have an unhappy effect upon the social affections." In short, "Our political harmony is therefore concerned in a uniformity of language"—just as it is in a federal constitution (*DEL*, 19–20).[46] However, when Webster referred, more emphatically, to "*universal undisputed practice*," he was encouraging a nationalist rejection of British models and learned opinion. For example: "Writers upon the subject of propriety in our language, have objected to the use of *means*, with the article *a* and the definitive pronouns singular, *this* and *that*," he wrote, "but we have the authority of almost unanimous national practice in speaking" to the contrary, so "neither Johnson, Lowth, nor any other person, however learned, has a right to say that the phrases are not *good English*" (*DEL*, 201, 203–204, 205). Common usage versus local usage; common usage versus imposed usage. The former assumes the absence of linguistic consensus; the latter, its presence.

To be sure, Webster was not consistent in his terminology, and I have made these distinctions more sharply than he probably would have allowed or even have recognized. But his call for a national language clearly performed these two separate functions, and the reasonings that underlie these functions appear to be mutually exclusive. On one hand, he wanted to eradicate regional (and ethnic) differences in the spirit of national unity—as if a recognizably American difference did not already exist. Common usage is ostensibly the rule of first resort to displace local usage, "and in disputed points, where people differ in opinion and practice, *analogy* should always decide the controversy" (*DEL*, 28). On the other hand, he wanted to overthrow British cultural dominance by patriotically asserting American linguistic difference—as if the difference (undisputed usage) were already there, *always* already there. Here analogy—the principle of prior purity—is not conceived as a practical supplement to usage, but as its mirror image. Their distinctive roles are blurred and their origins mystified: "the unanimous consent of a nation [common usage], and a fixed principle interwoven with the very construction of a language, coeval and coextensive with it [analogy], are like the common laws of a land, or the immutable rules of morality, the propriety of which every man, however refractory, is forced to acknowledge, and to which most men will readily submit." They are self-evident truths, "founded in the very nature of things, and remain unmoved and unchanged, amidst all the fluctuations of human affairs and the revolutions of time" (*DEL*, 29). For Michaelis, common usage and correctness were separate issues: by the very nature of their development, "the languages of nations are the repositories" of an "immense heap of truths and errors," and scholars had to accommodate themselves to that fact.[47] But Webster could not. Although he could admit that analogy and common usage sometimes work at cross purposes (as in the case of *means*), he could also—and more emphatically—assert their radical identity. "The people are right," he declared, "and a critical investigation of the subject, warrants me in saying, that common practice, even among the unlearned, is generally defensible on the principles of analogy" (*DEL*, viii).

"The people are right": through their agency the tensions between common usage and analogy can be resolved. But who are the people? Certainly not the shadowy "multitude," whose "negligence and ignorance," Webster tells us at one point, somehow threaten both analogy and common usage (*DEL*, 29). Nor the whiners, drawlers, and imitators of foreign fashions. Which brings us—and Webster—to John Horne Tooke.[48] Like Condillac's *Essay* and Michaelis's *On the Influence*, Tooke's *Diversions of Purley* (with its revisionary reading of Locke and its radical reduction of all parts of speech to nouns and verbs) justified Webster in his rejection of the "mountains of learned rubbish" generated by his favorite British villains, Lowth, Harris, Johnson, and so on. "I say that a little more reflection and a great deal less reading, a little more attention to common sense, and less blind prejudice for his Greek commentators," wrote Tooke, "would have made Mr. Harris a much better Grammarian, if not perhaps a Philosopher."[49] But it was Tooke's insistence on the Anglo-Saxon roots of the English language and the revelatory power of etymology that provided Webster with the myth by which he could potentially sustain the tensions that structure the *Dissertations*. Tooke's Saxonism implicitly underwrote the pattern of resistance to foreign dominance (Roman, Norman) that informs the history of the English language in the first dissertation and helped Webster shape American linguistic history into a final, open-ended chapter of a narrative of the Anglo-Saxon spirit. Webster was able to identify "the people" as those who have most faithfully maintained the traditions of their stalwart British ancestors: "On examining the language [etymologically], and comparing the practice of speaking among the yeomanry of this country, with the stile of Shakespear and Addison," he wrote at the end of the fourth (overtly Tookean) dissertation, "I am constrained to declare that the people of America, *in particular the English descendants* [italics mine], speak the most *pure English* now known in the world" (*DEL*, 288). Condillac and Michaelis are thus brought together under the aegis of Horne Tooke: analogy and common usage are joined in etymology. *These* people—genealogically defined and delimited—are right.

If, ultimately, Tooke merely substituted his own pedantry for the pedantry of his opponents, his philology was nonetheless contentiously antiauthoritarian, both philosophically and politically.[50] Webster's was nothing of the sort. Indeed, for all his adulation of the man for whom "the discovery of the true theory of the construction of language, seems to have been reserved," he still felt the need to apologize for the "exceptionable" nature of "particular instances of the writer's spirit and manner" (*DEL*, 181–182). His stated purpose in the *Dissertations* was to stabilize and consolidate, not to disrupt and overturn. Webster's populism is qualified by his concern for propriety and purity: he celebrated the American yeomanry only after he compared their speech to Shakespearean and Addisonian models and to the analogies derived by his own and Tooke's etymological labors. And only after he effectually excluded all but the "unmixed English descendants" (*DEL*, 240). Saxonism in the *Dissertations* is a strategy of exclusion and control: for the American to turn his country's history into Saxon genealogy was to rob the new republic of perhaps its most threatening force, limiting change within certain predetermined cultural and racial parameters.[51] Moreover, it resolved the conflict between common usage and analogy only provisionally, only in the restricted space and time occupied by a pure-blooded and pure-tongued American yeoman, somewhere between the country Webster saw and the nation he envisioned. Elsewhere in the text, the American people remained a more recalcitrant bunch: their minds still needed to be unshackled, their character had yet to be established, their foreign idioms and local dialects continued to present major obstacles to linguistic unity. In effect, the ambiguities inherent in Webster's use of "the people" define the American fiction of the *Dissertations*.

Tocqueville's account of the democratization of the English language greatly oversimplifies the matter of American cultural creation. For him, the meaning of America was clear and distinct, and cultural creation was an unproblematic, almost formulaic matter of representation. For Webster, the meaning of America was elusive and obscure. The true America was absent. Still, it seemed inevitable, almost palpable, and Webster's plan for a national language rushed in to fill the void, to make America's cultural destiny manifest. Formed by competing rhetorical structures and held together by enabling ambiguities, both the *Grammatical Institute* and the *Dissertations* should thus be seen as intriguing imaginative achievements, cultural fictions embodying Webster's confused, yet powerful, vision of America.

CHAPTER TWO

"A Fine Ambiguity":
Longfellow, Language,
and Literary History

WE MAY NOT think of *ambiguity*—the term of tribute usually reserved for Poe, Hawthorne, and Melville—as the proper adjective for describing a poet and scholar like Henry Wadsworth Longfellow. On the contrary, reviewers and critics since the nineteenth century have remarked upon the clarity, ease, and polish—the gentleness and gentility—of both his life and his verse; the word used over and again to characterize him has always been *simplicity*, not *ambiguity*. "He seems to have been always a man who felt very, very simply," wrote William Dean Howells, "and he spoke as simply as he felt." This, I should note, by way of compliment. "Longfellow wished above everything to be true," Howells explained, "and the constant pressure of his genius was towards clarifying his emotion and simplifying his word."[1] To be sure, Howells noted as well that, despite the smoothness and tranquillity which seemed to mark the poet, "his life included in its course all the sorrow and all the tragedy that can educate a man to sympathy with other human lives."[2] And Edward Wagenknecht, following Howells, has tried to bring Longfellow more in line with contemporary tastes by arguing that, in effect, he "cherished the virtues of simplicity in literature and in life, and he always wanted everything as simple as possible," *because* he was "a very complex man—at once a scholar and a gentle worldling, yet with something primitive and elemental about him too."[3] In a recent, last-ditch effort to revive Longfellow's reputation, Steven Allaback has even suggested that, rather than attempting to transform Longfellow into a more complex (and hence, academically palatable) figure, we stop apologizing for him and learn to value the quality of Longfellow's writing for what it is, "a wise, distilled, and earned simplicity."[4] Clearly, this sort of effort has not resonated well in the academic community: Longfellow remains for most the poet of simplicity (read: insipidity), his reputation is unambiguously low, and Jane Tompkins's sense that "Longfellow is now on the verge of a revival" has proven wholly unfounded.[5]

Still, it was no less a keen observer and critic than Henry James who noted a "fine ambiguity" in Longfellow, and in a context that is particularly significant for this study. James was describing "the way in which [Longfellow's] 'European' culture and his native kept house together." The poet's "large, quiet, pleasant, easy solution" to the international plot of his life perplexed James: "If it seemed a piece of the old world smoothly fitted into the new," he wrote, "so it might quite as well have been a piece of the new fitted, just as intimately, into the old." He could propose only a tentative (and characteristically Jamesian) explanation, that Longfellow had "worked up his American consciousness to that mystic point—one of those which poets alone have the secret—at which it could feel nothing but continuity and congruity with his European."[6] Clearly, the author who had built his "house of fiction" upon a foundation of cultural confrontation, of the *incongruity* of Old World and New, had expected more hostility and less harmony. But Longfellow had managed his "complex fate" well, and it left James mystified and bemused.

The question of national character is, of course, central to the history of Longfellow criticism. Although contemporaneous critics and reviewers could agree about his simplicity, they could not agree about his Americanness. Some thought him quintessentially American, that his was "the voice of this epoch of national progress," that it was "evident that Longfellow . . . possesses the national quality to a degree to which none of the others attained," that he was, indeed, the "true American laureate, the poet of our people," clearly more so than Bryant, Whittier, Emerson, Lowell, or (and especially) Whitman (*LAC*, 141, 327). Others could not disagree more emphatically: "Mr. Longfellow was [decidedly] not a national poet"; his "muse . . . owes little or none of her success to those great national sources of inspiration"; "his Americanism was an accident, his natural disposition leading him really to an emigration in thought and sentiment to the other side of the Atlantic"; indeed, his character had been "denationalized" (*LAC*, 136, 34, 239, 55). Still others recognized and were troubled by what seemed to be divided loyalties. Although his writing may be at times "overcharged with foreign sentiment," one critic apologized, "in his sympathies he was a true American" (*LAC*, 152). Howells's defenses were, perhaps, more astute, certainly more inventive. At one point he argued that Longfellow's "very love of what was old, and strange and far affirmed him citizen of a country where he dwelt perforce amidst what was new, and known, and near" (*LAC*, 352). At another point, drawing upon Longfellow's own comments in the 1840s, he explained that the poet "acted upon the belief . . . that we could not be really American without being in the best sense European; that unless we brought to our New World life the literature of the Old World, we should not know or say ourselves aright."[7] But James's brief, enigmatic remarks avoid rationalization and justification. He refused to decide the question. What intrigued him most about Longfellow's nationalism was both its simplicity and its ambiguity. It was not the sort of ambiguity that Matthiessen or Feidelson valued, not a moral or epistemological ambiguity, but a cultural ambiguity, "a subtle and very special, but wholly spontaneous, fusion of the native and the foreign," as Newton Arvin would describe it a half-century later, that defined, for James, Longfellow's *American* poetic consciousness.[8]

James's comments are particularly pertinent here because, biographically speaking, Longfellow's cultural ambiguity finds its origin in the study of language. For a quarter-century, as professor of modern languages first at Bowdoin College and then at Harvard, he studied and taught the languages of Europe in terms both of the interrelationship among nation, language, and literature and of the growth and development of national languages and literatures from medieval to modern times. The question I want to ask about Longfellow in this chapter has little to do with whether he was a good poet or a bad poet, major or minor, original or imitative. It has to do, rather, with how he imagined his writings culturally: principally, how he "worked up his American consciousness to that mystic point" of ambiguity in the scholarly essays he published and in the lectures he delivered as a professor of modern languages. Like Noah Webster's *Grammatical Institute of the English Language* and *Dissertations on the English Language*, Longfellow's academic writings themselves warrant literary consideration. Although the content of Webster's thought (his strident nationalism, his broad notion of literature, his exclusive focus on American English, his limited adoption of the theories of linguistic relativity) is diametrically opposed to Longfellow's immersion in the languages, literatures, and philosophies of Europe, and although Webster's perception of the absence of American political culture (his sense that America's government, along with its language and character, had yet to be formed) contrasts with Longfellow's strong sense of its presence, the same sort of enabling ambiguity— the capacity to sustain competing notions of what America was and what it meant—structures the writings of both. I want to argue that Longfellow's very simplicity needs to be understood as a complex cultural position informed by this "fine ambiguity."

"OUR NATIVE WRITERS"

Before Longfellow's first trip abroad, before he discovered the languages and literatures of Europe, before he learned of their histories and historians, a rudimentary form of the ambiguity could already be found in his writing—most noticeably in "Our Native Writers," the nationalist graduation address he delivered in 1825 to his classmates at Bowdoin. The address had great immediate personal significance to the student, for he himself had long before decided upon a literary career and had been pleading for his father's approval and support for over a year. "I have a particular and strong prejudice for one course of life," he wrote to his father in March of his junior year, "to which you I fear will not agree."[9] He resisted his father's urging to enter a more practical, lucrative profession and searched for some sort of compromise. "Let me reside one year at Cambridge,—let me study Belles Lettres," he specifically proposed. "After leaving Cambridge I would attach myself to some literary periodical publication, by which I could maintain myself and still enjoy the advantage of reading" (*LHWL*, 1:99, 94). He anticipated his father's practical objections. "Now I do not think that there is anything visionary or chimerical in my plan thus far," he explained. "There may be something visionary" in the fact that "I most eagerly aspire after future eminence in literature," that "my whole soul burns most ardently for it, and [that] every earthly thought centers in it," he admitted, "but I flatter myself, that I have prudence enough to keep my enthusiasm from defeating its own object by too great haste" (*LHWL*, 1:94–95). His father responded firmly and predictably. "A literary life, to one who has the means of support, must be very pleasant," he told his son. "But there is not wealth & munificence enough in this country to afford sufficient encouragement & patronage to merely [i.e., purely] literary men."[10] Longfellow responded with a mixture of resignation and (muted) defiance. "I can be a lawyer," he decided. "This will support my *real* existence, literature an *ideal* one" (*LHWL*, 1:104).

In the graduation address, Longfellow translated his disagreement with his father into broader nationalist terms. He reassured the audience that "palms [were] to be won by our native writers!—by those that have been nursed and brought up with us in the civil and religious freedom of our country."[11] But he warned that serious impediments stood in the way—the intimidating grandeur of English literature, for one, but Longfellow did not perceive this to be insurmountable. In fact, in "The Literary Spirit of Our Country," an essay similar in many ways to the oration and published earlier that year, he recognized that the "delicately finished model of English taste has always been the model by which we have fashioned our writings" and was willing to allow that "perhaps it is well, that it must for a time continue to be so." After all, "revolutions in letters are, indeed, the most gradual of all revolutions."[12] Clearly more imposing and debilitating were "the prevalent modes of thinking which characterize our country and our times." Longfellow observed that Americans were "a plain people that have had nothing to do with the mere pleasures and luxuries of life" and therefore "have an aversion to everything that is not practical, operative, and thorough-going" (*ONW*, 238). American literature was not yet fully developed, so it was being ignored in favor of the British. The young poet entered a plea with American entrepreneurs that, nevertheless, "if we would ever have a national literature, our native writers must be patronized" (*ONW*, 238). And he was—or claimed to be—optimistic that his plea would be answered.

The fact that the oration may be seen as a thinly veiled personal plea to his father should not distract us from—or detract from the signifi-cance of—the rhetoric in which his plea is couched. For as much as his correspondence with his father puts the biographical relevance of "Our Native Writers" into relief, so the oration reveals the ideological implica-tions of his filial rebellion. We still need to note, for instance, that the address sends conflicting cultural signals. On one hand, Longfellow re-grets the fact that "we cannot yet remove from our shelves every book which is not strictly and truly American" (*ONW*, 237), and, on the other hand, he encourages us to do so by quoting writers like Shake-speare ("the visage of the times," [*ONW*, 238]) and Scott ("This is my own, my native land," [*ONW*, 240]). On one hand, again, he can turn to advantage the perceived English reproach "that we have no finished scholars" by arguing deftly that "our very poverty in this respect will have a tendency to give a national character to our literature" because "we are thus thrown upon ourselves"; on the other hand, the address hardly lacks for classical allusion and calculated displays of erudition (*ONW*, 238). We could, of course, attribute these particular lapses to adolescent pretentiousness. Or we could see in them (from one point of view) Longfellow's still-evolving nationalism or (from another) the pre-conscious roots of his "denationalization." But, as with the various ex-planations of Webster's inconsistencies, these explain away more than they explain. We need, rather, to see the apparent lapses as part of a series of contradictory cultural assumptions held together by a funda-mental ambiguity in the meaning of the term *America*, an ambiguity that sustains the exclusionary force in the phrase "strictly and truly American." It allows the young Longfellow, in one breath, to define our "national literature" as "a literature associated and linked . . . with our institutions, our manners, our customs, in a word, with all that has helped to form whatever there is peculiar to us and the land in which we live" and, in the next breath, to identify the "prevalent" national charac-teristics as practical, thoroughly materialistic, and antiliterary (*ONW*, 237–238). It allows him to identify "our native writers" as "those who have been nursed and brought up . . . in the civil and religious freedom of our country" and to maintain nevertheless that poetry would spring only "in the hearts of those men whose love for the world's gain, for its business and its holiday has grown cold" (*ONW*, 237, 239). The logical inconsistency escaped him; in his mind he could (like Webster) separate the country he knew from the nation he envisioned, a nation whose "generous spirit" would engender "a rich development of poetic feeling" through "a genuine birth of enthusiasm" (*ONW*, 238, 239).

Tocqueville can once again serve as a convenient point of comparison. "The relations that exist between the social and political condition of a people and the genius of its authors are always numerous," Tocqueville explains; "whoever knows the one is never completely ignorant of the other." The dearth of American literature did not disturb the Frenchman, because he saw the lack as a result of the nature of American society. In the United States, men were practical, materialistic, acquisitive—they had no time for literary pursuits. If any literature were quintessentially American, it would be journalism—the genre of the here and now. Eventually, Americans would produce a more belletristic body of writing, but even so, Tocqueville predicted, it would take on the character of the American democracy: "Style will frequently be fantastic, incorrect, overburdened, and loose, almost always vehement and bold. Authors will aim at rapidity of execution more than at perfection of detail. Small productions will be more common than bulky books; there will be more wit than erudition, more imagination than profundity; and literary performances will bear the marks of an untutored and rude vigor of thought, frequently of great variety and singular fecundity. The object of authors will be to astonish rather than to please, and to stir the passions more than to charm the taste" (*DIA*, 2:62–63).

Although Longfellow clearly saw America in similar terms, he was not prepared for Tocqueville's conclusions. For him, literature was "polite literature"—polished, refined, elegant, correct, scholarly, exhibiting a refined taste—a literature antithetical to "all the vain cares that beset [men] in the crowded thoroughfares of life," nonpractical by definition (*ONW*, 238, 239).[13] For Tocqueville, following Condillac, "America" (equality of condition) redefined "literature"; for Longfellow, "literature" redefined "America"—only what is "noble and attractive in our national character will [or could] one day be associated with the sweet magic of Poetry" (*ONW*, 237). Only what is noble and attractive is "strictly and truly American." It is the pressure of this exclusionary force that leads Longfellow out of "the shadow of our free political institutions" to consider "the influence of national scenery in forming *the* poetical character," as if American poetry could only be national in topographic terms (*ONW*, 237, 239; italics mine).

Longfellow's nationalism here is clearly drawn from commonsense associationist psychology: in "The Literary Spirit of Our Country," he explains at some length how "climate and natural scenery have a powerful influence in forming the intellectual character of a nation," how by "intercourse and long familiarity" nature inspires us with "hallowed and associated feelings" which "we cherish and revere through life."[14] But his version of associationism excludes all but the natural environment: he avoids discussion of how American literature may be "associated and linked" with America's political and economic life. In effect, his associationism allows him to *dissociate* American poetry rhetorically from what he himself defines as the "prevalent modes of thinking" in America. Let me emphasize here that Longfellow was not, like Webster, working with a perceived absence, with political and economic institutions as yet unformed. "Our government has passed the ordeal of time," he wrote in "The Literary Spirit of Our Country," and "the same spirit that animated our fathers in their great struggle for freedom, still directs the popular mind to honourable enterprise."[15] Certainly he acted upon good authority, most prominently Wordsworth, when he considered the importance of nature to poetic development. And for the influence of climate on national character, Montesquieu. But prominent in Montesquieu's considerations was the effect of climate upon political formations.[16] And Wordsworth, though he sees nature as something apart from "the public way," antithetical to "getting and spending," did not really consider the idea of literary nationalism.[17] Longfellow seems to have conflated the two: "We may rejoice, then, in the hope of beauty and sublimity in our national literature, for no people are richer than we are in the treasures of nature" (*ONW*, 239). Nature here stands in for political culture, blurs the distinction between "American" and "literature," and, indeed, masks the ambiguity in the term "America" itself.[18]

A PHILOSOPHY OF THE MODERN LANGUAGES

Soon after commencement, Longfellow's life took an unexpected and extremely significant turn that would have far-reaching implications for his development as a writer. The trustees of Bowdoin College offered the young nationalist orator their newly established professorship in modern languages, with the proviso that he spend two years in Europe (at his own expense) to prepare for his duties. Whether or not the oration had a profound influence on his father, who happened to be one of the college's trustees, or whether he simply saw the professorship as an opportunity to prevent his son from becoming a poet and to set him upon a respectable career, he did agree to finance his son's stay abroad, and Longfellow departed for what turned out to be a three-year sojourn in France, Spain, Italy, and Germany on 15 May 1826.

The significance of this turn of events lay not in the irony of the young nationalist's leaving the country to study Old World culture. Longfellow's predilection for the study of foreign languages predated the offer from Bowdoin; he wrote to his father of his great admiration for Sir William Jones, for instance, in the same series of letters in which he apprised him of his literary aspirations.[19] The significance lay, rather, in the fact that the irony became lost in the ambiguity the American took with him to Europe, as it were, as part of his cultural baggage. Longfellow found his own literary nationalism echoed and reinforced in European literary nationalism. What he discovered in Europe was not simply Old World culture, not simply the languages and literatures he was to teach at Bowdoin, but a philosophical perspective that bore crucially upon his early literary and linguistic predilections and that he could adapt to fit his circumstances. Reading writers like Condillac, Michaelis, Friedrich and August Wilhelm Schlegel, Francesco Quadrion, and Simonde di Sismondi, he was introduced to a way of thinking about language and literature—about their history, their relation to nation and culture—that would both fortify his youthful patriotic leanings and allow him to embrace Old World culture by making his thinking about nationalism substantially more complex.[20]

Longfellow returned to Bowdoin convinced that the teaching of modern European languages entailed more than instructing his students how to speak and to write French and Spanish. He did teach elementary courses in foreign languages; he even translated and compiled several textbooks to aid him in that task.[21] But he was intent upon establishing the study of language as an intellectual discipline in its own right. He acquainted his students, for example, with various theories of the origin of language, from Aristotle through Origen to Rousseau.[22] But most strikingly, Longfellow wanted to introduce his students to what he called the "Philosophy of the Modern Languages," that is, to theories of linguistic and literary relativity. "In the philosophical study of the languages," he wrote in his notebook, "'we shall be led to observe, how Nations, like single men, have their peculiar ideas; how these ideas become the Genius of their language, since the symbol must of course correspond to its Archetype: etc.'"[23] One wonders what, if anything, Longfellow may have substituted for the "etc." in the lectures themselves, for Longfellow is quoting here from James Harris's *Hermes*. Harris, we recall, was a confirmed classicist and the archenemy of both Webster and Horne Tooke: he was interested in linguistic relativity only because it seemed to underscore what he already believed, that modern European languages were, philosophically considered, inferior to "THE GREEK TONGUE, [which] *from its Propriety and Universality, [is] made for all that is great, and all that is beautiful, in every Subject, and under every Form of writing.*"[24] In written form, the "etc." effectually supplants and rejects Harris's overriding intention in *Hermes*—to establish the philosophical foundation for a universal grammar grounded in classical linguistics. Longfellow may very well have admired Harris's intellectually sophisticated attempt to find meaning in grammar: after all, he would himself spend much time teaching grammar. But more clearly, in quoting Harris Longfellow indicated his difference from Harris, his intellectual readiness for a more purely relativist point of view. And it displays as well, just as significantly, his willingness to quote his sources out of context, to appropriate ideas for his own purposes, a practice that is characteristic of his scholarly work and through which he was able to express his Americanness.

The distance Longfellow had traveled since his graduation—along with his differences from Harris—becomes even more clear later on in the same notebook, where Longfellow seems to have been preparing a lecture with the Michaelis-like title "The Influence of National Character upon Language: and of Language upon National Character." Associationism is here left behind for the organicism of the continental Romantics. "A complexion is given to National character by climate—natural scenery—political situation and modes of life," he begins. "Hence arise peculiarities of thought and feeling." Because "language is but an expression of this—or in other words a palpable form in which these are presented to us—it must evidently correspond in its character to the character of a nation." The study of a language is, ultimately, the study of national character. He explains that, "according to the circumstances of its origin and progress—and the peculiar character of the people who speak" it, a language may "be cold, or passionate—grave or lively—majestic or trivial—slow or rapid—severe or voluptuary—rigid or flexible." Over time, in other words, a language's "progress towards perfection will be modified by the circumstances attending it" and by the degree to which "the ideas of a people become more enlarged and refined."[25] By studying languages comparatively and historically—that is, by mastering languages in order to read literature more critically—students could learn the history of the human mind and spirit.

The details and implications of Longfellow's "Philosophy of the Modern Languages" were worked out in his various college lectures and in a series of essays on modern European languages and literatures written for the *North American Review*.[26] But most generally and succinctly, they are expressed in the inaugural address he delivered at Bowdoin on 2 September 1830, *Origin and Growth of the Languages of Southern Europe and of Their Literature.* The history that seems to have influenced him (and which he draws upon) most in this lecture was Simonde de

Sismondi's *De la littérature du Midi de l'Europe*, and by comparing Longfellow to Sismondi we can begin to understand how Longfellow's "fine ambiguity" informed his adaptation of the new European learning.[27]

Sismondi begins his encyclopedic work by explaining that the rationale for his particular history, and for comparative literary study in general, lay in the natural growth and development of nations. He argues that only when a nation has reached a particular stage in its development is the study of foreign literature desirable. When nations are "in their infancy," he writes, they "are animated by a creative genius, which endows them with a poetry and literature of their own, while it renders them, at the same time, capable of splendid enterprises, susceptible of lofty passions, and disposed to great sacrifices." At this stage, "the literature of other nations is unknown to them" and, for their own benefit, should remain unknown (*LSE*, 1:25). For when "the literature of other countries . . . [is] adopted by a young nation with a sort of fanatical admiration," as it is likely to be, then "the spirit of imitation . . . extinguish[es] their natural vigour" (*LSE*, 1:27, 26). Even if servile imitation is avoided, however, the unself-conscious creativity of this early stage eventually passes. A time arrives when the "mind is no longer ignorant of itself," when "every thing is matter of observation, even to the mode of observing, and every thing is governed by rules, even to the art of imposing rules." During this second stage, "the spirit of analysis chills the imagination and the heart, and the soaring flight of genius is at an end." This is "the age of analysis and philosophy" (*LSE*, 1:28). And, Sismondi writes, it is the age in which Europe—and especially France—now finds itself.

At this point in history, Sismondi writes, comparative literary study is not only acceptable but essential. Nations must realize that "great authors are found in other languages" (*LSE*, 1:29):

> Let us learn to distinguish the genius of man from the genius of nations, and to raise ourselves to that height whence we may distinguish the rules which are derived from the essential principles of beauty, and which are common to all languages, from those which are adopted from great examples, which custom has sanctioned, refinement justified, and propriety still upholds; but which may, notwithstanding, amongst other nations, give place to other rules, depending upon other notions of propriety and other customs, sanctioned by other examples, and approved by the test of another, and, perhaps, not less perfect mode of analysis. (*LSE*, 1:30).

It is clear to Sismondi that the "genius of man can never again approach its noble origin, and recover the station which it held before the birth of prejudices" except "by elevating itself sufficiently above them to compare and analyse them all" (*LSE*, 1:29). The study of foreign languages and literatures is a cultural requisite for European nations, particularly the rationalistic French, who had fallen into the sin of chauvinistic neo-classicism. It was a way of rediscovering nationalism on a more liberal and universalist basis. The cure for self-knowledge, in short, is the knowledge of others.

According to Howard Mumford Jones, it was Sismondi's rhapsodic depiction of the first stage of national literary development—with its admonitory "better to leave them to themselves"—that inspired and encouraged the early champions of American literature. But as fond as Longfellow was of quoting from the literary historian, he does not make this particular part of Sismondi's argument his own—even though he had offered a similar argument himself five years earlier in "Our Native Writers." Most immediately, of course, it would have placed the newly installed professor of modern languages in a decidedly awkward position: if America and her literature were yet in their infancy, why study foreign culture? "It is better to leave them to themselves." For Longfellow, the matter was neither temperamentally nor ideologically so simple. His strategy is different from Sismondi's. The story Sismondi tells—or, more accurately, the mythological framework within which he wants us to read his history—is of original innocence, corruption, and rebirth. His cultural position is clear: he stands in the midst of European "prejudice" and at the threshold of transcendence. Longfellow's *American* position is more tenuous and his expression of it more ambiguous. His subject, like Sismondi's, is the fall of one culture and the origin and growth of another: specifically, "the decline of Roman literature; the origin of the modern languages; the state of the human mind and of society during the middle ages, and its influence on the revival of letters."[28] But his stated pedagogic purpose—"To trace the progress of the human mind through the progressive development of language; to learn how other nations thought, and felt, and spake; to enrich the understanding by opening upon it new sources of knowledge; and by speaking many tongues to become a citizen of the world"—lacks the moral immediacy of Sismondi's (*OGL*, 6). These are other languages, other cultures, other times. The nods here toward universalism ("the human mind"), provincialism ("other nations"), and cosmopolitanism ("citizen of the world") only underscore the cultural tenuousness of Longfellow's position.

When Longfellow turns to conclude his broad but detailed survey, he apologizes perfunctorily for having "done nothing but point out . . . the landmarks of that vast field of literature, which I hope ere long to explore with those whose situation leads them to rely upon my feeble endeavors." But he follows with another, more pointed, apology that throws much light on his cultural position: "I hope, farther, that I shall discharge these duties with becoming zeal" *but* "without investing them [the works of medieval literature] with an *importance* they do not deserve, or attributing to them a *duration* they cannot possess" (*OGL*, 111–112; italics mine). Importance and duration: in part Longfellow is apologizing for a new and ground-breaking discipline, the worth of whose primary materials was still in question, unlike the important and enduring classics of Greece and Rome, whose curricular status was secure. Yet the apology follows, and seems curiously to draw back from, Longfellow's overarching argument (taken, perhaps, from A. W. Schlegel) that "the spirit of modern literature" is marked by a "religious feeling," a "constant grasping after the things of another and higher world," while ancient literature is characterized by its this-worldliness: "heaven was an earthly heaven, and the eye could take in at a glance the sensual paradise of the Elysian Fields" (*OGL*, 110).[29] This drawing back may be explained by the fact that, in large part, Longfellow was apologizing as an American, preparing the way for his country's role in the literary and intellectual history of the world.

Let me explain further by turning to the closing lines of his address, a passage, ironically enough, quoted from Sismondi:

"For who may say," I speak in the language of an eminent literary historian, "who may say that Europe itself shall not in a few ages become as wild and deserted as the hills of Mauritania, the sand of Egypt, and the valleys of Anatolia? Who may say, that in some new land . . . *nations with other manners, other languages, and other thoughts shall not arise once more to renew the human race, and to study the past as we have studied it:* nations who hearing with astonishment of our existence, that our knowledge was as extensive as their own, and that we like themselves placed our trust in the stability of fame, shall pity our impotent efforts, and recall the names of Newton, of Racine, and of Tasso, as examples of the vain struggles of man to snatch that immortality of glory, which fate has refused to bestow?" (*OGL*, 112–113).

The emphases are mine, but the ellipsis is Longfellow's. Sismondi, who included these remarks at the close of a chapter on Arabic literature, had certain exotic "new land[s]" in mind, "those lofty regions, whence the Oronoco and the river of the Amazons have their source, or, perhaps, in the impregnable mountain-fastnesses of New Holland." But Longfellow chose to leave the identity of the "new land" suggestively ambiguous. Furthermore, Sismondi had identified Europe in the passage as the place "whither the empire of letters and of science has been transported" and had included "other religions" in his enumeration of "other manners, other languages, other thoughts" (*LSE*, 1:70). Longfellow dropped these—patriotically, reverently, and silently. Moreover, for Sismondi, "Europe" is identified with the writer's "we." For Longfellow, the relationship between historian and subject matter is more complex, his place in history less clear: he explicitly announces that he assumes the eminent historian's voice in order to distance himself from it. The ellipsis, in effect, marks a historical and cultural ambiguity. Clearly, it leaves room for America. But the question the passage asks is not completely rhetorical (at least for Longfellow), and its outlook is more melancholy and cautionary than congratulatory and hopeful.

The ambiguity in Longfellow's borrowed peroration turns us back upon the linguistic and literary history sketched in the address, especially upon the social, political, and intellectual conditions that, Longfellow tells us, influenced the origin and growth of—and are reflected in—European languages and literatures. Longfellow's position is defined by the stories he tells. Theoretically, he writes, certain conditions must be met before national languages can be established, before they can be perfected to a degree that would allow for literary production, and before literature can flourish. The most basic conditions for the development of a language are social stability (reflected most prominently in the growth of agriculture) and political unity, and the story he tells of the origin of the modern languages is a story of war and peace. "From the fifth to the tenth century the South of Europe was the scene of continual wars," Longfellow explains, and for those five centuries "the South of Europe may be said to have been without a language" (OGL, 22, 25). Only "after the long vicissitudes of war," when "the northern invader . . . felt that the luxuriant though uncultivated fields around him had become his country and his home, the soil was again tilled," and "society began once more to assume something like harmonious order," only then did the "illformed" admixtures of Latin and northern languages assume "the regularity of . . . uniform dialect[s]" and "those [languages] now spoken from the mouth of the Tagus to the mountains of Calabria" arise "out of the wreck of all language" (OGL, 27–30). The Provençal was the first of the Romance languages to develop, for instance, because the kingdom of Provence was "sheltered by the Alps on one side and on the other by the Pyrenees and the Mediterranean" and, alone of all her less sheltered neighbors, "had reposed in peace for nearly two centuries." "This repose," Longfellow explains, "was favorable to the development and the cultivation of a newly formed language, and to the revival of letters" (OGL, 31–32).

When he turns his attention next to "the origin of the literature of these several nations," Longfellow repeats his story of decline and rise, not as a narrative of war and peace, but as a movement from slavery to freedom. And his primary concern is not social and political institutions but the intellectual consequences of those institutions. "From the seventh century to the middle of the tenth," he writes, "the human mind had reached its lowest point of degradation." "Europe groaned beneath the triple tyranny of her Kings, her feudal lords, and her licentious priesthood" and the "human mind had become hoodwinked and enslaved" (*OGL*, 42–44). However, sometime during the eleventh century, the "aspiring and immortal principle of the human mind . . . burst its cerements, and struggled to be free" (*OGL*, 53). Longfellow identifies the primary institutional causes of this intellectual liberation as, on one hand, chivalry, which "introduced gentleness of manners, high minded feelings, and a refinement of honour and courtesy, unknown amid the convulsions of feudal anarchy," and, on the other hand, the Crusades, which spread "universal terror" all over Europe. Significantly, Longfellow halts his brief "political history" without explaining how the Crusades, which he portrays in a wholly negative light, contributed to the intellectual liberation of modern Europe, but he does insist that both constitute "the spirit of the age" and that their combined "influence upon the origin of modern literature in the succeeding centuries was immediate, vast, and powerful" (*OGL*, 56–59).

Significantly, that is, because he immediately follows his description of the "ill-directed zeal" of the crusaders' "undisciplined army," not with an announced description of the influence of the spirit of the age upon medieval literature, but with theoretical reflections upon the origin of poetry, reflections which reintroduce the theme of repose and tranquillity as they interrupt the narrative flow of the address, reflections that are more reminiscent of Pope than of Sismondi.[30] Longfellow admits, of course, that any attempt to sketch the origin of poetry is necessarily speculative since "we have only vague and uncertain traditions" to draw upon. "Doubtless," he nevertheless concludes, poetry "originated amid the scenes of pastoral life, and in the quiet and repose of a golden age." *Doubtless*, because "in all ages poets have loved the woodland shades" and because there is "something congenial in the soft melancholy of the groves which pervades the heart, and delights the imagination"—as if poetry always manifested not the spirit of its age but of an ideal golden age, when "life itself was an ecologue [*sic*]" and poetry itself only "added new charms to the simplicity and repose of bucolic life." Only in "later days," he presumes, did poetry sing "the praises of Grecian and Roman heroes, and [peal] in the war-song of the Gothic Scald": the belatedness of this sort of poetry underscores its inferiority (*OGL*, 61–63). Not only is Longfellow's clear valorization of the pastoral marked in these passages, but his inclusion of these remarks at this point in the address indicates his discomfort with the fact that the earliest modern poetry he was aware of was martial in character, as if his narrative of literary history had to begin with pastoral whether the history itself began that way or not.

In other words, Longfellow seems to insist that the value of poetry is both relative and absolute. Let me stress that this is not so much a contradiction as it is an ambiguity—the same sort of ambiguity that informed "Our Native Writers." Longfellow is quite ready to insist upon literary relativity, that "poetry is but the thoughts and feelings of a people, and [that] we give it the appellation of national, only when the character of a nation shines visibly and clearly through it," no matter what that character is (*OGL*, 63–64). From the scholar's point of view, the study of literary history and the study of political history are one. Indeed, Longfellow can sound, at times, very much like Tocqueville:

> If a national literature is animated with a martial ardour, and reflects the fame of heroes and the pomp of war, we may rationally infer, that the nation to which it belongs, was at that period of its history at least, a warlike people skilled in arms, and habituated to the stir of camps and the sound of battle. Or, if the poetry of a country be of a gentle pastoral kind, it conveys to our mind the image of a people enjoying the delights of peace, and gathering unmolested the fruits of their vineyards and the products of their fields. Again, if the history of a nation is one of war and revolution, we should have no doubt that whatever literature it might possess would resound with the praises of its heroes and the achievement of its arms: or if we read in history that a people had long turned its swords into ploughshares and its spears into pruning hooks, we may naturally infer that its literature is redolent with the charms of pastoral scenes and the delights of pastoral life. (*OGL*, 65–67)

But the rhetoric of the passage, the counterpoint of martial and pastoral, strengthened by the description of the origins of poetry that immediately precedes it in the text, undercuts—or rather gives direction to—the relativistic philosophical assumptions that sustain it. The conflict of values becomes even more apparent when Longfellow specifically describes the influence of the Moors on the poetry of Spain. Although "the spirit of the warrior is visible in a great portion of the Spanish romances," he writes, "in others the knight throws down his spear and unclasps his helmet." In these works, the "sound of the Moorish flute mingles with the brazen voice of the trumpet," but the relative value of the two strains is not lost in the mingling: "the rough feelings of the chieftain give way to gentler affections and more peaceful dreams" (*OGL*, 90).

My point is that we need to read Longfellow's inaugural address as an imaginative attempt to make sense of the origins of modern European language and literature—an attempt made in order to define America's place in linguistic and literary history, the place marked by the elliptical ambiguity in his closing paragraph. To accomplish this, he tells, in effect, two sorts of stories. The first is a historical tale of cultural progress: war followed by peace, slavery by freedom, illiteracy by literacy, and, most broadly, paganism by Christianity. The final chapter of this story—the rise of American culture—is what is hinted at in Longfellow's closing passage. The second story is mythological rather than historical: it begins in a golden, pre-Christian (though Longfellow does not explicitly refer to it as such) age of pastoral. If anything, it is a story of decline: life can never again be so simple, poetry never so purely poetical. Even so, pastoral values are eternal, and modern poetry can, at its best, echo them: pastoral is the origin of poetry and its recurring point of arrival.[31] When America is shadowed forth in the Sismondian closing paragraph, these values are shadowed forth as well. To put this another way, pastoral's function in the inaugural address is similar to that of natural scenery in the commencement oration: it follows within the expository line of the text, but it does not follow from the logic the text seems to be setting forth. I do not mean to ignore the difference between the sublime and the bucolic that distinguishes "Our Native Writers" from *Origin and Growth*. (Indeed, Longfellow would distance himself from the sublimity-and-grandeur school of American poetics first in "Defence of Poetry" and then, more emphatically, in *Kavanagh*.) But I do wish to suggest that in both works the relationship between literature and society is obscured—and the meaning of America thus made ambiguous—by a turning away from society, and from theories that see literature as a reflection or embodiment of the spirit of the age, a turn toward the notion of an unchanging nature and "the enduring requirements for great art."

AMERICAN LITERATURE

I should make clear that America is only an implied presence in *Origin and Growth*. It is referred to in an offhand manner at the very beginning of the address, when Longfellow sets forth his pedagogic philosophy—he remarks that "he who bends in a right direction the pliant disposition of the young, and trains up the ductile mind to a vigorous and healthy growth, does something for the welfare of his country and something for the great interests of humanity"—and again, more suggestively, when it is shadowed forth in the elliptical quotation from Sismondi at the end (*OGL*, 4). But in his 1832 "Defence of Poetry"—an updating of Sir Philip Sidney's *The Defence of Poesy* occasioned by the publication of a new edition of the work issued in 1831—Longfellow applies his new learning directly to America and its literature. In effect, "Defence of Poetry" can be seen both as a significant postgraduate, Continentalized revision of "Our Native Writers" and "The Literary Spirit of Our Country" and, since Sidney is expressly presented as one of the "connecting links between the ages of chivalry and our own," as an American sequel to *Origin and Growth*.[32]

Given the divided nature of Longfellow's approach to literary and linguistic history, it should not be surprising that the essay is divided into two parts, about equal in length, and argues two different theses: the first part defends poetry in general against "the popular doctrine of utility"; the second argues that "our native poets [should] give a more national character to their writings" (*DOP*, 60, 74). Nor should it surprise us, given the thematic importance of pastoralism in *Origin and Growth*, that each part begins with a pointed reference to pastoral. In the first, Longfellow prefaces his attack against American utilitarianism by mentioning Sidney's "little known, and still less read" *Arcadia* as one of his "most celebrated productions" and lamenting that "for now the pastoral reed seems entirely thrown aside," that the "shepherd's song,—the sound of the oaten pipe, and the scenes of pastoral loves and jealousies, are no becoming themes for the spirit of the age" (*DOP*, 57). In the second, he introduces his call for literary nationalism with a passage on the pastoral origins of poetry virtually identical with that of his inaugural address. Along with repeated references to Sidney and *The Defence of Poesy*, these invocations of the pastoral are what give a sense of coherence to the essay's two essentially disparate parts.

Disparate, because to defend its two theses, Longfellow must, as in *Origin and Growth*, define poetry in mutually exclusive ways. In the first part, poetry is defined as antithetical to "the spirit of the age," an age "clamorous for utility,—for visible, tangible utility,—for bare, brawny, muscular utility" (*DOP*, 59). In the second part, he describes the "intimate connexion of poetry with the manners, customs, and characters of nations" (*DOP*, 67). And only a *sense* of coherence, because he never explicitly addresses the problem.

Longfellow's strategy in the first part begins with a redefinition of terms. He argues that "we are much led astray by this word utility" because its "meaning is so vague, and so often misunderstood and misapplied." Utility should not be understood to apply only "to those acquisitions and pursuits, which are of immediate and visible profit to ourselves and the community" but to the less tangible rewards of poetry. Of course, poetry "will not till our lands, nor freight our ships, nor fill our granaries and our coffers," he admits, "but [it] will enrich the heart, freight the understanding, and make up the garnered fulness of the mind," and these are valuable, too (*DOP*, 60–61). Moreover, Longfellow goes so far as to argue that these intangible profits are *more* valuable than material gain, especially on a national level. Americans who boast of their country's material progress or even of her natural grandeur are working under a misconception of what "the true glory of a nation consists." In a striking departure from "Our Native Writers," Longfellow writes that national glory does not consist "in the extent of its territory, the pomp of its forests, the majesty of its rivers, the height of its mountains, and the beauty of its sky." Rather, "the true glory of a nation is moral and intellectual pre-eminence"; it lies "in the extent of its mental power,—the majesty of its intellect,—the height and depth and purity of its *moral* nature" (*DOP*, 59; italics mine). To this nationalist end, poetry is particularly useful, and "whoever in the solitude of his chamber, and by even a single effort of his mind, has added to the intellectual pre-eminence of his country, has not lived in vain, nor to himself alone" (*DOP*, 61).

Let me clarify Longfellow's argument and his rhetorical strategy in the first part a bit further by comparing two aspects of the essay to its Renaissance model. First of all, Sidney's *Defence of Poesy* was addressed to the Elizabethan nobility, that is, to potential patrons who formed an educated elite (Longfellow even quotes Sidney's "Thus your names shall flourish in the printers' shops" near the beginning of his essay), and he argued only against those "that professing learning inveigh against poetry," those, in other words, who respect philosophers and historians, in particular, but who berate poets.[33] His overall thesis is that poetry does what philosophy and history do, only better. But Longfellow, writing in "a pecuniary society under democratic patronage," could not adopt that strategy.[34] His targets were all those "in our active community" who inveighed against *all* learning, and he compared them to the Gothic barbarians who associated "a love of letters and the fine arts" with "the corruption and degeneracy of the Western Empire" (*DOP*, 61).[35] And his argument is that the poetic or contemplative life must join with the active life to form a balanced individual and, by extension, a well-regulated society. Second, Sidney lists as one of "the most important imputations laid to the poor poets" that "both in other nations and in ours, before poets did soften us, we were full of courage, given to martial exercises, the pillars of manlike liberty, and not lulled asleep in shady idleness with poets' pastimes." His response is that, to begin with, only perverse poetry corrupts (as corrupt medicine poisons) and that, more significant, poetry can hardly be said to debilitate soldiers because it has always been "the companion of camps."[36] Longfellow echoes both charge and refutation but with important differences that follow from the differences in his socioeconomic situation and his understanding of literary history. He writes that anti-intellectual Americans "think, that the learning of books is not wisdom; that study unfits a man for action;

that poetry and nonsense are convertible terms; that literature begets an effeminate and craven spirit; in a word, that the dust and cobwebs of a library are a kind of armor, which will not stand long against the hard knocks of 'the bone and muscle of the State,' and the 'huge two-fisted sway' of the stump orator" (*DOP*, 62). So far, mutatis mutandis, Sidney: Longfellow's concern here is primarily with the marketplace and the political arena, not the field of battle, but militarism remains important as a trope, and he adduces, among others, the historical figure of Sidney himself, soldier and scholar, as proof that "poetry neither enervates the mind nor unfits us for the practical duties of life" (*DOP*, 63). However, although he can argue like Sidney that poetry demoralizes only when it is abused, he can argue neither that poetry mixes well with business and politics nor (recalling its pastoral origins) that it can be associated with militarism. Indeed, he prefers to maintain the distinction between the active and meditative realms, a preference embodied stylistically in the oppositional structure of many of the sentences through which the argument is put forth.[37]

For Longfellow conceives of poetry in opposition to the practical life or, perhaps more accurately, as a corrective to it. "Man must have his hours of meditation as well as of action," he writes. "There are times, when both body and mind are worn down by the severity of daily toil," when "the spirit longs for the waters of Shiloah, that go softly," when man needs to leave "the beaten, dusty thoroughfare of business" and "the soul abstracts herself from the world." These times "are often those of the greatest utility [properly redefined] to ourselves and others," and these are the times for poetry (*DOP*, 63–64). It is in the context of this conception of poetry that Longfellow invokes Sidney's neo-Aristotelian refutation of the Platonic argument that poetry is by its very nature false and, moreover, politically harmful. Even though "poetry is nothing but fiction," he writes, "still . . . the impressions we receive can be erroneous so far only, as the views presented to the mind are garbled and false to nature." He concludes "that the natural tendency of poetry is to give us correct moral impressions, and thereby advance the cause of truth and the improvement of society" (*DOP*, 66). Poetry is true to nature, in other words, because it is fictional in fact, because the poet is able to abstract "correct moral impressions" from experience. Poetry is thus defined not only against "the spirit of the age"—against business, politics, materialism, and so on—but also against the physical world and mundane experience.

So when Longfellow introduces the "intimate connexion of poetry with the manners, customs, and characters of nations" in the second part of the essay, he must somehow reconcile this other "very important view of the subject" with the explicit assertion that the age is antipoetic.

To this end he recalls, as he did in *Origin and Growth*, the origin of poetry "amid the scenes of pastoral life, and in the quiet repose of a golden age." And, as in the earlier address, the invocation of the pastoral performs a critical expository, if not a thoroughly logical, function. On one hand, it reaffirms the relation of poetry to repose and underscores the difference between that originary golden age and the Age of Jackson, an age in which, we recall, no one reads Sidney's *Arcadia* any longer. On the other hand, it blurs the metasocial nature of poetry by depicting a time when "life itself was an eclogue," that is, when poetry did not relieve the pressures of life, did not remove man from the world, but reflected it back to him in an enhanced version. It is through this double function that the passage on pastoral serves as a crucial transition to Longfellow's argument "that now, whilst we are forming our literature, we should make it as original, characteristic, and national as possible" (*DOP*, 69).

Longfellow needs to argue that American literature should both reflect and affect the spirit of the age. Or, to put this another way, he seems to understand the phrase "spirit of the age" in two different ways, both as the existential quality that characterizes a particular period (pastoralism, militarism, utilitarianism) and as that period's essential spirituality, regardless of the particular quality that characterizes it materially. Literature, as an intellectual product, can and must reflect both. Hence the two theoretical distinctions Longfellow introduces in the second part of the essay. First, drawing both upon Sidney's distinction between history and poetry (that while history records the real, poetry depicts the ideal) and upon Friedrich Schlegel's definition of literature "as the voice which gives expression to human intellect,—as the aggregate mass of symbols, in which the spirit of an age or the character of a nation is shadowed forth," he offers a composite distinction between the "history of a nation," which "is the external symbol of its character" and from which we need to "reason back to the spirit of the age that fashioned its shadowy outline," and national poetry, which is "the spirit of the age itself,—embodied in the forms of language, and speaking in a voice that is audible to the external as well as the internal sense." He is thus able to argue that even when works of literature seem unrealistic, when they consist of "exaggerated facts, or vague traditions, or inventions entirely apocryphal," they nevertheless can be said to "represent the spirit of the ages which produced them" (*DOP*, 68). Most broadly, this distinction introduces an enabling ambiguity into the discussion: by allowing for a difference between the spirit of the age and its existential character, he can imply both difference and identity in the relation between American literature and American life.

The second distinction concerns the definition of national literature:

Longfellow argues that the term does not apply to "every mental effort made by the inhabitants of a country, through the medium of the press" but only those works which are marked by "those distinguishing features, which literature receives from the spirit of a nation,—from its scenery and climate, its historic recollections, its Government, its various institutions,—from all those national peculiarities, which are the result of no positive institutions, and, in a word, from the thousand external circumstances, which either directly or indirectly exert an influence" (*DOP*, 69–70). This distinction, first of all, allows Longfellow an exclusionary power, to withhold the appellation "national" from those works which do not seem to him truly American. Second, it makes the term "national"—and hence "American"—contingent upon so many diverse and unmeasurable variables as to render the term wholly subjective and, effectually, to beg the question of Americanness altogether. It is very telling that, when Longfellow offers "a few illustrations of the influence of external causes upon . . . the general complexion of literary performances," he turns not to political institutions but once again to "natural scenery and climate" and considers the relative affinities of the English, Italians, Spanish, and Portuguese to the pastoral (*DOP*, 70).

I do not mean to suggest either that these distinctions in themselves logically resolve the contradiction at the very heart of the "Defence of Poetry" or that they mask a lack of logical rigor. I mean, rather, that Longfellow does not conceive of his two approaches to poetry as discrepant and that the ambiguities introduced by these distinctions allow him to sustain the contradiction. First of all, by granting literary history an integrity of its own apart from "any record of mere events," he is able to merge the idea of the spiritual "utility" of poetry described in the first part of the essay with the theory of literary relativity outlined in the second. Because literature maintains an ambiguous relation to the actualities of national life, its historicity frees it from pure reflectionality and endows it with an affective (and meliorative) power, while still presenting an unmediated picture of a nation's spirit at any particular age. So conceived, American literature need not be a contradiction in terms. Clearly, Longfellow cannot go so far as to imagine, with Shelley, that "poets are the unacknowledged legislators of the world."[38] But he can conceive that poetry can contribute to the molding of a nation's character and that the "impressions produced by poetry upon national character at any period, are again re-produced, and give a more pronounced and individual character to the poetry of a subsequent period" (*DOP*, 67). And in this way, he can grant poetry "far greater importance in itself, and in its bearing upon society, than the majority of mankind would be willing to allow" (*DOP*, 69). In other words, literature's efficacy lies in its historicity, as its character lies in its nationality. Hence the absolutely crucial importance, for Longfellow, of the golden age of pastoral: the two definitions of poetry can merge in literary history only as long as poetry originates when "life itself was an eclogue."

Second, the ambiguities enable Longfellow to reject the various prescriptive recommendations of other literary nationalists—for instance, "that the war-whoop should ring in every line, and every page be rife with scalps, tomahawks, and wampum"—and to "whisper" to prospective American authors that the "whole secret" of literary nationalism "lies in Sidney's maxim,—'Look in thy heart and write'" (*DOP*, 69). Most directly, Longfellow's "whisper" is an admonition against "any pre-conceived notions of what poetry ought to be, caught by reading many books, and imitating many models." But its broader significance lies in the fact that it diverts attention from the definition of "American" as "utilitarian" and projects the meaning of America onto the level of language. To be American, poets have simply "to write more naturally, to write from their own feelings and impressions, from the influence of what they see around them" (*DOP*, 75). The potential incompatibility of internal "feelings" and external "influence" is blurred in the language of poetry. True Americanness is measured not so much in content or theme or national origin as in the simplicity of style and diction. Preconception and imitation are by definition un-American because they corrupt language itself. "Instead of ideas," imitative writers "give us merely the signs of ideas." In "these days of verbiage," they "erect a great bridge of words, pompous and imposing, where there is hardly a drop of thought to trickle beneath" (*DOP*, 75, 77, 75). Hence the ironic suggestions that Wordsworth, whose poetry embodies "republican simplicity," may be more American than his American imitators and that Sidney and his Elizabethan contemporaries, whose writings exhibit "a strength of expression, a clearness, and force and raciness of thought," can provide inspirational reading for aspiring American writers (*DOP*, 76, 77).

Clearly, Longfellow did not see the irony of closing his remarks on literary nationalism with Wordsworth and, in particular, the Elizabethans. Indeed, considering the fact that the essay begins with Sidney, it makes perfect *literary* sense for Longfellow to provide closure by directing American poets to "leave the present age, and go back to the olden time," to read "the whole body of English classical literature" (*DOP*, 77). Nor did he see his admonition "to write more naturally" inconsistent with his exhortation to read the best of English literature. Both are conditioned by his understanding of literary history. Poetry begets poetry: a poet should write from personal experience, should "throw his fetters off, and relying on himself alone, fathom the recesses of his own mind, and bring up rich pearls from the secret depths of thought," but the experience from which he draws must include the experience of reading poetry (*DOP*, 78). And since "the human mind is so constituted, that all men receive to a greater or less degree a complexion from those with whom they are conversant, the [American] writer who means to school himself to poetic composition"—and poetry is an art that must be learned—"should be very careful what authors he studies." Especially "in these practical days, whose spirit has so unsparingly levelled to the even surface of utility the bold irregularities of human genius, and lopped off the luxuriance of poetic feeling," American writers must necessarily turn to the poetry of other countries, particularly (since poetic education includes the study of "style and diction") England (*DOP*, 76–77). After all, Longfellow would probably argue, Americans may be without a literature of their own and, like the Gothic barbarians, may even be hostile to the study of letters, but America is not, strictly speaking, a nation arising out of barbarism. It need not create a new language and a new culture out of the ruins of the old. Thus, just as Webster turned to the language used in England between the reigns of Elizabeth and Anne as the model for American English, so Longfellow turned to the literature of that period for models of American literature.

To be sure, this argument is only implicit in the "Defence of Poetry," as it is elliptical in *Origin and Growth*. For Longfellow, the precise nature of American literature—that is, its relation to America and to the European literary traditions that preceded it—remains ambiguous, defined only as competing theories of poetry or narratives of progress and decline, and obscured by recommendations of "naturalness." My point is that Longfellow's cultural imagination is characterized by his ability to maintain the ambiguity. Its persistence throughout his career may be measured by the broad scope of Longfellow's writings, by the continuing controversy over his Americanness, and, most notably, by the seemingly renunciatory nature of his only major statement about literary nationalism published after the "Defence of Poetry," which may be found in the twentieth chapter of his "prose pastoral," *Kavanagh* (1849).[39]

The critique is articulated by Mr. Churchill, the schoolmaster (and novelist manqué) of a fictional New England town called Fairmeadow, in a conversation with a visitor named Mr. Hathaway (a caricature of Cornelius Matthews, the originator of the Young America movement), who, "in rather a florid and exuberant manner," solicits Mr. Churchill for contributions to a new magazine he intends to publish in order "to foster and patronize" American literature:[40]

> "I think, Mr. Churchill," said he, "that we want a national literature commensurate with our mountains and rivers,—commensurate with Niagara, and the Alleghenies, and the Great Lakes! . . . We want a national epic that shall correspond to the size of the country; that shall be to all other

epics what Banvard's Panorama of the Mississippi is to all other paint-
ings,—the largest in the world! . . . We want a national drama in which
scope enough shall be given to our gigantic ideas, and to the unparalleled
activity and progress of our people! . . . In a word, we want a national literature altogether shaggy and unshorn, that shall shake the earth, like a herd
of buffaloes thundering over the prairies!" (*KAT*, 84–85).

Churchill responds to Hathaway's bombast by accusing him of "con-
founding things that have no analogy," American literature and the
country's natural resources. For him, literature is by definition "rather
an image of the spiritual world, than of the physical . . . of the internal,
rather than the external" (*KAT*, 85). Moreover, literature cannot really
be "savage and wild" because it is "the result of culture and intellectual
refinement" (*KAT*, 87). He does not mean "to deny the influence of
scenery on the mind" but refuses to equate natural wonders with great
poetry or to reduce the influence of the one on the other to a simple
causality (*KAT*, 85).

Much of this may be found in the "Defence of Poetry." But here
Longfellow allows Mr. Churchill to disavow literary nationalism (when
"carried too far") by offering two different "universalist" arguments.
The first is grounded in the belief that what "is best in the great poets of
all countries is not what is national in them, but what is *universal*," that
poetic value transcends political boundaries. A great poet's "roots" may
be firmly planted in his "native soil," but his "branches wave in the un-
patriotic air, that speaks the same language unto all men" (*KAT*, 86;
italics mine). Building upon this organic analogy, he argues that "a national literature is not the growth of a day" but must be nourished for
centuries. American literature "is growing slowly but surely, striking its
roots downward, and its branches upward, as is natural." Extravagant,
chauvinistic campaigns want "to invert it, and try to make it grow with
its roots in the air" (*KAT*, 87). But neither trees nor literature grow that
way. "Let us be natural," he says, "and we shall be national enough"
(*KAT*, 86). The second argument is based on the postulate that "our
literature can be strictly national only so far as our character and modes
of thought differ from those of other nations." However, since, on one
hand, "we are very like the English," American literature must necessarily be a "continuation" (but not an imitation) of British literature (*KAT*,
86). And since, on the other hand, "the blood of all nations is mingling
with our own, so will their thought and feelings finally mingle in our
literature." German "tenderness," Spanish "passion," and French "vi-
vacity" will merge with "our solid English sense" to give to American
literature a "*universality*, so much to be desired" (*KAT*, 87; italics
mine). Here "universal" actually means something more like "cosmo-

politan." Poetic value is not measured by its transcendence but by its inclusiveness. But in neither argument is it measured by the exclusivity of nationalism.

Churchill's response is understood by critics as Longfellow's repudiation of the literary nationalism of his youth.[41] As we have seen, however, many of these ideas may already be found in Longfellow's earlier writings: the conceptual distinction between scenery and literature, the call for naturalness, the idea that a national literature must slowly develop over time, even the sense that true literature has an essence which transcends national distinctions. From the very beginning, Longfellow had been uncomfortable with the notion of an American literature "commensurate" (the term is both Hathaway's and, we should recall, Matthiessen's) with American institutions, and the discomfort manifested itself in the ambiguities of the early writings. What is remarkable about Longfellow's argument in *Kavanagh* is that in his very rejection of nationalism he is unable to dispel the ambiguities. By conjoining the "melting pot" theory of American literary nationalism (and the complementary notion of American literature as a continuation of the British) with the idea of transcendent poetic value, Longfellow reformulates the ambiguities of the earlier writings on a broader theoretical foundation. The distinction between the two universalist arguments is blurred by the ambiguity of "universal" and merges in the Crèvecoeur-like description of the course of American history. So construed, universalism is nationalism rightly understood.[42]

My argument has been that Longfellow's American imagination (as manifested in the ambiguities of "Our Native Writers") informed his study of the origin and growth of the languages and literatures of Europe and that his European scholarship—his readings in Sismondi, Schlegel, and others—enriched but did not "denationalize" his American imagination. The universalism of *Kavanagh*—nationalism conceived in ambiguity—may be seen as the theoretical culmination of Longfellow's scholarship: it is evident in Churchill's argument that Longfellow had "worked his American consciousness to that mystic point" and had transformed the ambiguities of the earlier writings into the "fine ambiguity" that James recognized. To be sure, the ideological differences between Webster's and Longfellow's American imaginations are conspicuous. Whereas Webster envisioned literary nationalism as a second American revolution, Longfellow saw it as a reemergence of pastoralism. Whereas Webster brought together the principles of common usage and analogy in pure Saxon genealogy, Longfellow joined nationalism and universalism as ethnic pluralism. For all the differences between them, however, and for all the logical inconsistencies in their thought, both could claim true Americanness and others would recognize their claims. And it is finally through these differences and inconsistencies, through these ambiguities, that the Americanness and literariness of their writings need to be measured.

"A Tongue According":
Whitman and the Literature
of Language Study

IN THE FOREWORD to his edition of Whitman's *An American Primer*, Horace Traubel records a comment by the author on the subject of language, a comment invoked over and again by scholars ever since it became the starting point for Matthiessen's account of Whitman's poetry in *American Renaissance*. "This subject of language interests me—interests me: I never quite get it out of my head," the poet is reported to have said. "I sometimes think the Leaves is only a language experiment—that it is an attempt to give the spirit, the body, the man, new words, new potentialities of speech—an American, a cosmopolitan (the best of America is the best cosmopolitanism) range of self-expression." Whitman continued, as if to explain himself: "The new world, the new times, the new peoples, the new vista, need a tongue according—yes, what is more, will have such a tongue—will not be satisfied until it is evolved."[1]

To Matthiessen, whose thesis concerned the development of a mode of literary expression in the nineteenth century that was both artistic *and* American (hence the exclusion of Webster on one count, Poe on the other, and Longfellow on both), this statement surely presented itself as an epitome of the motives he attributed to all five of his authors—"to give fulfilment to the potentialities freed by the Revolution, to provide a culture commensurate with America's political opportunity"—and goes far toward explaining his decision to close the volume with Whitman. For all his recognition of its tragic aspects, the age was, finally, that of Emerson and Whitman—not Hawthorne and Melville, nor even Thoreau. Whitman's poetry *fulfilled* "Emerson's doctrine of expression" and closes the book, as it were, on antebellum literature (*AR*, 523). The statement quoted by Traubel formed a bridge between Whitman's own theoretical interest in language and his artistic use of language, between *An American Primer* on one hand and *Leaves of Grass* on the other: Matthiessen called the section on Whitman "Only a Language Experiment," and he offered the *Primer* as a proof text for his critical method, to see "how much we can learn about Whitman just by examining his [poetic] diction" (*AR*, 517).

Matthiessen subordinates theory to practice at the same time that he valorizes the poetry as a manifestation of doctrine. I have already commented upon this critical strategy in my introduction, so I will not elaborate further here. But I should say that, as a result of this strategy, the imagination which informs *An American Primer* and Whitman's other linguistic writings is never examined in *American Renaissance* and has remained largely unexamined. The reason lies primarily in Matthiessen's and our own disciplinary prejudices. But part of the blame must be placed with Traubel himself. He called the *Primer* "a challenge rather than a finished fight": in it, Whitman was "laying his plans" rather "than undertaking to perfect them." He characterized the *Primer* as "a mass of more or less disjointed notes" that were never intended for publication and considered it unfair to "pass them under severe review" (*D&N*, 3:728n). To be sure, Traubel spoke on good authority: Whitman had himself disparaged the *Primer*, telling him that its material "was first intended for a lecture: then when [he] gave up the idea of lecturing it was intended for a book: now, as it stands, it is neither a lecture nor a book." Still, Whitman's deprecatory comments contain an intriguing equivocation. Although he characterized the *Primer* as "only a sketch-piece," that is, "a few rough touches here and there, not rounding up the theme—rather showing what may be made of it," he also remarked that he often thought "the Leaves themselves are much the same sort of thing: a passage way to something rather than a thing in itself concluded: not the best that might be done but the best it is necessary to do for the present, to break the ground." And Traubel himself was led to conclude that, in spite of its unfinished state, the *Primer* should be considered "a part of Whitman's serious literary product, of marked significance" (*D&N*, 3:729n). In this chapter, I will look at Whitman's early linguistic writings, *An American Primer* being only the best known among them, not as theories of language that help to illustrate his poetic practice, but as literary embodiments, in and of themselves, of his linguistic imagination, whose stylistic correlate is the very disjointedness Traubel found so troubling.

It is unclear from Traubel's foreword exactly when the "language experiment" comment was made: Matthiessen assumes it was made in the late 1880s, when, infirm and living on Mickle Street in Camden, Whitman was looking back over three decades of work on *Leaves of Grass*. If so, we can add a note of irony to the insights the statement provides into the poet's linguistic imagination. For it might just as well have been made early on, in the years between the appearance of the first and third editions of *Leaves of Grass*, between 1855 and 1860, when Whitman seems to have spent the most time and energy thinking, studying, and writing

about language.[2] On the whole, its tone is prospective, its mood opta-
tive. It speaks of a new nation and a new language coming into being, of
the inevitability of the progress and evolution of both. Yet there is a
curious and significant tension between the two major sentences of
Whitman's comment, between Whitman's conscious "attempt" through
his "language experiment" to fulfill the linguistic needs of "the new
world, the new times, the new peoples, the new vista" and the evolu-
tionary process that, he suggests, will inevitably satisfy them. Matthiessen obscures the tension by reversing the order of the sentences, effectually misconstruing the statement, and by drawing upon other statements
from the *Primer* itself to buttress his reading. Whitman, he writes, "believed that the fresh opportunities for the English tongue in America
were immense, offering themselves in the whole range of American
facts," and that "his poems, by cleaving to these facts, could thereby
release 'new potentialities' of expression for our native character" (*AR*,
517). Whereas Matthiessen moves from the growth of American English
to *Leaves of Grass*, Whitman actually moves from *Leaves of Grass* to the
growth of American English. Matthiessen's concern is with the "potentialities" for *poetic* language, for expressing "our native character" in literature. Whitman's focus is upon language itself: he sees his poetry as a
conscious, individual contribution to the unconscious, communal, evo-
lutionary process of the English language in the United States—however problematic that concept may be. The difference is significant indeed. And it allows us to turn away from Whitman's poetic diction to
the imagination that informs his linguistic writings.

That imagination is structured in large part by the very tension that
Matthiessen effaced, the tension between the tentativeness of "experiment" and the certainty of "evolved," between intentionality and deter-
minism, prophecy and history, a sense of being (in the words of "Song
of Myself") "both in and out of the game."[3] It is a tension embodied in
the personified grouping of world, times, peoples, and vista; inscribed in
the processual ambiguity of the phrase "will not be satisfied until"; and
informed by the open-endedness of "potentialities." In other words,
Whitman projects his belief in the manifest destiny of American English—an understanding drawn primarily from his various readings in
the study of language, his education in Democratic political thought,
and his conversion to the Emersonian persuasion—onto the American
people. A characteristic Whitmanian imaginative leap, to be sure: "what
I assume you shall assume" (*LOG*, 25). But this act of projection must
also be seen to occupy a particular, adversarial position within the discourse on American English in mid-nineteenth-century America. Of
course, Whitman would deny, from time to time, the contestational nature of his linguistic pronouncements. As early as 1855, for instance, in

what was to become the fourth section of "Song of Myself"—the section in which he considers the nature of "the Me Myself" and sees himself "both in and out of the game"—the speaker seems to renounce controversy altogether: "Backward I see in my own days where I sweated through fog with linguists and contenders, / I have no mockings or arguments. . . . I witness and wait" (*LOG*, 28). But Whitman's denial is itself a mode of contestation, very much a part of his linguistic imagination, and these lines—conjoined only by a comma, the temporal distance measured by "Backward" obscured—manifest the same sort of tension that may be seen in the later "language experiment" comment.

To put this another way, Whitman's interest in language was twofold: he was interested not only in language—in, say, the meaning and sound of words—but in the study of language as an activity unto itself. "Hast thou never thought," he wrote in an early manuscript fragment, "how there are certain studies & researches . . . almost as necessary for thee, for thy body & soul, as food, as good air, as human association and friendship? and that this very one of Names (*Language*), is one of them?" He described with apparent relish "the satisfaction[,] the ease, the pleasure, the sanity, the growth upward, and the mellowing vigor, expansion, (I say the *democracy*) of such study!" Here he is not specific about the nature of this democratic study of language, except that it was to be "taken leisurely—no haste—always eligible—fed by all times, all occasions—truly a sane & exhilarating pursuit." But he was clear as to what it was not, pointedly ruling out "college courses, or technisms," explaining that the study of language was not "to be taken up as an ungracious duty for school hours, or conned by rote from text books, or, reported from the lectures of the professors—not to be got through with in the crude seasons of youth or early manhood or womanhood, & then laid aside."[4] Plainly, both the form and the content of Whitman's linguistic writings were conceived in the context of, and in clear opposition to, contemporaneous linguistic literature (lectures, textbooks, and so on): to understand Whitman's writings on language, therefore, we cannot simply distill ideas from them but need to analyze them in all their textual and intertextual complexity. We need to see them as literature.[5]

We know that Whitman's theoretical interest in the study of language—in particular of American English—reached its peak between 1855 and 1860. Sometime late in 1855, some months after the initial publication of *Leaves of Grass*, Whitman met William Swinton, then a teacher at Mount Washington Collegiate Institute and a writer for the *New York Times*, who tutored the poet in French (Swinton was translating Rousseau's *Confessions* at the time) and introduced him to what has been

termed "the discovery of language," the rise of comparative and historical linguistic scholarship that began with Sir William Jones's researches
into the affinities between Sanskrit and the European languages.[6] During this half-decade, Whitman began a notebook of jottings and clippings entitled "Words," published a magazine article on the subject of
American English called "America's Mightiest Inheritance," sketched
another brief essay on "Our Language and Literature," drafted *An
American Primer*, and collaborated with his friend Swinton (as a ghostwriter) on *Rambles among Words*.

In fact, Whitman's intense fascination with the development in America of "a tongue according" must have begun even before he met Swinton, for it already appears in print in a paragraph toward the end of his
long preface to the 1855 edition of *Leaves of Grass*:

> The English language befriends the grand American expression . . . it is
> brawny enough and limber and full enough. On the tough stock of a race
> who through all change of circumstances was never without the idea of
> political liberty, which is the animus of all liberty, it has attracted the terms
> of daintier and gayer and subtler and more elegant tongues. It is the power-
> ful language of resistance . . . it is the dialect of common sense. It is the
> speech of the proud and melancholy races and of all who aspire. It is the
> chosen tongue to express growth faith self-esteem freedom justice equality
> friendliness amplitude prudence decision and courage. It is the medium
> that shall well nigh express the inexpressible. (*LOG*, 22–23)[7]

In this passage, Whitman displays a rudimentary awareness of several issues in the contemporaneous comparative and historical study of the
English language. The first concerns the organic connection between
national character and national language, the same issue that captured
Longfellow's imagination: Whitman first expresses the connection in the
personification of the initial two clauses and elaborates the political, intellectual, and moral attributes of both nation and language as the passage continues. A second appertains to the putative differences between
American English and British English: significantly, both the political
and linguistic differences between the two nations—differences that are
essential to Webster, Tocqueville, and countless other commentators
and were clearly known to Whitman—are underplayed here; the political
animosity which led Jefferson to characterize the British and the Americans as two separate "peoples" is swept under the designation "race"
and the controversial issue of Americanisms is smoothed over by the
verb "befriends." A third relates to the growth of English and its resulting composite nature—its "tough" Anglo-Saxon "stock" and the "dain-
tier and gayer and subtler and more elegant tongues" that were later
engrafted.

These sorts of theoretical considerations, which combine to form what we might call a mythology of American English, inform Whitman's linguistic writings, and I will elaborate below upon the interplay of the various strains in Whitman's imagination. But they constitute only one aspect of his study of language, one discourse (broadly construed) into which his writings enter and in terms of which they must be understood. Another crucial aspect—less theoretical and more practical—must also be considered, and it has, to paraphrase Emerson on Whitman's poetic career, an even longer foreground. In the broadest sense, it may very well stretch back into his childhood, when, between 1825 and 1830, he attended public school in Brooklyn. It almost certainly extends into the formative years between 1836 and 1840, when Whitman taught school on Long Island and participated in a local debating society. Only a teenager, hired to teach basic language skills (along with arithmetic and geography) to the sons of farmers—it was most likely then that Whitman first "sweated through fog with linguists" and developed an early antipathy to textbooks like Webster's *Blue-Back Speller* and Lindley Murray's *English Grammar* and, in general, to what Dennis Baron calls the "schoolmastering" of the language.[8] "Drawing language into line by rigid grammatical rules, is the theory of the martinet applied to the processes of the spirit," he later wrote in his "Words" notebook. "It is for small school-masters, not for great souls." Commenting on Murray's popular *Grammar* in particular, he wrote, "The fault [is] that he fails to understand those points where the language is the strongest, and where [the] developements [*sic*] should [be] most encouraged, namely, in being *elliptic* and *idiomatic.*—Murray would make of the young men merely a correct and careful set of writers under laws.—He would deprive writing of its life—there would be nothing voluntary and insouciant left.—"[9] It was clear to him that "not only the Dictionary of the English Language, but the Grammar of it, has yet to be written" (*D&N*, 3:666–667). Comments like these run through Whitman's linguistic writings. They indicate not only a general familiarity with popular textbooks and dictionaries but also his reformist intentions (however vague and unrealized) to replace the current primers, grammars, and dictionaries with ones of his own devising.[10] They constitute the antielitist, antigenteel aspect of Whitman's linguistic thought that Mencken much admired and go far toward explaining what Whitman meant by "language *experiment.*" If we are to make sense of his linguistic imagination, the philosophical aspect of Whitman's study of language, in all its complexity, needs to be understood to stand in problematic relation to this reformist aspect of his thought. For Whitman, the Americanness of his writings on language is defined by its attempt to incorporate the two disparate discourses.

"AMERICA'S MIGHTIEST INHERITANCE"

Whitman's various writings and jottings on language display a broad and eclectic (but plainly unsystematic) knowledge of nineteenth-century linguistic discourse. He was clearly enthralled by comparative and historical philology and appears to have read with some thoroughness (thanks to Swinton) both Christian Charles Josias Bunsen's *Outlines of Universal History, Applied to Language and Religion* and Maximilian Schele de Vere's *Outlines of Comparative Philology* and to have had some acquaintance with the thought of Jacob Grimm, Wilhelm von Humboldt, George P. Marsh, Max Müller, and Friedrich Schlegel. He was aware as well of the major lexicographers from Johnson through Webster and Worcester and the controversies that attended their work. And he knew the elementary textbooks, from Lindley Murray's popular *English Grammar* to the Anglo-Saxon–based *Hand-book of English Orthography*. He took notes on what he read, commented on what he learned, and included these writings, along with clipped items on language and philology from newspapers and reviews and long lists of words and phrases, in his "Words" notebook. From all these sources, Whitman intended to compose some sort of major American work on language—an alternative textbook, perhaps, or a dictionary or phrase book, or a series of lectures. In his notebook he jotted down possible titles: "Lessons En Passant," "Lessons Accouché," "Arousing Lessons," "Hints and Lessons," "Travelling Lessons," "Transcendental Lessons," "American Lessons," "Walt Whitman's Lessons" (*D&N*, 3:685, 712). But his plans never came to fruition.

The writings we do have—published or unpublished, finished or fragmentary—display many similarities in substance, structure, and phraseology, as if they were successive versions of the one unrealized work. Yet we need to understand each as a separate literary "experiment," each as an attempt (not always successful) to give form to his many, seemingly desultory and sometimes contradictory thoughts about language, a form that would promulge his sense of the manifest destiny of the English language in America, that would both narrate his mythology of the language and propagate his linguistic and pedagogic reforms. Consider first "America's Mightiest Inheritance," an article published in *Life Illustrated* on 12 April 1856, in relation to the unpublished essay "Our Language & Literature," thought to have been written about the same time.[11] In both, Whitman introduces the English language as "our most precious inheritance," a "bequest . . . that subordinates any perfection of politics, erudition, science, metaphysics, inventions, poems, the judiciary, printing, steam-power, mails, architecture, or what not" (*D&N*,

3:809; *NYD*, 55). In both he is vague as to the reasons for its preeminence, although they are clearly related (echoing the 1855 preface) to its being "so long in growing, so sturdy and fluent, so appropriate to our America and the genius of its inhabitants" and to its not being "a polished fossil language, but the true broad fluid language of democracy" (*NYD*, 55; *D&N*, 3:809). In both, as well, Whitman joins his cultural celebration of the English language to a reformist lamentation of its failure to live up to its promise in America. Indeed, the polemical thrust of each essay depends upon the perceived gap between linguistic promise and fulfillment and the cultural imperative that derives from it.

Yet the two essays remain substantially different imaginative expressions of the relation between America and its "tongue according." The unpublished essay is the simpler of the two. In it, the celebratory introduction is brief and explicitly conditional. English "has the nature and adaptability so well to serve us" but only "when we make it what it *must be* made." And clearly, Whitman argues, our inherited language "*has yet to be* acclimated here" (*D&N*, 3:809; italics mine). The tension between the two auxiliary verbs I have emphasized—between "must be" and "has yet to be"—generates the reformist proposals that constitute the body of the essay, and the conditions for the resolution of the tension are characterized by the nationalist terms in which those proposals are formulated: the antagonists in his linguistic drama are "English grammarians" and "ultra-marine critics and schoolmasters," and Whitman's attacks are reminiscent of Webster's denunciations of Dilworth in the *Grammatical Institute* and of Harris and Lowth in *Dissertations on the English Language*. These men and "those who follow them here" are "dazzled by the lustre of the classical tongues, whose spirit is different from ours" and know nothing of "the law of the living structure of language in its largest sense" which may be seen in "the common speech of the people" (*D&N*, 3:809–810). Whitman complains that "a kind of smell—betrays every passage of elegant writing, old and new in British works," that "the perfect . . . sanity and beauty of nature are . . . unknown and unattempted in all the literature of England," as if he had never read Wordsworth, or Carlyle, or Cobbett—or Shakespeare (*D&N*, 3:810–811). He calls for "a far more complete dictionary to be written—and the grammar boldly compelled to serve the real genius underneath our speech, which is not what the schoolmen suppose, but wild, intractable, suggestive—perhaps in time, made a free world's language" (*D&N*, 3:810). Employing the organic metaphor he used in the 1855 preface, he writes that the "life-spirit" of the United States "must be engrafted upon their inherited language" (*D&N*, 3:811). The English language has escaped the depravity of England, has arrived in the American asylum, and can now await its destiny: "The tendencies of other [i.e., foreign] minds, when viewing languages, politics, religion, literature, &c[. has been to] consider one or all of them as arbitrarily established, and as thus better than we are, and thus to rule us," Whitman explains in his peroration, but "the American mind *shall* boldly penetrate the interiors of all, and treat them as servants, only great because they forego us, and [are] sternly to be discarded the day we are ready for superior expressions" (*D&N*, 3:811; italics mine). The tension between "must" and "has yet" is resolved in the confidence of "shall." In short, "Our Language and Literature" draws its rhetorical force from a primary, controlling opposition of English and American culture, an opposition that subsumes and defines in its political terms a series of more or less common Romantic oppositions (common, that is, both to British and American writers): books and talk, elegant and common, artificial and natural, past and future, dead and living, ruled and free. The meaning of American English, as a literary symbol, takes shape in terms of these oppositions.

Despite the similarity of its point of departure and its rhetoric of promise and fulfillment, "America's Mightiest Inheritance" does not draw its rhetorical force from Websterian Anglophobia. To the contrary, the ideological antagonism is completely muted. While Whitman certainly does not repudiate his linguistic chauvinism, he formulates the conceptual grounds upon which his nationalism is brought forth in significantly more complex terms. The result is a notably more intricate text. To begin with, the delineation of the mythology of American English in the *Life Illustrated* article is considerably longer and more detailed than in "Our Language and Literature," and it is more thoroughly informed by Whitman's growing interest in the field of comparative philology. Significantly, what seems a self-evident truth in the manuscript essay, as well as in the 1855 preface—the superiority of the English language—is here underwritten, ironically, by a quotation from a foreign authority, "Grimm, the German scholar," who characterizes English as "a *universal* language, with whose richness, sound sense, and flexibility, those of none other can for a moment be compared" (*NYD*, 55–56; italics mine).

Whitman lifted this quotation from Grimm—and a substantial part of the article itself—from the introductory sections of the *Hand-book of English Orthography* published in New York in 1852 as part of a new series of elementary textbooks called "The American System of Education."[12] He was no doubt attracted to the *Hand-book*'s nationalism and revisionism, and it provided him with brief, accessible synopses of the history of the English language and of the general conclusions of the historical linguists. Without any apparent compunction, he took what he needed, molded it to his purposes, combined it with ideas culled from elsewhere (like Schele de Vere's *Outlines*), and rejected that which he could not use or with which he did not agree—most obviously and significantly, its valorization of writing over speech and its virulent strain of Anglo-Saxonism. Like the *Hand-book*, "America's Mightiest Inheritance" is structured as a series of short sections, each dealing with one aspect of a larger thesis. But rather than form a logical sequence to facilitate the learning of a complex, technical subject, Whitman's sections are strung together so as to complicate and mystify our notions of American English. He uses the quotation from Grimm, for instance, to introduce two distinct, if complementary, themes, which are developed contrapuntally in the text: first, the "universal" character of the English language; second, the importance of comparative philology as method.

As in Longfellow's *Kavanagh*, moreover, universalism here shows two faces, thus further complicating Whitman's exposition. Most simply, it appears as the composite nature of the language:

> *Contributions and Parts.*—The Anglo-Saxon stock of our language, the most important part, the root and strong speech of the native English for many centuries, mainly serves for sensible objects, specific thoughts and actions, home, and domestic life; it has the best words for manliness, friendship, and the education of childhood. The Celtic contribution consists much of proper nouns, given by the earlier inhabitants of Britain to towns, lands, woods, and mountains. The French contribution is large; the words refer to taste and the arts, poetry, manners, finesse, and law. Latin and Greek contributions refer to religion, science, the judiciary, medicine, and all learned nomenclature. (*NYD*, 58)[13]

Its composite character, Whitman argues, has given it both "elasticity" and "perfect precision," and is a manifestation of its capacity for unlimited growth. At times, like the authors of the *Hand-book*, Whitman describes this capacity in quasi-imperialist terms, relating it to the commercial character of its speakers: "The intercourse of trade with other countries annually brings back, and has long brought, words as well as wares; the best of these, in time, become familiar, and have a home look. . . . Whatever we want, wherever we want any addition, we seize upon the terms that fit the want, and appropriate them to our use" (*NYD*, 56–57). At other times, as I will explain, the capacity is described more in terms of an ethnic melting pot. "The best of America," as he would later put it to Traubel, "is the best cosmopolitanism."

Universality also refers to the primitive origins of the English language, not simply to the well-known history of migration to, and conquest of, the British Isles beginning, say, when the "*Angles* . . . passed from Germany to Britannia" and gave the "name to this mighty dialect, by naming the wonderful nation of whom it took shape"—the history, in other words, that explains its composite nature—but to the earlier history uncovered by the "modern corps" of "language searchers," who "go unerringly back, taking the English, and all other speech, to the vale of Kashmere, to the Sanskrit and the sacred Zend, the nursing-breasts of all the lore that comes home to us." This history adds little or nothing to the familiar explanation of the unique composition and capacities of the English language. To the contrary, its "farther retrospect" stresses the underlying similarity of all Indo-European languages, not their differences: English shares its Asian heritage with all modern European languages. This, indeed, is where the *Hand-book* leaves the matter. But Whitman insists that the common ancestry of European and Asian languages—understood against the background of the migrations of the Celtic, Gothic, and Slavic peoples from Asia to Europe—constitutes a significant prehistory of English in particular: "To these three enormous movements the English language recurs as one recurs to the events of forefathers," he writes; "it, too, is of Asiatic transmission" (*NYD*, 56–57).

"America's Mightiest Inheritance" (like much of Whitman's writing, both poetry and prose) is thus composed less as a piece of logical exposition than as a chain of separate and distinct observations and assertions, the transitions between them more often implied than explicitly stated, the overall argument accumulating rather than developing. Whitman presents these two histories, these two senses of universalism, in separate, alternating, juxtaposed sections: he narrates the composite history in a section entitled "*Stocks and Grafts of the English Language*," follows it with an explanation of Indo-European linguistic history in "*Asiatic Stock—Movements of Races*," and then returns to further elaborate the composite history in "*Composition and Parts.*" What is suggested by this structure is a larger historical principle of coherence, a principle Whitman hints at with the only tangible link among these disparate sections, his American method of dating historical events: the Anglo-Saxon migration to Britain occurred "in the year 1326 before American Independence" and the Celts entered Europe "thirty-four hundred years before the American era, or year I of these States" (*NYD*, 56, 57).[14] This link situates "the American era" not simply in regard to British history but within the larger history of the world (thereby effacing the merely political opposition between the United States and Great Britain that structures "Our Language and Literature") and gives ideological force to the statement that concludes the "farther retrospect" and comes closest to explaining why English is the nation's "mightiest inheritance": "You see how the history of language is the most curious and instructive of any history, and embraces the whole of the rest. It is the history of the movements and developments of men and women over the entire earth.

In its doings every thing appears to move from east to west as the light does" (*NYD*, 57). Only later in the article does he make the principle explicit: "The English language seems curiously to have flowed through the ages, especially toward America, for present use, and for centuries and centuries of future use; it is so composed of all the varieties that preceded it, and so absorbs what is needed by it" (*NYD*, 59). Here Whitman conjoins the composite nature of the English language with its Indo-European affinities and establishes American English as the culmination of the history of all languages and its best hope for the future. For Whitman, the history of American English is a story of epic, indeed mythic proportions: what began in diversification and dispersal ends in reunification, a gathering in of the exiles.

The structure of "America's Mightiest Inheritance," and thus its argument, is complicated still further by the two sections that immediately precede and follow the three which narrate the language's history, "*Language cannot be Traced to First Origins*" and "*Only Language Endures.*" These sections, whose source is not in the *Hand-book*, define the extent and limits of linguistic historiography and envelop Whitman's already complex narration in paradox. On one hand, although scholars (like Grimm and the other "language searchers") can elucidate the transmission of language in remarkable detail, the full historicity of language remains beyond their reach. "We go back to Hindostan; we decipher the hieroglyphics of Assyria and Egypt; we come onward to Hebrew and Greek records," Whitman writes, "but we know no more of actual origins than before" (*NYD*, 56). On the other hand, language is clearly the most accessible and enduring of all historical artifacts. "There are, doubtless," Whitman writes, "now in use every hour along the banks of the Hudson, the St. Lawrence, the Sacramento, and the Colorado—as by the Rhone, the Tiber, the Thames, and the Seine—words but little modified, or not modified at all, from the same use and sound and meaning they had twenty thousand years ago, in empires whose names have long been rubbed out from the memories of the earth" (*NYD*, 58). Language both embodies and transcends history. In Whitman's words: "Language makes chronology petty; it ante-dates all, and brings the farthest history close to the tips of our ears" (*NYD*, 56). To be sure, this paradox only enhances the prestige of historical linguistics, of the English language, and of America as the final repository of both.

Taken together, then, these five sections—"*Language cannot be Traced to First Origins*," "*Stock and Grafts of English Speech*," "*Asiatic Stock—Movements of Races*," "*Contributions and Parts*," and "*Only Language Endures*"—form an elaborate, multiplotted, interlinked narrative that suggests, but never fully explains, why the English language is "America's Mightiest Inheritance." But these sections do not constitute the article in its entirety, nor is Whitman's rhetorical strategy wholly contained within this narrative. Taken separately, each section can be shown to have an immediate strategy and argument of its own that complements the historical narrative and contributes to the reformist argument articulated in the closing three sections: *"Diffuse and Showy Use of Language," "A Perfect English Dictionary has yet to be Written,"* and *"Meanness of the Tuition of Schools."*

Take, for example, the section entitled *"Language cannot be Traced to First Origins."* The section may be divided into rhetorical halves. In the first Whitman remarks upon the futility of theorizing about the origin of language, an argument common among comparative philologists: indeed comparative philology may even be said to have grown out of the ruins of the speculative eighteenth-century discourse on the origin of language.[15] Whitman's argument echoes Humboldt:

> A connected chain of languages had rolled on for millennia before it got to the point which our sparse lore designates as the oldest. . . . All process of becoming in nature, most particularly its organic and living aspects, slips beyond the grasp of our observation. . . . We can follow the manifold changes which the Roman language underwent during its decline; we can add the mixtures due to immigrant hordes: none of it explains the origin of the living germ which in diverse forms meanwhile unfolded into the organisms of new languages.[16]

It echoes as well, and perhaps more directly, Schele de Vere's *Outlines of Comparative Philology*, which introduces its subject by summarizing and rejecting the various theories of the origin of language and presenting "the opinion shared by the highest authorities, that the circle of original language was closed before the dawn of history." Schele de Vere concludes—as Humboldt does not—that "human power alone, cannot produce or create a language."[17] And in the second half of the section, Whitman concludes similarly: "No art, no power, no grammar, no combination or process can originate a language; it grows purely of itself and incarnates everything." The phrase "of itself" is not elaborated upon in the article, though it clearly relates to Humboldt's organicism. Whitman uses it in opposition to deliberate efforts to change language, and the phrase accrues meaning in the sentences that follow it: "It is said of Dante, Shakspeare [*sic*], Luther, and one or two others, that they created their languages anew; this is foolish talk. Great writers penetrate the idioms of their races, and use them with simplicity and power. The masters are they who embody the rude materials of the people and give them the best forms for the place and time" (*NYD*, 56).[18] In other words, Whitman transforms the position of the comparative philologists into a reformist argument for a populist linguistics, a version of Michaelis's "language is a democracy." Language, for Whitman, is quintessentially "of the people" and thus, by definition, wholly natural—"of itself."

This line of argument, implicit in the early, theoretical sections of the article, is elaborated later, when Whitman turns abruptly from the English language to American letters, from his celebration of the history and character of "America's Mightiest Inheritance" to a consideration of three areas in which Americans have failed to make the most of it: literature, lexicography, and pedagogy. Unlike in "Our Language and Literature," where British villains bear the brunt of Whitman's invective, here the villains are homegrown writers, public speakers, scholars, and teachers, and the term "America" is made to suffer the strain of self-contradiction and possible failure. Americans must take responsibility for their own words. In the section entitled "*Diffuse and Showy Use of Language*," for instance, he berates those *American* writers and speakers who, "without exception, lack the self-denial to reject showy words and images, and employ terms in their beautiful exact meanings, using only what is applicable." American writing, in particular, is uniformly "diffuse and artificial": the writers "bow, defer . . . [are] subdued to other men's or nation's models." Even journalistic writing, which Tocqueville had seen as quintessentially democratic, Whitman judges to have "no precision, no ease, no blood, no vibration of the living voice in the living ear." While the authors of the *Hand-book* argued (in support of orthographic study), "The spoken word perishes: the written word abides forever," Whitman makes the value of the written word dependent upon its affinity with the spoken word (an argument he elaborates in *An American Primer*).[19] And in this vein he remarks that "illiterate people"—perforce speakers rather than writers—"are not one quarter as guilty" of perverting the promise. Furthermore, corrupt, imitative American writing "will fall dead on the American soul," and "we wait for writers that favor the mass of the people, body and brain" (*NYD*, 58–59). Whitman's argument here echoes countless other charges of literary deference and imitativeness, including Webster's, Longfellow's, and, of course, Emerson's. It even upholds Tocqueville's distinction between American writers and the general American populace (although Tocqueville, like Longfellow, had only "polite" literature in mind). What sets it apart is the clear radical-democratic bias, the implicit identification of "the American soul" with, alternately, "illiterate people" and "the mass of the people": the ambiguity inherent in the term "America" allows Whitman to maintain a distinction between "American writers" and "the American soul," and, with the use of the open-ended term "wait," to turn contradiction into a moral and political imperative.

For Whitman, waiting connotes purpose and direction: the distance between promise and fulfillment is bridged by the advent in America of the new philosophy of language, heretofore embodied in the work of grammarians like Grimm, now announced prophetically in *Life Illustrated*. Accordingly, the following two sections return to the theme of comparative philology. In "*A Perfect Dictionary has yet to be Written*," Whitman surveys the history of lexicography: "Dr. Johnson did well; Sheridan, Walker, Perry, Ash, Bailey, Kenrick, Smart, and the rest, all assisted; Webster and Worcester have done well." Nevertheless, "the dictionary, rising stately and complete, out of a full appreciation of the philosophy of language, and the unspeakable grandeur of the English dialect, has still to be made." And just as English "seems curiously to have flowed through the ages, especially toward America," so the perfect dictionary is "to be made by some coming American worthy the sublime work" (*NYD*, 59). The fulfillment of the promise lies, in short, in the confluence of two historical movements, *translatio linguae* and *translatio studii*.

Furthermore, this confluence is characterized by reformulation of *translatio imperii*. The authors of the *Hand-book* had compared the course of empire to the growth of American English in terms Whitman must have applauded: "Like the American nation [the English language] gathers to itself the elements of power from the four quarters of the globe," they explained. "It is the asylum of free thought and song." But they had valorized English in purely ethnocentric terms: "Its various elements are points of union between it and all other languages," the authors asserted, "and hold out a fresh promise of readily Anglicizing the mind of the world."[20] For Whitman, the ethnocentricity of "the unspeakable grandeur of the English dialect" could only be understood in the context of "a *full* appreciation of the philosophy of language" (*NYD*, 59; italics mine). "The immense diversity of race, temperament, character—the copious streams of humanity constantly flowing hither—must reappear in free, rich growths of speech," he would explain in *Rambles among Words*, and "not merely in the copious new verbal contributions the various idioms may bring, but in the entire spirit of the Language—moulded more and more to a large hospitality and impartiality."

In *Rambles*, as in "Our Language & Literature," Whitman blames the corruption of linguistic philosophy on "English scholars and literateurs" who "have discouraged and cramped the spontaneous expansions of the Language" with their "pitiful cant" about Anglo-Saxon.[21] But in the concluding section of "America's Mightiest Inheritance," "*Meanness of the Tuition of Schools*," Whitman lashes out (as in the earlier section) against American pedagogues—including the authors of the *Hand-book*. "The study of language, dictionaries, 'grammar,' etc., as pursued in the public and other schools of New York, Boston, Brooklyn, and elsewhere through the States," he writes, "is worth nothing but the scornful and unrestrained laughter of contempt." The reason is simple: "Probably not one teacher of them all is possessed of the few great simple leading principles of the mighty science of speech." The solution, too, is apparently simple: "Read the works of modern language-searchers—that majestic and small brotherhood." The literature of comparative philology "will open and enlarge your mind" because it embodies true universality and largeness of soul. "You will see," he writes, "interwoven like the network of veins, regardless of different continents, colors, barbarisms, civilizations, all the races of men and women on whom the sun shines and the night drops shadows." In this passage, we are granted a glimpse of one of the sources of Whitman's own fascination with the science of language, an epiphany of linguistic universalism: "Discrepancies fall into line. All are of one moral as well as physical blood—the blood of language" (*NYD*, 59–60). These lines echo the sentiments of Max Müller (in a passage Bunsen quotes at the close of his first volume and Whitman copied into his notebook):

> And if now we gaze from our native shores over the vast ocean of human speech . . . —if we gaze, and hearken to the strange sounds rushing past our ears in unbroken strains, it seems no longer a wild tumult . . . and the more intensely we listen, the more all discords melt away into higher harmonies, till at last we hear but one majestic trichord, or a mighty unison, as at the end of a sacred symphony.
>
> Such visions will float through the study of the grammarian, and in the midst of toilsome researches his heart will suddenly beat, as he feels the conviction growing upon him that men are brethren in the simplest sense of the word—the children of the same father—whatever their country, their colour, their language, and their faith.[22]

Still, for Whitman, such visions of universal brotherhood do not wholly mitigate American exceptionalism. For him the "mighty unison" of all languages and the "unspeakable grandeur" of American English are one. He positions himself, in effect, somewhere between Müller and the authors of the *Hand-book*.[23]

My point is this: in "America's Mightiest Inheritance," Whitman takes on the role of redactor, gathering passages and ideas from a variety of writers representing different discourses and assembling them into a whole intended to be more than the sum of its parts. The intricate structure of "America's Mightiest Inheritance" reflects Whitman's sense of both the complex history of American English and the difficult synthesis that faced the American linguist. The ever-receding past must correspond to the limitless future; the manifest diversity of races and dialects must be made to mirror back the underlying unity of mankind and of language; the zeal of the reformer must incorporate the patience of the observer: all furnish their parts toward the "unspeakable grandeur" of American English.

AN AMERICAN PRIMER

Although it is difficult to confine Whitman's writings within too restrictive generic categories, it may nevertheless be said by way of contrast that "America's Mightiest Inheritance" is primarily philosophical and that *An American Primer* is practical. Although the *Primer* begins with the "great observation" that as "humanity is one, under its amazing diversities, language is one under its," the title plainly invites comparison with those elementary textbooks intended to instruct young students in reading, writing, and speaking. Like Webster and Murray, Whitman claims as his province the traditional areas of spelling, grammar, diction, and pronunciation. He writes of "the renovated English speech in America" and points out the language's weaknesses and its strengths, where usage has gone awry, and what improvements can be made in both language and discourse (*D&N*, 3:732). Still, Whitman's style is too playful and diffuse, or, in his own terms, "elliptical" and "insouciant," for the *Primer* to be considered formally as a textbook. Even in its unfinished state, the work seems to have been fashioned deliberately as a prospectus for a textbook grounded in his American version of the new philology—the "Real Grammar" and "Real Dictionary" to which he repeatedly refers in his linguistic writings—that, by its own logic, could never be completed. The "mass of more or less disjointed notes" (as Traubel put it) that the manuscript comprises reveals a revisionist literary strategy and an alternative pedagogic stance both expansive and evasive, an attempt to enter into the discourse of the grammatical "martinets" and to appropriate it, not only to challenge their ideas but to create a pastiche of their genre.

Consider, for instance, Whitman's remarks on spelling, an issue he deems "subordinate" but nevertheless feels compelled to comment upon in some (if comparatively limited) detail. In one brief passage bearing no overt or necessary relation to those preceding or following it, Whitman alludes to the major orthographic debates of his day, from the Webster-Worcester controversy over the spelling of words like *hono[u]r* and *almanac[k]* to the various efforts (by Franklin, Webster, and others) to reform spelling on natural or scientific principles. His overall tone is dismissive: true American pedagogy recognizes that this sort of punctiliousness and perfectionism is petty. "For many hundred years," he writes at the end of the passage, "there was nothing like settled spelling in most . . ." (*D&N*, 3:740; ellipses mine). This uncompleted sentence distances us from the controversies as it places them in historical perspective. Still, it keeps them within view. For Whitman, spelling is not unimportant: it may be "subordinate," but it remains an aspect of language that cannot be ignored. He is too fond of word lists, too fascinated by etymology, too proud, perhaps, of his own literacy (his spelling is, by and large, impeccable) to reject it out of hand, and the structure of the paragraph reflects his ambivalent view. "Morbidness for nice spelling, and tenacity for or against some one letter or so, [may mean] dandyism and impotence in literature," but "the great writers must have digested all these things,—passed lexicons, etymologies, orthographies, through them.—and extracted the nutriment." Whitman's rhetorical strategy here is to declare his opposition to strict, arbitrary doctrines of correctness but to allow the issues some play and, at all cost, to avoid resolution and closure. Even though "modern taste is for brevity and for ranging words in spelling-classes," Whitman feels that English words "can never be ranged in spelling-classes"—or, at least, they "probably" cannot. "The Phonetic Spelling . . . may in time prevail"; indeed, "it surely will prevail"—that is, "if it is best it should" (*D&N*, 3:740). Hence the double significance of Whitman's historical close. He witnesses and waits.

Consider, too, Whitman's remarks on grammar. "Alas," he writes, "the forms of grammar are never persistently obeyed, and cannot be" (*D&N*, 3:734). *Alas:* dispensing with the invective of "Our Language & Literature" and sidestepping the particular issues that had preoccupied Webster and Murray—most significantly, whether English, with all its irregularities, can be reduced to strict rules at all—Whitman declares all questions of grammar moot. He is not like the despairing grammarians whom Webster chastised in 1783: "They study the language enough to find the difficulties of it—-they tell us that it is impossible to reduce it to order—-that it is to be learnt only by the ear—-they lament the disorder and dismiss it without a remedy" (*GI*, 5). Nor can he agree with Murray that language is "purely a species of fashion" and that grammar is nothing but "a collection of general observations methodically digested, and comprising all the modes previously and independently established, by which the significations, derivations, and combinations of words in that language, are ascertained."[24] Clearly, he observes, something there is that doesn't like grammatical forms. But, like spelling, grammar cannot simply be dismissed: it is intrinsic and indispensible to language, and the various forms and laws compiled and adjudicated in the various textbooks are its manifestations, albeit imperfect. "The Real Grammar," Whitman writes, "will be that which declares itself a nucleus of the *spirit* of the laws, with liberty to carry out the spirit of the laws, even by violating them" (italics mine). But only, he adds, "if necessary." If unnecessary, the laws stand. Similarly, he asserts, "The English Language is grandly lawless like the race who use it," and then he qualifies, "Or Perhaps – or rather breaks out of the little ? laws to enter truly the higher ones[—]It is so instinct with that which underlies laws, and the purports of laws, it refuses all petty interruptions in its way" (*D&N*, 3:735). Whitman's strategy is to make bold revisionist statements and then to draw back from them, leaving the matter essentially as it stood, although, as with spelling, our perspective has been noticeably broadened. We stand, with Whitman, "both in and out of the game."

Whitman's remarks on spelling and grammar are brief intercalations in *An American Primer*, one manuscript page devoted to each subject, a sign he was firmly ensconced in the discourse of the martinet-schoolmasters he despised. More prominent in the argument of the *Primer*, and more central to its literary strategy, is the matter of diction. It was clear to commentators since the mid-eighteenth century that Americans were developing a dialect different from that spoken by the British. Questions about the propriety of the new dialect took on the form of a political controversy during the Revolution; indeed, the controversy may be said to have begun formally when John Witherspoon, complaining about the sad state of American public discourse, coined the term *Americanism* in 1781.[25] Not only was the language spoken in the United States different from that spoken in Great Britain, many argued, but it was also qualitatively inferior. Americans had clearly "departed from the standard of the language," wrote John Pickering in 1816. "We have formed some *new* words; and to some *old* ones, that are still used in England, we have affixed *new significations*, while others, which have long been *obsolete* in England, are still retained *in common use* with us." Pickering considered these differences—noted by many students of the English language in America, from Webster to Tocqueville—to be "corruptions" and concluded that "the English language is not spoken and written in America, with the same degree of purity that is to be found in the writers and orators of England."[26]

Noah Webster responded to Pickering with characteristic vehemence. "To arrest the progress of a language is . . . impossible," he wrote; "and, if possible, would be a misfortune." Agreeing (uncharacteristically) with Jefferson, he wrote "that a language must keep pace with improvements in knowledge, and that no definable limits can be assigned to a living language, because such limits cannot be assigned to future discoveries and advances in science." Sensing that the criticism of Americanisms included within it an element of class prejudice, he added that "the terms used by the common people of a country, are as genuine and legitimate, as those used by the poet and historian, and as necessary, nay, more necessary, in proportion as the cultivation of the earth and the mechanical arts are more necessary to a nation, than history and poetry; and as subsistence and comfort are more necessary than refinement and luxury." He argued that the benefits of words "are often perceived . . . instinctively by a nation" and that "rarely, indeed, do we find a new word introduced into a language, which is entirely useless." Most often, "the use of new terms is dictated by necessity or utility; sometimes to express shades of difference . . . ; sometimes to express an idea with more force; and sometimes to express a combination of ideas, by a single word, which, otherwise, would require a circumlocution." In short, Webster believed, the cavils of critics like Pickering were grounded in a false assumption, "that the language has arrived to its *ne plus* of perfection—that it is incapable of improvement—and that it is our duty to limit its progress."[27]

An American Primer is Whitman's official entry, as it were, into the debate over Americanisms. He agrees with Webster on most major points—and goes beyond him on others. As the scope of American progress is unlimited, so the copiousness of American English is ever increasing. "In America an immense number of new words are needed, to embody the new political facts," Whitman writes, "also words to answer the modern, rapidly spreading, faith, of the vital equality of women with men," as well as "the copious trains of facts, and flanges of facts, feelings, arguments, and adjectival facts, growing out of all knowledges" (*D&N*, 3:736–737). He agrees with Webster as well that no word is extraneous, that "each word of the [hundred thousand (Whitman's estimate)] that now compose the English language, has its own meaning" and that "there are no two words the same any more than there are two persons the same." He foresees a lexicon as broad and inclusive (and as expansionist) as the American territories, as varied as the occupations of its inhabitants, as extensive as nature and history and human experience: he includes pages and pages consisting of little else than catalogs of words and word groups—"Canada Words / Yankee Words / Mannahatta Words, / . . . Mexican and Nicaraguan Words, / California Words, / . . . Carpenter's words / Mason's words / Blacksmith's words / . . . Words of the Laws of the Earth / . . . Words of the Body, Senses, Limbs, Surface, Interior, / . . . Words of Feebleness, Nausea, Sickness, Ennui, Repugnance, and the like" (*D&N*, 3:747–750). Whitman's sweeping exuberance challenges the generic constraints of all but his theoretical "Real Dictionary," whose rhetorical power lies precisely in its unlimited fecundity and fluidity, that is, in its remaining unrealized.

Not all areas of American life seem to be caught up, however, in the "procreant urge" of American English. In some areas—"Law, (Medicine), Religion, the Army, the personnel of the Army and Navy, the

Arts"—speakers and writers seem to "stand on their old stock of words, without increase" (*D&N*, 3:734). The names of American places, institutions, and people still "commemorate the old myths" and should be changed to "commemorate things belonging to America, and dating thence" (*D&N*, 3:755). The "Anglo-Saxon breed," Whitman writes, "has less of the words of the various phases of friendship and love than any other race" (*D&N*, 3:751). In polite literature and conversation, there "have not yet been served up, by resistless consent, words to be freely used in books, rooms, at table, any where, to specifically mean the act male and female." Whitman feels that the resistance to neology, or the repression of words already in existence, is unnatural, that "the blank left by Words wanted, but unsupplied has sometimes an unnamably putrid cadaverous meaning." But even these must be seen in historical perspective: "When the time comes for them to represent any thing or any state of things, the words will surely follow." After all, "the glory and superb rose hue of the English language" is "that it favors growth as the skin does – that it can soon become, wherever that is needed, the tough skin of a superior man or woman—" (*D&N*, 3:745–746).

When Whitman wrote to Emerson in the notorious open letter of 1856 that the United States had "the perfectest of dialects," he was in effect joining Webster in challenging the notion, articulated in one form by Condillac and in another by Pickering, that languages can arrive at a state of perfection in which all its forms are fixed and from which all deviations must be considered corruptions.[28] For Whitman, perfection could only mean perfectibility, a perpetual state of growth and change, and stasis could only mean stagnation and corruption—not only for language but for people. In fact, Whitman's most significant deviation from Webster on this matter is his refusal (following Herder, Humboldt, and, perhaps most immediately, Emerson) to consider language as an entity apart from the people who spoke it or the things it signified. Perfection and corruption are moral states, not linguistic states. Or, perhaps more precisely, they are linguistic by virtue of the fact that they are moral. "The corruption of man," Emerson wrote, "is *followed* by the corruption of language."[29] Whitman's formulation echoes Emerson's but is simpler and allows for a broader range of possibilities: "Words follow character" (*D&N*, 3:732). At certain points in the *Primer*, this principle emerges as Whitman's politicized, ethnocentric version of the widely held notion that national language reflects national character: "The races that in their realities are supple, obedient, cringing have hundreds of words to express hundreds of forms of acts, thoughts, flanges, of those realities. . . . The English tongue is full of strong words native or adopted to express the blood-born passion of the race for rudeness and resistance, as against polish and all acts to give in" (*D&N*, 3:738). At other points, it seems to refer to individual character and individual usage and, in this, to follow closely Emerson's notion of "rotten diction," when "simplicity of character and the sovereignty of ideas is broken up by the prevalence of secondary desires . . . and old words are perverted to stand for things which are not."[30] Whitman's formulation is cast in the affirmative: "A perfect user of words uses things – they exude in power and beauty from him – miracles from his hands – miracles from his mouth"; and again, "A perfect writer would make words sing, dance, kiss, do the male and female act, bear children, weep bleed, rage, stab, steal, fire cannon, steer ships, sack cities, charge with cavalry or infantry, or do anything that man or woman or the natural powers can do" (*D&N*, 3:740, 742). His model is "Christ, the divine son, who went about speaking perfect words, no patois – whose life was perfect" (*D&N*, 3:744). In Whitman's imagination, of course, these two applications of the principle, national and moral, are two sides of the same coin: American nationality is morality raised to the highest level. Christ is the type of which America is the fulfillment. "The Americans are going to be," he believed, "the most perfect users of words" (*D&N*, 3:732).

They are also "going to be," Whitman writes, "the most fluent and melodious voiced people in the world" (*D&N*, 3:732). Given Whitman's well-known interest in opera and oratory, it should not be surprising that his utter fascination with words and names is matched by an abiding preoccupation with voice: "nothing is more important than names," "nothing is better than a superb vocalism" (*D&N*, 3:754, 752). Indeed, except for the significant intercalations on spelling or grammar, Whitman apparently intended to weave *An American Primer* together primarily from the two separate thematic strands of words and voice to form a single, seamless, organic fabric; or, perhaps more accurately, to sew together diverse scraps of comments, observations, and lists into a patchwork quilt of American English. In any case, Whitman jumps from the one subject to the other, as if they were interchangeable or, perhaps, as if one necessarily depended upon the other. Indeed, although he actually devotes more space to vocabulary, he privileges speech (and valorizes writing that approaches speech) and, hence, voice. "Pronunciation is the *stamina* of language"—its strength, vital principle, generative ability—"it is language" (*D&N*, 3:739; italics mine).

In the schoolmaster's discourse, pronunciation was an integral part of language study, and one of the most crucial from a sociopolitical standpoint. The way a person spoke marked him in terms of class and region. Webster, for instance, felt strongly that it was essential "for the reputation of Americans to unite in destroying provincial and local distinctions, in resisting the stream of corruptions that is ever flowing from ignorance and pride, and in establishing one uniform standard of elegant pronunciation" (*GI*, 7n). John Adams believed that a uniform standard of pronunciation would have "a happy effect upon the union of the

States."[31] Whitman observed that in 1856 ("the 80th year of These States") there was "much diversity in the ways of pronouncing" words and argued that language "cannot be left loosely to float – to fly away" but "must coh[e]re" (*D&N*, 3:738). Yet he did not argue for standardization: as with spelling, grammar, and lexicography, he undoes the genre as he makes it his own. "The subtle charm of beautiful pronunciation is not in dictionaries[,] grammars, marks of accent, formulas of a language or any laws or rules," he argues, but "in perfect, flexible vocal organs, and in a developed harmonious soul" (*D&N*, 3:745). Indeed, "all the rules of the accents and inflections of words drop before a perfect voice – that may follow the rules, or be ignorant of them – it is indifferent which" (*D&N*, 3:739). Voices, too, "follow character" (*D&N*, 3:752). "All sorts of physical, moral, and mental deformities are inevitably returned in the voice," he explains. "Drinking brandy, gin, beer, is generally fatal to the perfection of the voice; – Meanness of mind, the same; – Gluttony, in eating, of course the same; a thinned habit of body, or a rank habit of body – masturbation, inordinate going with women, rot the voice." On the other hand, "no man can have a great vocalism, who has no experience . . . with woman and . . . who has no experience with man. – The final fibre and charm of the voice, follows the chaste drench of love" (*D&N*, 3:738, 737). Americans are going to have the world's most perfect voices, but not until they attain perfect physical, spiritual, and (implicitly) political health. New Englanders are singled out (as they are by Webster) for their "nasal and offensive" pronunciation, and, curiously, Whitman makes no mention at all of America's well-known oratory, except for an occasional reference to "the stump speech" and its "limber, lashing—fierce words" (*D&N*, 3:737, 746). The best American voices are found in unlikelier places. Thus, "the voices of the native healthy substrata of Mannahatta young men, especially the drivers of horses, and all whose work leads to free loud calling and commanding" are equal to those of the "great Italian singers" (*D&N*, 3:737). And thus, the "nigger dialect," with its "wide open pronunciations, as *yallah*, for yellow – *massah* for master – and [its instinct] for rounding off the corners of words" adumbrates "the future theory of the modification of all the words of the English language, for musical purposes, for a native grand opera in America" (*D&N*, 3:748).

The broader political implications of Whitman's remarks on voice and diction may best be understood through a brief consideration of "The Eighteenth Presidency!"—a political manifesto written and printed by Whitman in 1856 but never published—in which he caustically denounces the corruption of American partisan politics and of political discourse. The manifesto is structured as a series of questions and answers addressed by the "Voice of Walt Whitman to each Young Man in the Nation, North, South, East and West," two of which stand out as particularly central to Whitman's argument here and in the *Primer*: "Who are the Nation?" and "Where is the real America?" (*NUM*, 6:2120, 2123). He answers the first simply, directly, and by the numbers—"the great mass of mechanics, farmers, men following the water, and all laboring persons," who, he estimates, "constitute some six millions of the inhabitants of These States." Men of other professions—"merchants, lawyers, doctors, teachers, and priests"—together number only a half-million, and slave owners add another 350,000. All told, laborers outnumber all the others by more than six to one. Yet the nation's government is conducted solely by members of the minority classes of professionals and slave owners and not by those of "the American nation, the people" (*NUM*, 6:2120). Hence Whitman's second question—and the unacceptable answer: the real America "does not appear in the government. It does not appear at all in the Presidency" (*NUM*, 6:2123). He confronts the current political situation with a prediction: "The young genius of America is not going to be emasculated and strangled just as it arrives toward manly age" but "shall live, and yet baffle the politicians and the three hundred and fifty thousand masters of slaves." For a "new race copiously appears, with resolute tread, soon to confront Presidents, Congresses and parties, to look them sternly in the face, to stand no nonsense; American young men, the offspring and proof of These States, the West the same as the East, and the South alike with the North" (*NUM*, 6:2125).

Two related aspects of the rhetoric of "The Eighteenth Presidency!" are particularly relevant to an understanding of the rhetoric of *An American Primer*. First of all, it demonstrates plainly the characteristic way Whitman, for all his poetic inclination to embrace and include, uses the term "America" to delimit and exclude. The "real America" is defined by youth, labor, and "the spirit of . . . manliness and common-sense" and in opposition to "*limber-tongued* lawyers, very *fluent but empty*, feeble old men, professional politicians, dandies, dyspeptics, and so forth" (*NUM*, 6:2123, 2121; italics mine). The lines are clearly drawn here, and they include a linguistic component. Whence, the second aspect: Whitman relates the shameful state of (un-)American politics to corrupt modes of address. "In the South," he writes, "no end of blusterers, braggarts, windy, melodramatic, continually screaming in falsetto, a nuisance to These States, their own just as much as any" (*NUM*, 6:2122). And in the North, a "parcel of windy . . . liars are bawling in your ears the easily spoken words Democracy and the democratic party." Politicians may be glib, or they may be loud and shrill, but, either way, their words are meaningless. They employ, to use Emerson's term, "rotten diction," words radically cut off from their referents. Some, for instance, "are using the great word Americanism without yet feeling the first aspiration of it," Whitman claims, "as the great word Religion has been

used, probably loudest and oftenest used, by men that made indiscriminate massacres at night, and filled the world so full with hatreds, hor-
rors, partialities, exclusions, bloody revenges, penal conscience laws and
test-oaths" (*NUM*, 6:2127–2128).

Whitman's accusations here need to be clearly understood. He is not
here bemoaning the democratization of American political rhetoric, a
common complaint after the Revolution and, perhaps even more commonly, after the election of 1840. "Do you suppose the liberties and the
brawn of These States have to do only with delicate lady-words? with
gloved gentleman-words?" he asks in the *Primer*. "Bad Presidents, bad
judges, bad clients, bad editors, owners of slaves, and the long ranks of
Northern political suckers, monopolists, infidels (robbers, traitors, sub-
orned,) castrated persons, impotent persons, shaved persons, supple-
jacks, ecclesiastics, men not fond of women, women not fond of men,
cry down the use of strong, cutting, beautiful rude words" (*D&N*,
3:746). But the "appetite of the people of These States in popular
speeches and writings, is for unhemmed lattitude [*sic*], coarseness, di-
rectness, live epithets, expletives, words of opprobrium, resistance," and
he admits, "I have the taste myself" (*D&N*, 3:741). The "Voice of Walt
Whitman" that we hear in "The Eighteenth Presidency!" is just this sort
of voice: "The President," he writes in one particularly vitriolic passage,
"eats dirt and excrement for his daily meals, likes it, and tries to force it
on The States" (*NUM*, 6:2123). However we may see a distinction
without a difference between this sort of rhetoric and that of his adver-
saries, Whitman clearly believed one was both moral and American and
the other was neither, that one proceeded from the character of the people and embodied what he called "the Theory of These States" and the
other did not. Language follows politics.

The revisionist pedagogy of *An American Primer* is grounded both in
the linguistic philosophy of "America's Mightiest Inheritance" and in
the political imperatives of "The Eighteenth Presidency!": its literary
strategy is to bring them both to bear upon the discourse of Webster
and Murray. Or, to put this another way, the *Primer* occupies a crucial
point of intersection, where the theory and practice of American English
meet and their differences are made to correspond, where the revulsion
Whitman feels at the "rotten diction" of American politicians merges
with the "exultation" he experiences when he considers the "ease, defin-
iteness, and power" of "the tongue that spurns laws" (*D&N*, 3:753). At
certain points in the text, Whitman gives vent to the strain of his awkward position between past and future, myth and reality, evolution and
reform. "The past hundred centuries have confided much to me," he
writes, "yet they mock me, frowning." He wants to be "done with many
of the words of the past hundred centuries"; he is "mad that their

poems, bibles, words, still rule and represent the earth, and are not—superceded" (*D&N*, 3:739). But he realizes that "it is no small thing; no quick growth; not a matter of rubbing out one word and writing another" (*D&N*, 3:755). The very form of the *Primer*—its patchwork quality, its tendency to equivocation, its uncertain genre, perhaps even its incompleteness—is defined by the tension inscribed in Whitman's self-admonition: "I must not,—will not, be impatient" (*D&N*, 3:739).

Narrowly construed, *An American Primer* and "America's Mightiest Inheritance" each represent a different aspect of Whitman's linguistic imagination. In one, he plays the schoolmaster; in the other, the philosopher. In one he prescribes; in the other he describes. More broadly construed, however, they are mirror images, reflecting back upon each other the same vision of a language (and a nation) teeming with potentialities, even at those points where their discourses seem most disparate and each seems most internally inconsistent, where what *is* comes up against what *ought to be*. It is this open-ended vision, this blurring of the categories of time and space, that gives coherent form to all the multifarious and disjointed elements of Whitman's linguistic writings. As he later wrote in *Rambles among Words*, "The English has vast vista in it—vast vista in America."[32] The second hemistich qualifies the first, and the caesural dash becomes, in Whitman's hand, a prosodic device of tremendous significance, marking the ambiguous, relation between language and nation that informs the way Whitman imagines both language and the study of language. Like Webster and Longfellow, for all the political, philosophical, and literary differences among them—and I need not replay them here—he too cannot imagine "a tongue according" without coming flush up against the recalcitrant, unassimilable facts of American life, and, like them, he too finds ready at hand to mask them the ambiguous, malleable term "America." What distinguishes Whitman from the others is not that his "America" is more real, or that his language is more representative, or that he is more able to "fulfill the potential freed by the Revolution" and to "provide a culture commensurate with America's political opportunity," but that he embraces contradiction and transforms what is in them an unconscious habit of vision into a deliberate literary strategy.

Part Two

THE PHILOSOPHY OF
LANGUAGE IN AMERICA

Consensus through Ambiguity:
Why Language Matters to
The Federalist

WHEN JOHN ADAMS urged Congress in 1780 to form "the American Academy for refining, improving, and ascertaining the English language," it was evident to him, as it was to many of the Revolutionary fathers, that language was the indispensable medium of a government whose authority rested on the consent of the governed. In practical terms, this meant for Adams himself that, along with the academy's formation, serious attention should be paid to the art of eloquence, "the instrument for recommending men to their fellow citizens, and the principal means of advancement through the various ranks and offices of society."[1] For Thomas Jefferson, who would later become his most prominent political adversary, it meant otherwise, that, above all, it was necessary "to give [the people] full information of their affairs thro' the channel of the public papers, & to contrive that those papers should penetrate the whole mass of the people."[2] These divergent points of view clearly reflect the profound differences among Revolutionary statesmen about the nature and viability of self-government: while Jefferson believed, for instance, that "newspapers without a government" were preferable to "a government without newspapers," James Madison doubted that the press held "a remedial power . . . over the spirit of party," and Fisher Ames worried that the press "left the understanding of the mass of men exactly where it found it," indeed, that it "inspired ignorance with presumption, so that those who cannot be governed by reason are no longer awed by authority."[3] Still, just as clearly as they reflect these ideological differences, the divergencies bespeak an even profounder consensus, that the state of the union depended upon the state of the language.

Because it seemed to them that Americans had, in the words of Alexander Hamilton, "to decide the important question, whether societies of men are really capable or not, of establishing good government from reflection and choice, or whether they are forever destined to depend, for their political constitutions, on accident and force," language reform was an issue that occupied the minds of many of the most prominent figures of the generation.[4] To be sure, just as they were divided over the efficacy of a free press, so Americans were hardly of one voice on the question of language reform. John Witherspoon, on one hand, could bemoan "hav[ing] heard in this country, in the senate, at the bar, and from the pulpit, and see[ing] daily in dissertations from the press, errors in grammar, improprieties and vulgarisms, which hardly any person of the same class in point of rank and literature would have fallen into in Great Britain."[5] Jefferson, on the other hand, could declare himself "no friend . . . to what is called *Purism*, but a zealous one to the *Neology*," for only by inventing new words could a language express "every shade of idea, distinctly perceived by the mind."[6] Again, while they may have disagreed about the character and composition of American English, all generally seemed to share the belief that it was necessary to achieve clarity and precision in public discourse—or, at least, to strive for it, for they differed as well on the extent to which such an achievement was indeed possible.

For those who thought about language from this perspective, the fundamental questions were not about language as a cultural product, as they were for Webster, but about language as a constitutive part of the American social and political systems. These questions form a distinct strain in the study of language in post-Revolutionary America, although they overlap at times with questions of literary nationalism and linguistic relativity. In this chapter I will elaborate further upon the intellectual underpinnings of the political situation that faced the generation of Adams and Jefferson and suggest the imaginative consequences of the fact that so much political significance was placed upon the use of language. My focus will be a single text, *The Federalist*, the most remarkable (and problematic) work of political literature produced in eighteenth-century America.

Remarkable, that is, both in conception and execution. Consider the circumstances of its production. After the delegates to the Philadelphia convention completed their intense deliberations in September 1787 and their revisionary document made its way to the states for all-but-certain ratification, Alexander Hamilton, the sole signer from New York, returned home to prepare for political battle. Hamilton knew that opposition in this crucial state was widespread and formidable, and he conceived of *The Federalist* as a propaganda effort of prodigious proportions. Enlisting the aid of John Jay and James Madison and writing under the pen name of "Publius," Hamilton published in several New York newspapers (often simultaneously) a series of eighty-four essays (in book form, eighty-five) that together scrupulously and methodically analyze the Constitution and defend it against all comers. From October 1787 to August 1788, New Yorkers were inundated with the dignified and determined prose of Publius. In *The Federalist*, the full significance of language to the debates about self-government becomes apparent. My purpose here will be not only to explain the linguistic philosophy that may be gleaned from Publius's pages but, more important, to describe how that philosophy—or, more accurately, those philosophies—figured imaginatively in the rhetorical strategy of the authors. I hope to show, in fact, that under the pressure of heated debate and necessary compromise, James Madison was forced to abandon the predominant linguistic theory of the founders (that of the Scottish Commonsense philosophers) and to call upon a more radical view of language (Locke's) to defend the Constitution against charges of obscurity and duplicity.

As early as 1788, George Washington predicted, "When the transient circumstances and fugitive performances which attended this crisis [of the Philadelphia convention and its aftermath] shall have disappeared, [*The Federalist*] will merit the notice of posterity, because in it are candidly and ably discussed the principles of freedom and the topics of government—which will be always interesting to mankind so long as they shall be connected in civil society." And in 1825, when Jefferson was formulating a list of required texts for the law school of the University of Virginia, he listed second, after his own Declaration of Independence, "the book known by the title of 'The Federalist,' being an authority to which appeal is habitually made by all, and rarely declined or denied by any as evidence of the general opinion of those who framed, and of those who accepted the Constitution of the US. on questions as to its genuine meaning."[7] Still today, *The Federalist* retains a certain pristine authority among teachers and historians who, like Clinton Rossiter, rate the work "third only to the Declaration of Independence and the Constitution itself among all the sacred writings of American political history."[8] The amount of secondary literature on *The Federalist* is staggering.

Yet, over the years, literary critics have had remarkably little to say about it. When Robert Spiller and the editors of the monumental *Literary History of the United States* looked for someone to write the chapter on the "Philosopher-Statesmen of the Republic" (Madison and Hamilton prominent among them) they chose not a literary critic but a historian, Adrienne Koch, whose thesis in that chapter sheds much light, I think, on the marked critical silence. The founding fathers, she wrote, "were primarily devoted to the issues and principles growing out of a serious national undertaking." For these practical men, "the methods of belles-lettres were inadequate to the urgent demand for clear and effective expression." To be sure, they "wrote their state papers, their reports, their tracts, and their letters with some care for the form as well as the content, but they subordinated the formal demands of art to the immediate need for communication." Madison, for instance, "never forsook the rounded and urbane prose line," but he "never hesitated to put communication and content above consideration of style or form"; and Hamilton, while he "did not hesitate to employ rhetorical ornament and insistent, obvious rhythm," nonetheless firmly believed that, above all, writing should have "'force in the idea rather than in the expression.'" Indeed, Koch concluded, the place of these philosopher-statesmen in American literary history is secured, in effect, by the fact that they resisted the seductions of style, that, because their minds were focused so intently on the problems and potentialities before them, they force us to "study their ideas and actions" rather than the polish of their words.[9]

Koch's estimation, such as it is, of the stylistic concerns of Hamilton and Madison is intriguing because, for all the supposed clarity of style of *The Federalist*, scholars have been unable to agree upon what it means. "Depending on the degrees of wisdom and influence attributed to *The Federalist* and the Constitution," David Epstein remarks, "the book has been available for patriotic appreciation of the American regime's fundamental principles, for critical revelation of the regime's essential deficiencies, or for melancholy or satisfied contemplation of the subsequent degradation or improvement of that regime." Indeed, many of its best-known commentators have found ambiguity and duplicity in its arguments. Charles Beard saw Publius's discussions of "the principles of freedom" as a thinly veiled, antidemocratic defense of economic privilege, and Robert A. Dahl, agreeing with Beard, painstakingly deconstructed the putative logic of "Madisonian Democracy." Albert Furtwangler has recently argued that each of the authors "wrote contrary to his convictions, avoided revealing his hand, expressed his dissatisfaction about the work as a whole, and contributed a share that merged indistinguishably with writings he would later disclaim." In short, the "author" of *The Federalist*, in Garry Wills's words, "has for long been a rather bedraggled figure, his argument in disarray, his defenders unable to agree on any remedy for this situation." But the discordant chorus of scholarly voices we hear when we survey twentieth-century interpretations of *The Federalist* would have us learn more about the politics of interpretation, perhaps, than about the ambiguities in the document itself, for even those who find equivocation and incoherence in *The Federalist* do not consider the possibility that, for all their lip service to the ideal of clarity and precision, the authors relied heavily for their rhetorical strategy on language's capacity for ambiguity.[10]

My argument is that the writers of *The Federalist*—Madison in particular—thought about language quite a lot, not simply in practical terms (how best to explain something) but in complex theoretical terms, not fleetingly in regard to an occasional rhetorical flourish but profoundly, as it came to bear upon the fate of the nation under the proposed constitution. I will focus on a short passage that occurs in *The Federalist* No. 37, toward the end of a long paragraph analyzing the difficulties faced by the convention in distinguishing between the domains of the federal and state governments:

> The use of words is to express ideas. Perspicuity therefore requires not only that the ideas should be distinctly formed, but that they should be expressed by words distinctly and exclusively appropriated to them. But no language is so copious as to supply words and phrases for every complex idea, or so correct as not to include many equivocally denoting different ideas. Hence, it must happen, that however accurately objects may be discriminated in themselves, and however accurately the discrimination may be considered, the definition of them may be rendered inaccurate by the inaccuracy of the terms in which it is delivered. And this unavoidable inaccuracy must be greater or less, according to the complexity and novelty of the objects defined. When the Almighty himself condescends to address mankind in their own language, his meaning, luminous as it must be, is rendered dim and doubtful, by the cloudy medium through which it is communicated. (37.179–180)

How, Publius (here Madison) argues, could the delegates be expected to define unambiguously the boundaries between the state and federal governments, if all definitions, ultimately, are inaccurate?

It is a peculiar argument. Certainly, if we take it at face value, it complicates Koch's and all other uncritical evaluations of Madison's style: if language is a "cloudy medium," how could it also be clear and direct? But more important, this frank admission of diminished expectations presents a potentially devastating rebuff to Publius'—or anyone else's— defense of the Constitution, more devastating, in fact, than any of the antifederalist complaints lodged against it. For language matters to *The Federalist* in such fundamental and thoroughgoing ways that if scholars have, for the most part, overlooked it as an issue in their understanding of the text, it is only because its importance is so obvious, informing and sustaining the convention's undertaking. Language matters, first of all, because *The Federalist* urges Americans to place their trust in a written constitution. The significance of this circumstance cannot be overemphasized: even a cursory reading through the records of the convention or the debates over ratification makes it clear how attuned Americans were in 1787 to the power of words—to the ability of particular words, phrases, formulations to restrain or let loose the forces of anarchy or tyranny. They had entered the lists against Great Britain singing the praises of an unwritten constitution grounded in precedent and supported by the substantial institutions of Parliament and the monarchy (however limited). They claimed the rights of Englishmen guaranteed by that constitution—and they were (they felt) betrayed. The general ineffectiveness of the written Articles of Confederation was, as Hamilton put it, "unequivocal," yet they still believed, federalist and antifederalist alike, that written constitutions could expressly define and delimit the powers of government (1.2).[11] Language matters, too, because *The Federalist* is an exercise in interpretation; it presents itself (despite this particular passage) confident in its ability to render the meaning of the Constitution and often explicitly challenges the validity of antifederalist counterconstructions. Not long after publication, *The Federalist* became, in Thomas Jefferson's words, "an authority to which appeal is habitually made by all, and rarely declined or denied by any as evidence of the general opinion of those who framed, and of those who accepted the Constitution of the US. on questions as to its genuine meaning."[12] And, finally, language matters to *The Federalist* because its composition and publication speak to the importance and the efficacy of argument in the workings of self-government. In other words, the felt need for *The Federalist* argues that, as the founders perceived it, language had become both the source and avenue of all political authority in the new republic, that the fate of the nation depended upon how well and to what purpose people used words.[13]

Given the importance of language to the work in general, it should not be surprising that Madison gave some thought to the question of language's ability to render meanings. But the extent of the author's willingness to allow the fundamental ambiguity of words to surface in his defense of the Constitution and then to remain unchallenged should give us pause. If language was so unavoidably inaccurate, what trust could be placed in any constitution—indeed, in any document whatsoever? What credence could be given to Madison's and Hamilton's and Jay's construction? And of what worth was the debate over ratification? I am not suggesting that Madison wanted us to ask these questions. In fact, I will suggest the opposite. Madison was skillful enough as a writer to turn this potentially disastrous passage to his immediate advantage. In other words, this passage serves a rhetorical purpose. By presenting the passage out of context, I have obscured that purpose: the remainder of this chapter represents an effort to read the passage back into context—in fact, back into a number of contexts (philosophical and historical)—and in so doing gradually work it back into No. 37. This recontextualization will, I hope, not only show that Madison was a far more subtle and complicated literary craftsman than we have heretofore imagined, but also that language was, in crucial ways, one of Publius's major concerns.

THE PHILOSOPHY OF LANGUAGE

Any of *The Federalist*'s early readers generally familiar with contemporary philosophical discourse would have possessed an adequate frame of reference for understanding Madison's passage.[14] Language matters in many ways to seventeenth- and eighteenth-century philosophical discourse, most simply and generally, because it was seen to be the source of much philosophical confusion. "Although we think we govern our words," wrote Francis Bacon in *The Advancement of Learning*, "certain it is that words, as a Tartar's bow, do shoot back upon the understanding of the wisest, and mightily entangle and pervert the judgment." Through the use of words men could accomplish much—indeed, had accomplished much: they could, as Thomas Hobbes put it, "register their Thoughts; recall them when they are past; and also declare them to one another for mutuall utility and conversation." Without words, "there had been amongst men, neither Common-wealth, nor Society, nor Contract, nor Peace, no more than amongst Lyons, Bears, and Wolves." But language could do no more than its nature allowed, and by abusing language, by failing to recognize its limitations, men had stumbled in their efforts to understand the universe around them. "Nature it selfe cannot erre," Hobbes wrote; "and as men abound in copiousnesse of language; so they [may] become more wise, or more mad than ordinary." Philosophers, it seems, had become madder than most. "Nothing is more usual," wrote Madison's beloved David Hume, "than for philosophers . . . to engage in disputes of words, while they imagine, that they are handling controversies of the deepest importance and concern." To avoid linguistic ambiguity, Bacon had suggested that writers "imitate the wisdom of the mathematicians, in setting down in the very beginning the definitions of our words and terms." Hobbes agreed. The authors of the *Port-Royal Logic* saw an even more profound problem and suggested that the "best way to avoid confusion of Words . . . is to make a new Language, and to coin new Words, to belong only to those Ideas, which they are assigned to signify."[15] Hence Madison: "Perspicuity therefore requires . . . that the ideas should be . . . expressed by words distinctly and exclusively appropriated to them." Such was the accepted wisdom on prose style: "Proper words," as Swift wrote, "in proper places."[16] And this, Koch would argue, is what distinguishes Madison's style.

But the problem of language, Madison knew, was more complicated than the many stylistic recommendations of this sort would suggest. For, in the century preceding *The Federalist*, language became the object, more than simply the tool, of philosophical inquiry. John Locke's third book of the *Essay concerning Human Understanding* is in many ways the most important analysis of language in the period, and his account of his own awakening to the importance of language is salient to a contextual understanding of the remainder of Madison's passage:

> I must confess, then, that, when I first began this Discourse of the Understanding, and a good while after, I had not the least thought that any consideration of words was at all necessary to it. But when, having passed over the original and composition of our ideas, I began to examine the extent and certainty of our knowledge, I found it had so near a connexion with words, that, unless their force and manner of signification were first well observed, there could be very little said clearly and pertinently concerning knowledge: which being conversant about truth had constantly to do with propositions. And though it terminated in things, yet it was for the most part so much by the intervention of words, that they seemed scarce separable from our general knowledge.[17]

Locke argued that a good dictionary would not, in itself, solve the problem of ambiguity, would not shift the object of discourse from words back to things. This is because words are not signs of things at all, and at issue was not what words meant but how they signified. Words are "articulate sounds" used as "signs of internal conceptions," or ideas, which are, in turn, signs of ordinary sense perceptions (*CHU*, 3). The use of language is to communicate these ideas (not simply to express them, as Madison would have it). Particular sounds become words, "not by any natural connexion" between them and things or ideas, but arbitrarily, "by a voluntary imposition" (*CHU*, 8). The more abstract and complex our ideas, the more difficult it is to be sure that our words are communicating them. "Hence it comes to pass," Locke wrote, "that men's names of very compound ideas, such as for the most part are moral words, have seldom in two different men the same precise signification; since one man's complex idea seldom agrees with another's, and often differs from his own—from that which he had yesterday, or will have tomorrow" (*CHU*, 107). Words for concrete substances often fare no better. *Gold*, for instance, never signifies the "real essence" of any thing or sort of thing, but only its "nominal essence," the particular qualities of the substance that we have perceived and have chosen, by abstraction, to be signified by the word. We cannot be certain (for philosophical purposes) that the nominal essence we have in our heads is in anyone else's. Locke concluded: "If we consider, in the fallacies men put upon themselves, as well as others, and the mistakes in men's disputes and notions, how great a part is owing to words, and their uncertain or mistaken significations, we shall have reason to think this no small obstacle in the way of knowledge" (*CHU*, 119). "Nor is it to be wondered,"

Locke suggested at the close of his consideration "Of the Imperfection of Words," "that the will of God, when clothed in words, should be liable to that doubt and uncertainty which unavoidably attends that sort of conveyance, when even his Son, whilst clothed in flesh, was subject to all the frailties and inconveniences of human nature, sin excepted" (*CHU*, 120).

In short, language mattered to Locke because all philosophical (and theological) discourse was subject to its intrinsic imperfections, and, to this extent, Madison's critique of language in No. 37 may be seen to be firmly in the Lockean tradition—indeed, derived from Locke's text itself, down to its skeptical approach to biblical hermeneutics. To this extent, but no further. The stated purpose of Locke's critique was to overcome the imperfections of language and to reform the abuses. Locke was "not so vain as to think that any one can pretend to attempt the perfect reforming the languages of the world, no not so much as of his own country, without rendering himself ridiculous." But he did believe that "those who pretend seriously to search after or maintain truth, should think themselves obliged to study how they might deliver themselves without obscurity, doubtfulness, or equivocation, to which men's words are naturally liable, *if care not be taken*" (*CHU*, 148–149; italics mine). He offers a series of rules, a manual of style (of sorts) for philosophers. For instance: "A man shall take care to use no word without a signification, no name without an idea for which he makes it stand." Another: "It is not enough a man uses his words as signs of some ideas: those he annexes them to, if they be simple, must be clear and distinct; if complex[, like moral words, they] must be determinate" (*CHU*, 152). And so on. Locke conceded that, "after all, the provision of words is so scanty in respect to that infinite variety of thoughts, that men, wanting terms to suit their precise notions, will, notwithstanding their utmost caution, be forced to use the same word in somewhat different senses." So far, Madison. But, unlike Madison, he believed that "the import of the discourse will, for the most part, if there be no designed fallacy, sufficiently lead candid and intelligent readers into the true meaning of it" (*CHU*, 164). He did not, like Madison, despair of reasonable accuracy.

Moreover, Locke carefully distinguished two uses "for the communicating of our thoughts to others," one "*Civil*," the other "*Philosophical*." He made it clear that his critique of language was aimed primarily at philosophers, admitting that "a great deal less exactness will serve in the one than in the other" (*CHU*, 104–105). Not that civil language was unimportant: it was "the great instrument and common tie of society" and thus bore an analogous relationship to, and indeed constituted, the social contract that, Locke argued in *The Second Treatise of Govern-*

ment, structured civil society, authorized all governments, and, when necessary, justified revolution (*CHU*, 3). Theoretically, then, "every man has so inviolable a liberty to make words stand for what ideas he pleases"; but men must give up that liberty in order to become socialized, because "words . . . being no man's private possession, but the common measure of commerce and communication, it is not for any one at pleasure to change the stamp they are current in, nor alter the ideas they are affixed to" (*CHU*, 12, 154). For most civil matters, an informal consent is sufficient, and "common use regulates the meaning of words pretty well" (*CHU*, 108). However, when we deal with writings "that contain either truths we are required to believe, or laws we are to obey, and draw inconveniences on us when we mistake or transgress," and when "we see that, in the interpretation of laws, whether divine or human, there is no end; comments beget comments, and explications make new matter for explications; and of limiting, distinguishing, varying the signification of these moral words there is no end," then, Locke wrote, we are apt to become "anxious" (*CHU*, 109–110). And, by extension, our civil liberties are threatened. Still, there are remedies. Most simply, to be specific in drafting laws and to avoid commentary and disputation. Political things—governmental structures, legal documents—are clearly "artificial things," produced by men, and we can "so settle the signification of the names whereby the species of artificial things are distinguished, with less doubt, obscurity, and equivocation than we can in things natural, whose differences and operations depend upon contrivances beyond the reach of our discoveries" (*CHU*, 89–90). No commentaries, no constructions are necessary. "What have the greatest part of the comments . . . upon the laws of . . . man served for," Locke asked, "but to make the meaning more doubtful and perplex the sense?" Often, "a man of an ordinary capacity very well understands a text, or a law, that he reads, till he consults an expositor, or goes to counsel; who, by that time he hath done explaining them, makes the words signify either nothing at all, or what he pleases." Clearly, "the use of words [in political matters can and should be] made plain and direct; and that language, which was given us for the . . . bond of society, should not be employed to . . . unsettle people's rights" (*CHU*, 131).[18]

The issue of social language and its abuses is only of marginal concern in the *Essay concerning Human Understanding* and only of implied importance in the *Two Treatises on Government*, but it becomes central to the Scottish Commonsense moral philosophers, whose influence upon the founding fathers, we now know, was extremely significant. In the moral philosophies of Madison's teacher John Witherspoon and of Francis Hutcheson (from whom Witherspoon draws heavily), discussions of language are located amid their discussions of contracts, and the two subjects are inextricably interwoven and interdependent. "Words are," Witherspoon wrote, "the most natural and proper for giving immediate consent, and writing to perpetuate the memory of [a] transaction." And conversely, wrote Hutcheson, "our duties in the use of speech have a near affinity to those in contracts."[19] My point is, very simply, that for the moral philosophers, language mattered because the social, political, and economic order depended upon the proper use of language.

Hutcheson's and Witherspoon's discussions of language—and in particular its abuses—differ substantially from Locke's. Most important, they do not dwell upon the inherent imperfections of language. Thomas Reid, the founder of the Commonsense school, had agreed with Locke (and all the others) that "there is no greater impediment to the advancement of knowledge than the ambiguity of words." But he found no reason to distinguish between language's civil and philosophical uses. Even in philosophy, "common words . . . ought to be used in their common acceptation." Only when words "have different acceptations in common language, these, when it is necessary, ought to be distinguished." Distinguished, but not defined. "It is sufficient to define words that are uncommon, or that are used in an uncommon meaning," Reid argued, warning philosophers against "too fastidious a way of treating the common sense of mankind."[20] Certainly, Hutcheson and Witherspoon would add, common usage was an adequate standard for civil language.

Still, ambiguity was a concern. However, the problem "lies not in the words themselves," Witherspoon wrote, "but in the use of them as signs." Or, to be more exact, error does not arise from the radical lack of correspondence between words and things, or words and ideas, so much as from the potential disparity between language and intention. The issue, in other words, is not epistemological but moral. We are all naturally men (and women) of our words. "Truth is the natural production of the mind when it gets the capacity of communicating it," Hutcheson wrote (presaging Emerson's notion of "rotten diction"), while "dissimulation and disguise are plainly artificial effects of design and reflection." This natural inclination translates into a moral imperative, "the great rule of sincerity," as Witherspoon put it. When we are obliged to communicate to others (say, in a courtroom) we must "not only . . . speak truth but . . . reveal the whole truth." When we speak voluntarily, "we should speak nothing but what agrees with our sentiments." Moreover, in all ordinary situations, "we ought to use [words] in the least ambiguous manner possible." This means, first of all, "that all signs . . . should be used in the customary manner, without regard to antient obsolete meanings or etymologies." Furthermore, equivocation (double entendres, private meanings, evasive language) should be scrupulously avoided. In short: "Wherever we are under obligation to impart our sentiments, we are bound to use such words as we judge most proper and effectual for that purpose; and to use other words designedly which we foresee will deceive the hearers, tho' in some other way of interpretation they may be true, is [nothing less than] criminal."[21]

Madison, however, studiously avoided mentioning the possibility of overcoming imperfection. His argument in the passage proceeds in the opposite direction: his defense of the Constitution's imprecision demands that linguistic ambiguity be permanent and unavoidable. Language is not a transparent medium; words cannot point, unproblematically, to things. Madison bypassed the Commonsense affirmation of the validity of common usage (the approach he learned from Witherspoon at Princeton) in order to appropriate the more epistemologically difficult Locke. And then he chose not to follow Locke's argument through to its remedial end. And he did this, I repeat, in support of a written constitution. Language indeed matters to *The Federalist*, but not in the way Koch, or any of us, would have guessed.

THE RATIFICATION DEBATES

Let me move on at this point to the passage's immediate historical context, the debates over ratification. The antifederalist argument against the Constitution is fueled by the Lockean and Commonsense critiques of language. Consistently, the writers who opposed ratification found the convention's language ambiguous, misleading, equivocal. John DeWitt's cogent reformulation of the social compact theory of government epitomizes this sort of argument. He began familiarly enough: "A people, entering into society, surrender such a part of their natural rights, as shall be necessary for the existence of that society"; he underscored the fact that these natural rights "are so precious in themselves, that they would never be parted with, did not the preservation of the remainder require it." The act of surrender is potentially dangerous, because rulers are, almost by definition, power-hungry: they are men "who are very willing to receive [the rights entrusted to them], who are naturally fond of exercising of them, and whose passions are always striving to make a bad use of them." At this point language enters into the equation, for, to preserve their rights and neutralize the danger, men draw up "a written compact, expressing those [rights] which are given up, and the mode in which those reserved shall be secured." DeWitt explained: "Language is so easy of explanation, and so difficult is it by words to convey exact ideas, that the party to be governed cannot be too explicit. The line cannot be drawn with too much precision and accuracy. The necessity of this accuracy and this precision encreases in proportion to the greatness of the sacrifice and the numbers who make it."[22] Linguistic ambiguity was acknowledged—in terms both of the inherent imperfections of words and the insincerity of those who might interpret them— but it was not seen as an insurmountable problem. On the contrary, it was simply seen as a spur to accuracy. And so it was seen by all the writers I have surveyed from Bacon to Witherspoon.

Charges of ambiguity pervaded the political atmosphere in New York at the time Hamilton and Madison composed the first part of *The Federalist*. For example: the antifederalist *Letters of Cato* were published in the *New York Journal* between 17 September 1787 and 3 January 1788; in other words, they began to appear about a month before Hamilton's introductory essay and concluded a week before Madison published No. 37. In his first number he implored his fellow New Yorkers to be conscientious consumers, as it were, when shopping for a constitution. "The disposal of your reputation, and of your lives and property, is more momentous than a contract for a farm, or the sale of a bale of goods," he wrote; "in the former, if you are negligent or inattentive, the ambitious and despotic will entrap you in their toils, and bind you with the cord of power from which you, and your posterity, may never be freed." Make sure you read the fine print, he says in effect, before you sign. The subsequent letters apprised his readers in detail of the possible dangers. "Notwithstanding the great learning and abilities of the gentlemen who composed the convention," he wrote, "it may here be remarked with deference, that the construction of the first paragraph of the first section of the second article, is vague and inexplicit, and leaves the mind in doubt, as to the election of a president and vice-president." He wondered why "there is no explicit provision for their election in case of the expiration of their offices" and warned that "this inexplicitness perhaps may lead to establishment for life." Indeed, he later charged, "inexplicitness seems to pervade this whole political fabric." Of course, any compact *implies* that a magistrate should rule well, but history has shown that "mere implication was too feeble to restrain the unbridled ambition of a bad man, or afford security against negligence, cruelty, or any other defect of mind." Because America is a commercial society and commerce "begets luxury, the parent of inequality, the foe to virtue, and the enemy to restraint," even American magistrates cannot be expected to rule well without express limits set upon them. Do not set sail, he warned, upon a constitutional "sea of uncertainty."[23]

Both Madison and Hamilton were extremely sensitive to this sort of critique; the pages of *The Federalist* are replete with defenses of the Constitution's clarity. "Some who have not denied the necessity of the power of taxation, have grounded a very fierce attack against the Constitution on the language in which it is defined," Madison wrote. "But what colour can the objection have, when a specification of the objects alluded to by these general terms ['to lay and collect taxes'] immediately follows; and is not even separated by a longer pause than a semicolon" (41.209). The authors provide definitions when necessary, suggest rules for proper construction and even once resort to etymology—all in an attempt to refute the antifederalist charges of ambiguity. In fact, they turn these charges back against their accusers. "Under the confusion of names," wrote Madison, "it has been an easy task [for certain 'celebrated authors'] to transfer to a republic, observations applicable to a democracy only" and thereby to tarnish the republic's reputation (14.63). "Men upon too many occasions do not give their understandings fair play," Hamilton charged, "but yielding to some untoward bias they entangle themselves in words and confound themselves in subtleties" (31.148–49). All of which follows nicely from the Commonsense critique of ambiguous language and flies in the face of our passage. And all of which only serves to underscore how seriously Madison and Hamilton took the antifederalist charges.

THE RHETORIC OF AMBIGUITY

In effect, Publius offered two distinct and disparate critiques of language. The first was grounded in the Commonsense "rule of sincerity" and was directed against the abuses and distortions of the antifederalists; the second recapitulated unremediated Lockean philosophy and the Herculean labors of the convention. The first pervades both volumes of *The Federalist*; the second is restricted to No. 37. In fact, Madison's strategy in No. 37 was to shift, deliberately, from one critique to another, to translate us from the war of words in which Publius (whether he liked it or not) was embroiled to the near-mythic deliberations of the delegates. Let me emphasize that this is not a simple movement from ambiguity to clarity, but a movement from one sort of ambiguity to another, from one sort of fallibility to another—from the "misfortune, inseparable from human affairs" that political language invariably "betrays a predetermination or bias, which must render [the opinions it expresses] of little moment in the question" to the "unavoidable inaccuracy" of words that arises not in human affairs but is prior to them, sown in the very physiopsychological nature of man (37.176, 180).

No. 37 is a transitional paper, linking the critique of the Articles of Confederation to the analysis of the Constitution. Madison built upon its liminality, presenting it precisely as a digression from the central subject of the work. It was meant as a break in the text, a deliberate aside, a brief excursion into metapolitical territory, significant precisely because of its very marginality. It is composed of "reflections" on the work of the convention and amounts to an essay on the vicissitudes of constitution writing. Madison began with the postulate that the delegates, like all men, are fallible, but he measured that fallibility, not in terms of moral depravity (as he does, most familiarly, in the discussion of the causes of faction in No. 10) but in terms of a series of objective absences and ambiguities—he called them "difficulties"—completely out of the delegates' control (37.177). The series moves dramatically, carefully building difficulty upon difficulty, from particular to general, from difficulties specific to the convention (the absence of models to follow, the balancing of strong government with individual liberty) to universal epistemological difficulties that culminate in the critique of language. Throughout, as I have said, Madison was careful to present these as obstacles faced by the convention, not caused by it. He even underscored this point syntactically: "The use of words is to express ideas" is preferred to "Men use words to express ideas." Indeed, no one talks in the critique of language at all—except God. We have moved, in short, from a world in which language is ambiguous because it is used to disguise intentions to a world in which words are ambiguous because they cannot be otherwise.

We emerge from this philosophical interlude—this psychological melodrama of sorts—with our faith shaken, not only in words, but in the work of the convention. How could they possibly succeed? Who will save the country? Madison acted to restore our faith, ironically, by adding a fourth difficulty and bringing us back into the real world of practical politics, specifically, to the competing demands of the large and small states. "We may well suppose," he wrote, "that neither side would entirely yield to the other, and consequently that the struggle could be terminated only by compromise." No precise, objective delineations—just compromise, by definition imperfect, and, as it confuses word and intention, ambiguous. But Madison adroitly put this shortcoming to immediate advantage. Given the fact that the "history of almost all the great councils and consultations, held among mankind for reconciling their discordant opinions, assuaging their mutual jealousies, and adjusting their respective interests, is a history of factions, contentions, and disappointments; and may be classed among the most dark and degrading pictures which display the infirmities and depravities of the human character"—given this overwhelming fact, it is hardly surprising that "the Convention should have been forced into some deviations from that artificial structure and regular symmetry, which an abstract view of the subject might lead an ingenious theorist to bestow on a Constitution planned in his closet or his imagination." Indeed, the "real wonder" is that so many obstacles were overcome and that any compromise at all was achieved. Here, if not in the words of the Bible, may be seen clearly "a finger of that Almighty hand which has been so frequently and signally extended to our relief in the critical stages of the revolution" (37.180–181). Deus ex machina. The convention may not have succeeded in devising a perfect government, but no body of men—almost by definition—is able to do that. Indeed, to criticize the Constitution for its imperfections is to betray hypocrisy, haughtiness, and smallness of spirit; those who demand perfection are themselves the least perfect. What the convention did accomplish was a moral victory, to knit themselves together as one man, to make God's presence felt, not by defining precisely, but by recognizing their own fallibility, their own humanity, by substituting public virtue (permanent interest) for private interest.

In effect, Madison inverted—or retooled—the Commonsense critique of language, in which ambiguity disguises design and dissimulation. Here, ambiguity gives way to good intentions. If we must live with ambiguity—and we must—we can at least rely on virtue. And so interpretation becomes not a mode of distortion (as Locke would have had it) but a mode of remediation, a way of allowing free play to virtue. Language matters to Publius *because* it is ambiguous, because it forces readers to look beyond the letter to the spirit, in this case, beyond the language of the Constitution to the virtuous intentions of the delegates.

This is Publius's argument, however, not Madison's. No. 37 presents a picture of the convention he wanted us to see. His notes of the convention's proceedings tell a different story. Madison knew that the Constitution was ambiguous in parts, and he knew the reason had often little to do with the imperfections of words. His notes testify to the repeated wrangling over words and phrases. "Some verbal criticisms were raised agst. the first proposition," he recorded, "and it was agreed on motion of Mr. Butler seconded by Mr. Randolph, to pass on to the third, which underwent a discussion, less however on its general merits than on the force and extent of the particular terms *national* & *supreme*." And again: "Mr. Madison observing that the words '*or to the number of free inhabitants*,' might occasion debates which would divert the Committee from the general question whether the principle of representation should be changed, moved that they might be struck out." And so throughout. Benjamin Franklin's speech at the close of the convention, recorded in full by Madison and most certainly used as a model for No. 37, underscored the ambivalence of the delegates toward the document they had produced. Admitting his personal misgivings, but also his fallibility, Franklin called upon the delegates in the name of virtue and the public good to suppress their particular objections and reservations and to present the Constitution to the world in "our real or apparent unanimity," lest their enemies rejoice that their "councils [had been] confounded like those of the Builders of Babel." One document, one voice, even if the two did not accord with their individual sentiments. He moved that the words "Done in Convention by the unanimous consent of *the States* present" be appended and that all the delegates sign. Madison's comment provides a fitting coda to their collective work, as well as an appropriate preface to the labors of Publius: "This ambiguous form [i.e., 'the States' present] had been drawn up by Mr. G[ouverneur] M[orris] in order to gain the dissenting members."[24] Consensus through ambiguity—for the convention and, by extension, for *The Federalist* itself.

James Madison brought to *The Federalist* a profoundly complex sense of language. He understood from Locke and the Scottish philosophers that language was the fundamental bond of society and how important it was, in particular, for the new republic of the Unites States, a nation formed deliberately by compact and ruled by opinion. He recognized the intrinsic imperfections of language, how difficult it was for a man to communicate his ideas exactly, as well as the difficulties that accompanied the stylistic ideal of clarity and simplicity, of "proper words in proper places." He believed, too, that sincerity in language, as much as accuracy, was essential to social intercourse, but he learned at the convention, if he did not before, that equivocation and duplicity were part and parcel of political discourse. He knew that the debate over ratification would be a war of words, and he assumed the persona of Publius to enter the lists in defense of a compromise constitution, to speak other than he truly and completely believed.

Adrienne Koch's analysis of Madison's style in the *Literary History of the United States*, along with all the interpretations that similarly depend on the unproblematic relation between words and ideas, needs to be, at the very least, revaluated. We cannot study *The Federalist* without attending to style. We cannot study the ideas without confronting the words. The founders knew that language could do more than signify, that it could transform—transform dissensus into consensus; transform Madison, Hamilton, and Jay into Publius; transform a slave into two-thirds of a citizen. They knew, too, that the source of its strength was also the source of its weakness, and Madison, for one, could not imagine an easy way out of the bind. *The Federalist* reveals a world in which the philosophical ideals of truth, clarity, and virtue come up against the reality of falsehood, ambiguity, and faction, thus reflecting broadly the post-Revolutionary problem of conceiving of language as the foundation of all political process. No. 37 is as much a fictional response to this problem as, say, the tragedy of Charles Brockden Brown's *Wieland* or the satire of Hugh Henry Brackenridge's *Modern Chivalry*.[25] Thrown back upon the "cloudy medium" of language, Madison fashioned a political idyll, in which ambiguous words give way to virtue and which, like Longfellow's originary pastoral moment, defines the course of history precisely because it stands outside the ordinary course of human events.

But he imagines no alternative America and no alternative language. Constrained by the imperatives of Commonsense moral philosophy, undoubtedly convinced by them, he continued well into the nineteenth century to advocate the ideal of linguistic clarity, but with little apparent optimism. Evidently forgetting his experience at the convention, he complained over and again in later years that "the language of our Constitution [was] already undergoing interpretations unknown to its founders will" and cautioned that "if the meaning of the text be sought in the changeable meaning of the words composing it, it is evident that the shape and attributes of the government must partake of the changes to which the words and phrases of all living languages are constantly subject." He welcomed both William Cardell's proposal for a "National Philological Academy" and Webster's dictionary, but only tentatively. "To provide for the purity, the uniformity, and the stability of language, is of great importance under many aspects," he wrote, but due to "the nature of man and the progress of society," he had to admit, "few things are more difficult."[26] This was the legacy that the founders bequeathed to the next generation.

CHAPTER FIVE

Language in a
"Christian Commonwealth":
Horace Bushnell's
Cultural Criticism

EVER SINCE Charles Feidelson classified Horace Bushnell as a "version of Emerson," a growing number of scholars have sought to secure Bushnell's place in American intellectual history by revaluating his contributions to the development of American education, theology, philosophy, literature, and sociology, and a major focus of this "rediscovery" has been the controversial minister's views on language.[1] The work that most engaged Feidelson and continues to attract sustained critical interest is the same work that achieved its author's notoriety in his own century—*God in Christ* (1849), a radical reassessment of the Christian doctrine of the Trinity with an extended theoretical introduction, "Preliminary Dissertation on Language, as Related to Thought and Spirit."[2] Here Bushnell formally enters into the nineteenth-century discourse on language limned by Feidelson, taking issue with some of its most important voices: Locke (still influential), Humboldt, and the American A. B. Johnson, among others. Here he writes about the symbolic nature of language, the uses of ambiguity, and the limits of rational discourse—discussions that adumbrate much modern thought on the nature of language.[3] But the views expressed in the "Preliminary Dissertation," though central to an understanding of Bushnell's thought in particular and of American Romanticism in general, constitute only a portion of his philosophy of language. By isolating this essay, intended primarily for an audience of theologians, we overlook the major underlying intellectual concern of his ministerial career—to reformulate prevailing Enlightenment notions about the relation between language and society so as to re-present the role of language in the unfolding of America's political and spiritual destiny.[4]

Indeed, from the very beginning of his intellectual career, Bushnell's thinking about language was tied to social considerations. Having been "brought up in a country family, ignorant of any but country society, where cultivated language in conversation was unknown," he felt at a distinct disadvantage to his articulate classmates when he entered Yale

College in 1823. He proposed a problem for himself then, a problem fraught with implications both for his own intellectual development and, as he would soon see it, for the developing Jacksonian culture around him: "how to get a language and where?" To be sure, the incipient class consciousness that accompanied his early awareness of language soon vanished; after something of a conversion experience at Yale triggered by his reading of Coleridge's *Aids to Reflection*, the direction of his thinking about language and society took, in political if not in theological terms, a decidedly conservative turn. "My habit was only landscape before," he confessed, "but now I saw enough to convince me of a whole other world somewhere overhead." Persuaded of "the two-world range that belonged to [him]," he began to view the problems of the material world with one eye always toward the world of spirit, and of the spiritual with an eye toward the material.[5] This double vision provided the fundamental structure of Bushnell's linguistic thought—and allowed him, as it were, to imagine his way out of the philosophical bind bequeathed to him by Madison and the founders—as his initial difficulties with language (his provincial lack of polish and his vernacular vocabulary) grew into a sophisticated understanding of language as an instrument of public discourse. In fact, the locus of his career, especially in the decade leading up to *God in Christ*, may be described as a series of attempts to define, in terms of this double vision, his own role as an American man of letters and, at the same time, to reorient accordingly the languages of religious, political, and literary discourse in America.

LANGUAGE AND POLITICS

Horace Bushnell saw the "new spectacle" of the 1840 presidential campaign—when the Whigs abandoned their aristocratic image to appeal to the common man, as the Democrats had, with catchy slogans and patriotic ballyhoo—as a sign that America was in dire spiritual trouble. "The public mind is now so deeply absorbed in the politics of the country," he preached soon after the election, "that we can hardly get a hearing for the more spiritual truths of the Gospel." The language of politics—"the harangues of their great assemblies and the reports of their expresses"—had drowned out the Word of God.[6]

Four years later, Bushnell would warn his congregation, and the electorate at large, that "the divorce of politics from conscience and religion . . . must infallibly end, if not arrested, in the total wreck of our institutions and liberties."[7] He believed that without inner restraints the democracy could not be sustained—not the argument of *Federalist* 10, but a common belief among conservative Americans since the Revolution.

Still, to point to the minister's republican concerns is to obscure the precise motivation behind his jeremiads. Bushnell's political warnings were informed by a vision of America's spiritual destiny, a vision highlighted by a strong sense of personal and national mission. "The wilderness shall bud and blossom as the rose before us," he wrote, "and we will not cease, till a christian nation throws up its temples of worship on every hill and plain; till knowledge, virtue, and religion, blending their dignity and their healthful power, have filled our great country with a manly and a happy race of people, and the bands of a complete christian commonwealth are seen to span the continent."[8] The events of 1840 and 1844 threatened this vision. Bushnell was not concerned that Americans were manifestly a "political people"; in fact, he consistently praised "our great principle of self-government" (*AP*, 190). But his faith in America's political future was predicated upon the promise of "a complete christian commonwealth." This was the practical, political embodiment of the "two-world range" of his thought, defining the difference between his vision of America and, for our purposes here, Madison's. He feared that, in their enthusiasm for politics, Americans were completely shutting out the spiritual half of their dual heritage. As long as Americans remained religious, he could offer words of encouragement—even in the midst of economic depression. "There are too many prophetic signs admonishing us, that Almighty Providence is pre-engaged to make this a truly great nation," he declared during the financially disastrous year of 1837, "not to be cheered by them."[9] But the apparent wholesale segregation of religion and politics marked by the recent presidential campaigns was a real cause for concern.

The titles of the two "election sermons" I refer to—*American Politics* (1840) and *Politics under the Law of God* (1844)—are, in effect, interchangeable. Both rehearse the underlying argument of Bushnell's political writings: elsewhere politics may be played by its own rules, but in America it must conform to the law of the gospel. It was a delicate position to maintain. He certainly did not mean to suggest the abrogation of the First Amendment. On the contrary, the minister embraced the separation of church and state as an important extension of civil liberty, as well as a crucial step on the road to his "christian commonwealth." He claimed "no right to meddle," in his pulpit, "with any political questions, whether in regard to men or measures" (*AP*, 191). But each time he repeated this disclaimer during his ministry, it was as a prelude to a political sermon. He saw no contradiction in his stance. The First Amendment was, for him, an institutional, procedural matter; it involved the church, not religion. Which did not at all mean that he wanted, in the words of one politician, "to draw religion from her seat in the hearts and consciences of men, and to associate her with power, or parade her before the world."[10] On the contrary, the explicit goal of his ministry and the implicit burden of his philosophy of language was to close the conceptual gap between these two beliefs. The First Amendment reaffirmed for Bushnell the crucial role of religion, and his own role as a minister, in the unfolding of national destiny. To separate church and state meant to secure the church's domain. "Do save us one half of society," he demanded, "free of the broils, and bruises, and arts of demagogy." He envisioned "a place of quiet," where "the din of our public war" could not be heard but the spiritual truths of the gospel would ring clear (*AP*, 199). In America, no one could be coerced into accepting the Word, but through language, in particular sermonic language, religion could become "virtually incorporate in the principles and feelings of the people" (*TWW*, 16). And through language, Bushnell could enter the lists on an equal, if separate, footing with the political demagogues of the day.

A year previous to the notorious campaign of 1840, Bushnell had painted a different picture of the relationship between church and state. Addressing his congregation on the options, short of physical force, that were open to Americans opposed to slavery, he preached: "Our newspapers, secular and religious, will tell; our electors' meetings, and the voices of our speakers at Washington will tell; our pulpits will tell; and our prayers will go up together and tell in the ear of Him who is the slave's Friend."[11] Acting in unison, political and religious language could abolish the institution of slavery. To be sure, he was aware even then that when people organized for a political end, their language would suffer; that when no individual accepted responsibility for the organization, the language of power would subvert the language of truth. When people speak as a group, their "object is to swing a battering-ram against something, the resolution is drawn so as to hit, and the society pass it with acclamation." As a result of this verbal show of force, the resolution's "truth is doubtful and its bearing in some other direction most hostile to valuable and sacred interests" (*DSQ*, 19–20). But Bushnell was then confident that if Americans, as individuals, were moved "by a spontaneous and separate impulse, speaking, writing, preaching, voting," then "there would be moral grandeur in [their] position and [they] should be felt" (*DSQ*, 22).[12]

The campaigns of 1840 and 1844 made it clear to the minister that the normative political practices of his countrymen were themselves responsible for the general declension in political discourse and that a purely political solution was therefore impossible. A typical public pronouncement was "a false and base appeal," consisting essentially of "suggestions of selfishness" (*AP*, 194). "Duty, and the fear of God" were "so far subordinated to the power of party discipline" that political contests had been recognizably transformed into tests "of mere physical force, in which the masses are wielded as instruments of political adventure" (*PLG*, 7, 10, 7). The alliance of religion and politics, or morality and democracy, had been sundered by the ascendancy of the political side of American life. To combat the imbalance, Bushnell called for a tactical retreat, reemphasizing the distinction between church and state only to consolidate the church's strength. His goal was not to politicize religion. He wanted not to place the influence of the church behind any man or measure for partisan reasons but to place politics itself "under the law of God." His strategy called for a revitalization of religious language. "What then shall we do, since you turn away your ears so far from the great truths of God and eternity," he asked, "but go after you, carrying these truths with us, and endeavor *to surround you* with them in the daily strife of your political arena" (*AP*, 189; italics mine). The implications of this strategy of "surrounding" with language would play themselves out over the next decade and would issue, ultimately, in the detailed linguistic formulations of *God in Christ*.

LANGUAGE AND SOCIETY

Bushnell's antipolitical militancy declined after the election of 1844, in the wake of charges that he had overstepped his ministerial bounds by venturing into the political arena. Until his political activism was revived by the advent of the Civil War, the minister modified his rhetorical strategy. Instead of attacking the political system head-on, he subtly called into question the theoretical foundation upon which it stood: rather than depict society in terms of two radically opposed *spheres* of influence, the church and the state or politics and religion, he turned his attention toward *modes* of influence, conscious and unconscious, and reimagined the linguistic foundations of society. The embattled minister's focus on differing forms of public discourse in his early jeremiads soon grew into speculations on the nature of "man as a creature of language." An example of this shift in focus is the popular sermon *Unconscious Influence* (1846).[13] Its text, Bushnell admits, is an unlikely one: "Then went in that other disciple" (John 20:8). To put the verse into context: the Sunday after Christ's crucifixion and burial, Mary Magdalene discovered that the stone covering Christ's sepulcher had been removed. When she informed Peter and John, both disciples ran immediately to the site. John arrived first, gazed into the sepulcher, but refrained from entering. However, after Peter arrived and entered, John "went in also." Bushnell opens "this slight touch and turn of history" into "one of the most serious and fruitful chapters of Christian doctrine" (*UI*, 230). What convinced the hesitant John to follow the less reluctant Peter? Surely John did not deliberate and decide to follow Peter, nor did Peter consciously act to draw his fellow disciple after him. Rather, Bushnell suggests, they remained unconscious of their intentions. "And just so," he concludes, "unawares to himself, is every man the whole race through, laying hold of his fellow-man, to lead him where otherwise he would not go" (*UI*, 230).

The sermon moves from an unremarkable passage to a profound doctrine. According to one observer, Bushnell's preaching style was characterized precisely by this "wonderful skill in getting legitimately a text for his sermon, just where nobody else would look for it."[14] Viewed as a sermonic strategy, this style may be seen to reinforce the minister's message, for it involves the audience in a process of intellectual discovery by introducing them to unlooked-for meanings in Scripture. John's following Peter is significant precisely because it is an event that is easily passed over. By opening this passage, Bushnell is attempting to turn his congregation's attention away, for the moment, from the more prominent events of the Bible and to relocate significance "where nobody else would look for it." He finds "doctrine" in the interstices of the biblical text, in the suggestion that the apostles' actions were not deliberate. The meaning of Bushnell's sermon is tied to the audience's response to his exegetical technique, a technique not of explicating obscure passages but of making the texture of the Bible bristle with unconscious meaning. In effect, it redefines hermeneutics: Bushnell here is not concerned with articulated meaning but with the unarticulated assumptions that underlie the text. And those he finds underlying John 20:8 contradict those underlying the American polity. If the apostles' actions cannot be ascribed to volition, to what extent can we hold men responsible for their actions?

Reflecting on her response to *Unconscious Influence*, one parishioner remarked that "she was not a free moral agent for five years after hearing it."[15] Although the reaction is almost certainly exaggerated, Bushnell's purpose was well served by the comment. For he wanted to weaken the authority of the idea of free agency in America and thus to call into question the theoretical foundation of democratic government. If men are not in control of their lives, if they are not rational free agents, then what sort of power may be derived from the "consent of the governed"? How high a value can we place upon man's conscious political choices, if "men are ever touching unconsciously the springs of motion in each other"? Our individuality, our very political freedom, becomes suspect. Of what use is it that the structure of our society is built upon the foundation of the social compact, if our lives are governed "by a law of social contagion"? We consider ourselves free individuals, but actually we "overrun the boundaries of our personality—we flow together" (*UI*, 230). In effect, Bushnell was trying to establish that "half of society" he had asked for in his earlier political sermons. But the demarcations he earlier admitted to do not hold up under the theory of influences. The church cannot stand as an alternative to the state if, like the state, it purports to be a voluntary association. If the church directs itself to man's free choice, Bushnell argues, it "suffers in beauty and strength" (*UI*, 231). The purpose of *Unconscious Influence* is to establish the primacy of forces and influences "no human government can trace." The strategy is simple: once we admit that there are two modes of influence—conscious and unconscious—we must admit also that "public laws make men responsible only for what they do with a positive purpose, and take no account of the mischiefs or benefits that are communicated by their noxious or healthful example" (*UI*, 232). And once we admit to this, the insufficiency of the American political system to govern man becomes apparent.

Even more clearly than in his earlier political sermons, language is offered as the key to Bushnell's account of human interaction in *Unconscious Influence*, and his psycholinguistic formulations take on the "two world" pattern of his thought. "If we distinguish man as a creature of language, and thus qualified to communicate himself to others," he reasons, "there are in him two sets or kinds of language; one which is voluntary in the use, and one that is involuntary" (*UI*, 233). Voluntary language refers to "speech in the literal sense," and it represents "a door to the soul that we may open or shut at will." By definition, speech is limited to what we choose to say. It may reveal or conceal, be honest or manipulative, clear or ambiguous. In short, it may be controlled, and its influence may be "trace[d] and compute[d]" (*UI*, 232). But involuntary language—"that expression of the eye, the face, the look, the gait, the motion, the tone or cadence, which is sometimes called the natural language of the sentiments"—cannot be controlled.[16] It is "a door that stands open evermore, and reveals to others constantly, and often very clearly, the tempers, taste, and wishes of their hearts" (*UI*, 233). It is a language that cannot be manipulated and is generally unambiguous. Furthermore, there are "two inlets of impression" to receive the messages sent by man's two languages. First, "the ear and the understanding for the reception of speech." Like its delivery, the reception of speech is voluntary: one must attend to this sort of language in order for it to exert any influence. In effect, an implicit contract obtains in what modern sociologists call the "speech situation."[17] One man chooses to speak and another to listen. Without mutual consent, no communication occurs. But with the second kind of language, no such relationship exists. For, to receive "those sparks of emotion revealed [involuntarily] by looks, tones, manners, and conduct," "the sympathetic powers . . . have a certain wonderful capacity to . . . propagate in us whatsoever falls into their passive moulds from others." Unlike the understanding, which deals exclusively with verbal propositions, the sympathetic powers "catch the meaning of signs" unconsciously and involuntarily (*UI*, 234). And because no verbal propositions are involved, communication of the second sort is effected without the consent of the sender or receiver. The power of unconscious influence is thus coterminous with social life.

In these terms, the conceptual differences between Bushnell and Madison are readily apparent. Reasoning like Locke that society begins with language, Bushnell concludes that, considering "the double line of communication which man has with his fellow-men," we must speak in terms of two societies, coextensive and interrelated, but theoretically separate. Through rational language, or speech, "we are constituted members of a voluntary society": social contracts are drawn up, relationships are defined, and goods are exchanged. Bushnell concedes that society begins as a voluntary association. But as soon as contiguity is established, involuntary communication begins and men "become one mass, one consolidated social body, animated by one life." This involuntary society is, as it were, the soul of the body politic, and what is commonly known as national character issues from it. In other words, the spirit of any nation is a product of the involuntary communication among its members. No matter what ideology is professed or doctrine preached, it is of no real effect unless it has been incorporated into a man's character. If the language of the sentiments communicates "every thing that is warm, dignified, genial, and good in religion," then the goodness will propagate itself. But if "the spirit of gain, or pleasure, or appetite" underlies professions of benevolence, "you will almost fancy that you see the shapes of money in the eyes of the children" (*UI*, 235).

Bushnell's political motives should be clarified: his claims for dual citizenship evince his desire to register a fundamental critique of American society, and, at the same time, his unwillingness to do away with the very principles he is criticizing. His insistence on the primacy of involuntary society indicates his dissatisfaction with the fruits of Lockeanism in America, but the retention of the concept of the voluntary society speaks to the powerful influence that Lockean thought and values maintained in Jacksonian society. Bushnell's summary statement of dual citizenship is thus couched in a syntax of equivalence, registering the precise balance he seeks between political and spiritual America: "You are all, in a certain view, individuals, and separate as persons from each other: you are also, in a certain other view, parts of a common body, as truly as the parts of a stone" (*UI*, 235). In more practical terms, too, Bushnell's program for America is one of separation and balance. If Americans remain ignorant of unconscious influence, they will be unable to subdue the influence that partisan politics and a market economy exert on the national spirit. Appeals to the understanding cannot help, for Americans "dislike to be swayed by direct, voluntary influence." Careful of their rights as individuals, they "are jealous of such control" (*UI*, 238). Bushnell's purpose is, at least, "to awaken . . . a suspicion of the vast extent and moment of those [unconscious] influences, which are ever flowing out unbidden upon society, from your life and character" (*UI*, 231).

Bushnell's theory of influence and social interaction contains the germs of a theory of genre. "Histories and biographies," Bushnell writes, "make little account of the power men exert insensibly over each other. They tell how men have led armies, established empires, enacted laws, gained causes, sung, reasoned, and taught." In short, they are "always occupied in setting forth what [men] do with a purpose" (*UI*, 231–232). But no matter how thoroughly they accomplish their objectives, these genres can only give partial accounts. For, fully considered, the stories of the lives of men and nations are products of both the voluntary and involuntary forces that men exert upon each other. Some other literary form, Bushnell implies, must be conceived to reproduce in language the twofold character of social life. He does not here suggest alternative genres (as Hawthorne, say, would suggest romance), but he does offer the Bible as the paradigmatic integrated work—as evidenced by his exegesis of John 20:8—and presents his sermon, which exposes the importance of unconscious influence, as a prolegomenon of sorts to any future historiography.

In 1850—the year that saw the publication of Hawthorne's *The Scarlet Letter*, his fictional account of the Puritan fathers and their rebellious daughter—Bushnell published an oration called *The Fathers of New England*, in which the minister attempts to approach an integrated account of American history. (Significantly, he later retitled the piece "The Founders Great in Their Unconsciousness.") His immediate target is the national historiographical habit of projecting "the political successes in which, as Americans, we so properly indulge our pride" back upon the Puritans, holding them up "as a tribe of successful visionaries, coming over to this new world, in prophetic lunacy, to get up a great republic and renovate human society the world over."[18] The assumption underlying this prevalent view of American history is that the course of human events is determined by the conscious efforts of the participants. Bushnell comments that "our literature is at work, as in a trade, upon the manufacture" of democratic heroes, and he argues that this venture distorts both the true nature of the Puritan errand in particular and that of the "morally dynamic forces" of history in general (*FNE*, 10, 28). But most egregiously, the democratic vision of history defines the American corporate identity in strictly political terms. Bushnell's purpose in *The Fathers of New England* is to revamp American historiography, to turn aside from political events and to consider the unconscious, involuntary, "morally dynamic forces" that have shaped the nation's history.[19] Not that he wanted to discredit the country's political advances. Rather, Bushnell grounded his revisionism in this inclusive credo: "All kinds of progress, political and spiritual, coalesce and work together in our history" (*FNE*, 43). His present aim was to point to "the unconscious or undesigning agency of the fathers of New England, considered as authors of those great political and social issues which we just now look upon as the highest and crowning distinctions of our history" (*FNE*, 9).

In redefining historical categories to include the involuntary along with the voluntary, Bushnell also meant to offer parallel categories for political science. "We do not understand . . . the real greatness of our institutions," he argues, "when we look simply at the forms under which we hold our liberties" (*FNE*, 29). Considered "as foundations of civil order," the principles of social compact, majority rule, and laissez-faire are worthless without "a power of God entering into souls and reigning in them as a divine *instinct* of civil order." The democratic forms of government must combine with the "out of form" spirit of truth and justice, the body politic with the body of Christ, "creating thus a state—perpetual, beneficent, the safeguard of the homes and of industry, the condition of a public feeling and a consciously organic life" (*FNE*, 20, 21; italics mine). Liberty must be understood, not as license, but as self-control. The uniqueness of republican government is, not simply that it allows for the exercise of inalienable rights, but that it "substitut[es] a moral in place of a public control" (*FNE*, 32). In these political and historical terms, Bushnell revaluates the Puritan role in shaping American society. The fathers of New England did not undertake their migration "with any political objects in view; least of all as distinctly proposing to lay the foundations of a great republic." More accurately: "Their end was religion, simply and only religion" (*FNE*, 19). Indeed, many of their practices were unabashedly antidemocratic. But given Bushnell's notion of dual citizenship, of a nation comprising the forms of government and the "out of form" national character, the title "fathers" may still be justified. For the Puritan bequest to democratic America lay in their "simple fidelity to God" (*FNE*, 14). They brought to America the sense of moral responsibility without which democracy lapses into anarchy. They provided posterity with the spirit without which the letter of the Constitution remains meaningless or, as Bushnell would suggest during the Civil War, hopelessly (in Madisonian terms) ambiguous.

The religious militancy that characterizes Bushnell's sermons and orations earlier in the decade is abated in *Unconscious Influence* and *The Fathers of New England*, but the fundamental vision of a politically and spiritually integrated society remains. Whatever successes Americans have achieved are the results of, not simply the forms of democratic government, but the vivifying force of religious sentiment. Political liberty remains a hollow concept without the "morally dynamic force" of spiritual liberty. Bushnell reiterates his earlier support for the separation of church and state but reminds us that they are both simply "forms." He prophesies that "it will be found that, as church and state must be parted in the crumbling and disintegrating processes of [political] freedom; so, in freedom attained, they will coalesce again, not as church and state, but in such kind of unity as well nigh removes the distinction." In the fullness of time, Bushnell suggests, the distinction between voluntary and involuntary society, between conscious and unconscious influence, would dissolve in "the peace and love and world-wide brotherhood, established under moral ideas, and the eternal truths of God's eternal kingdom" (*FNE*, 43–44). In the meantime, the minister's role in this historical movement is to provide a language for American liberty, a rhetoric that would keep before the public the "two-world range" of their experience, alert them to the possible consequences of their actions, and remind them, in times of great political upheaval, that they are not, in any simple sense, the masters of their fate.

WORK AND PLAY

To appreciate better the peculiar balance Bushnell wanted to strike between religious and secular values in America and the precise way he decided to go about it, we should understand that the worldview expressed in *Unconscious Influence* and *The Fathers of New England* was not intended to diminish man's scope for voluntary action. In bringing to light the invisible network of relations that govern social interaction, Bushnell was employing a strategic device to mute the authority of the political and economic sphere but not to limit it in any concrete way. In fact, in a sermon entitled *Prosperity Our Duty* (1847), the Reverend Horace Bushnell shifts his emphasis drastically to the importance of man's exertions in the business world. "The great truth," he maintains, "is that God favors industry, and has made the most beautiful arrangements to bless it."[20]

The immediate event that prompted *Prosperity Our Duty* was the proposal, then before the voting public in Hartford, of a municipal project to build a water sluice that would bring the power of the Connecticut River from Windsor to Hartford. As in his earlier political sermons, Bushnell claimed not to be exceeding his ministerial limits. He admits, "It is not my office to advocate works of public improvement, nor to meddle in any respect with schemes which are purely secular and belong only to the province of business men." But he did little to mask his opinion. The text he chose for the sermon was 2 Chronicles 32:30: "This same Hezekiah also stopped the upper water-course of Gihon, and brought it straight down to the west side of the city of David. And Hezekiah prospered in all his work." Bushnell felt that his congregation would not be coerced, that they would not countenance his interference, yet he was wary of leaving the matter to the contingencies of an election. This ambivalence translated itself into a specific rhetorical strategy. Rather than plead the case of the specific project, he would try to place the voters "in the best possible attitude for the exercise of [their] own wisdom." This accomplished, he told his flock, "whatever you may undertake or decline you will undertake or decline for yourselves; it will only be more sure that you will not be false to any just enterprise or call of duty that comes before you" (*SIM*, 136).

For the minister who had pleaded for a sacred domain for God's truth apart from the broils of secular life, the urgency of tone in this sermon is remarkable. He told his congregants that the city had arrived at "a great and final crisis" in their economic development: "the opening of new avenues of trade and travel on every side of us has compelled the business of our city to change its form." Bushnell realized that such transitional periods are bound to be accompanied by "a degree of anxiety," but he did not counsel a retreat into the solace of the Word (*SIM*, 137). Rather, he implied that his listeners should seize the opportunity presented to them by the water sluice, for "it is the duty of every man to be a prosperous man, if by any reasonable effort he may" (*SIM*, 139). The awkwardness of his position did not escape him. "We are often required as ministers of truth," he admits, "to speak of the dangers of prosperity" (*SIM*, 138). But for Bushnell, prosperity itself is not morally dangerous; it is part and parcel of the "christian commonwealth" he envisioned. In the moral scheme of *Prosperity Our Duty*, money is not the root of all evil—the lack of money is. It should be noted, however, that financial decline is denigrated here, not poverty. For Bushnell, economic mobility is all-important; he excludes the alternative of a stable economy, and he explains his intentions in religious terms, by building a bridge between religion and economics. "An industrious, enterprising, hopeful, prosperous community is far more easily moved by the demands of duty and religion," Bushnell writes, "than one that is drooping and running down" (*SIM*, 139). A city experiencing financial decline will thus inevitably be subject to spiritual declension, and a city undergoing economic growth will be prone to moral elevation.

Bushnell is arguing for "a fixed connection between virtue and prosperity" (*SIM*, 143). Whereas in other works the minister tries rhetorically to separate the two, here he reverses himself and brings together the sacred and the profane. On one hand morality is a function of economic success; on the other hand "prosperity is the badge and flower of virtue" (*SIM*, 144). He defends his concern with business on the grounds that religion depends upon financial success; he promises that if his listeners were virtuous, they would be successful. The philosophical justification for these connections is less important here than the fact that Bushnell makes them. He can encourage financial exertion because, within the conceptual framework he constructs, it carries its own set of controls. Understanding Bushnell's intentions in these terms, we can better appreciate the disclaimer that concludes the sermon: "And let no one say that I have given you a discourse on the water project" (*SIM*, 157). Because virtue and prosperity are so integrally related, he has no need to address the issue directly. His language has been fashioned "to impart courage, to create public responsibility and public spirit; to impress a conviction of the value of talent and the ruinous and destructive power of vice; and thus to prompt us to united and vigorous action for all that concerns the common good" (*SIM*, 158). His purpose is to condition his audience for their role in the referendum. They remain free to vote as they will; he remains within the bounds of his pulpit. In a manner that parallels his division of voluntary and involuntary language, Bushnell opposes direct to indirect language—although, significantly, both categories here refer to verbal language. Politicians and businessmen speak directly: they argue specific measures in terms of immediate advantages and disadvantages, thereby diminishing the integrity of each individual's choice. But ministers speak indirectly, treading only upon the grounds upon which decisions are made, otherwise leaving each individual to determine the best course to follow. Bushnell can make the division, and can safely rely upon the voters' freedom, because he denies that any real division exists. His closing directions to his congregation speak to the integrity of secular and religious experience: "Go then every man to his own altar and live a godly life; every man to his work and do it manfully and well" (*SIM*, 158). Ultimately, the two are the same.

In *Prosperity Our Duty* Bushnell throws the full force of his ministerial weight behind the American work ethic and the ideology of progress. But the strategy of indirection he employs in the sermon functions for him as a mode of restraint. By serving up a version of the Puritan notion of "calling," the nineteenth-century minister translates American materialism into spiritual terms. Work is conceived as a form of religious devotion. In this way, acquisitiveness is encouraged; but because the internal source of acquisitiveness is understood as virtue, rather than greed, the character of materialism is transformed. Material and spiritual progress coalesce. The immediate purpose of the sermon was to get out the vote, but its ultimate goal was the ushering in of the "christian commonwealth."

The separation of spheres of experience in American life—religious and secular, spiritual and material—obtrudes into the *Prosperity Our Duty* only as background. Bushnell acknowledges the customary distinction between the City of God and the City of Man only to dissolve it. But it is a background that, in effect, structures the argument. Business and religion must be understood as separate spheres in order for the redefinition to occur. This is the strategy, too, of an oration delivered before the Phi Beta Kappa society in Cambridge, Massachusetts in August 1848, *Work and Play*.

The oration begins with an explanation of rhetorical strategy similar to those offered in *Prosperity Our Duty* and *Unconscious Influence*. Certain truths "require to be offered . . . by suggestion," so Bushnell aims to fashion his language, not to inform his audience of the truth, but to present certain ideas that will allow them to come to the truth on their own.[21] His intention, in other words, is to be ambiguous; for only through ambiguity can the full force of the truth be transmitted. He explains his aesthetic of suggestion, appropriately enough, with an illustration. Imagine a man of "thoughtful spirit" who, "in some interval of care and labour," returns home to find his children playing with a kitten on the floor. He is a man "worn by the toils of years" and "effectually tamed to the doom of a working creature," but observing "the unconscious activity, the exuberant life, the spirit of glee" displayed by his family, he is soothed. At this point the scene is transformed for the father, unconsciously, and he sees it as a "prophecy or symbol of another and higher kind of play, which is the noblest exercise and last end of man himself" (*WP*, 2–3). Its message is hardly formed, barely suggested. But, Bushnell remarks, it is remarkably effective. The sociological resonances of this aesthetic of suggestion are important, all the more so because they seem to call into question the ideology of *Prosperity Our Duty*. It is an aesthetic grounded in the disparate spheres of labor and leisure, "work" and "play." Clearly, work is not presented here as a form of devotion; on the contrary, it leads to spiritual decay. And play is offered as a type of spiritual fulfillment, not as a sort of depravity. To be sure, the oppositions of industry/dissolution and work/play are not exactly cognate. But there is no easy way of getting around the fact that in *Prosperity* Bushnell supports the work ethic and in *Work and Play* he inverts it.

It is a contradiction that can be resolved only through attention to Bushnell's larger rhetorical intentions.

"Work and play," Bushnell writes, "are the universal ordinance of God for the living races; in which they symbolize the fortune and interpret the errand of man. No creature lives that must not work, and may not play" (*WP*, 5). These categories are, again, sociological: they refer to man's activities on the job and at home. But Bushnell dissolves these categories and substitutes metaphysical ones instead, all in preparation for a redefinition of the "errand of man." Work is not what an individual does nine to five, as it were, but any "activity *for* an end." Play is to be understood, not in terms of relaxation, but in terms of "activity *as* an end" (*WP*, 6). Consciously, work is an "effort of will, and . . . play is impulsive, having its spring in some inspiration, or some exuberant fund of life at the back of the will" (*WP*, 7). Work "argues defect or insufficiency," but play argues completeness, "a joyous overflow of the soul's liberty" (*WP*, 9, 10). And yet he insists, "Let no one imagine that I derogate thus from the dignity of work" (*WP*, 11). For as he conceives it, work is above all a transitional activity, preparing for the "exalted" activity of play. Often, a soul "descends into selfishness and evil, which are only forms of work, there to learn the wisdom of goodness in the contrasts of distaste, weariness, and hunger" (*WP*, 13). Through this variant on the Puritan notion of preparation for salvation, Bushnell resolves the sociological problem of work. Business may be spiritually degrading, but if it is conducted as a means to "some loftier state of being—call it rest, retirement, competence, independence—no matter by what name, only be it a condition of use, ease, liberty, and pure enjoyment," then the work is sanctified. "And so we find the whole race at work to get rid of work," Bushnell remarks, "drudging themselves to-day in the hope of play to-morrow." And so American materialism becomes a type of spiritual aspiration: the "passion for money" may seem "sordid" and "selfish," but it has "its heat in the most central fires and divinest affinities of our nature" (*WP*, 15).

The metaphysics of work and play issue as well in a theory of genre. Bushnell understands "that profound passion for the drama" as a yearning for "the realization of play." For the drama presents "life in its feeling and activity, separated from its labours and historic results." In other words, the fictionality of drama is its highest recommendation, for the audience may experience "a life in which all the actings appear without the ends and simply as in play" (*WP*, 15–16). But a play is only *play* when it is read, Bushnell insists, not when it is acted. When we read, he explains, "we invent our own sceneries, clothe into form and expression each one of the characters, and play out our own liberty in them as freely, and sometimes as divinely, as they." The language of drama is ambiguous in a positive way, for it invites interpretation and creativity. But acted out, the drama loses that vital, liberating ambiguity. It becomes not a play but, as it were, an "*opera*," work: "men and women inspired through their memory, and acting out their inspirations by rote; panting into love, pumping at the fountains of grief, whipping out the passions into fury, and dying to fulfill the contract of the evening, by a forced holding of the breath." The mechanics of theatrical performance leave little room for free play. The power that the theater holds over the less-cultivated public, Bushnell argues, is only an intimation of, or preparation for, "that divine instinct of play, in which the summit of our nature is most clearly revealed" (*WP*, 17).

The literary correlatives of work and play are perhaps best understood in terms of the distinction between prose and poetry. If the author writes "for some use or end ulterior to the writing," if the reader senses that the writing is "only means to an end," the writing is prose. Poetry, on the other hand, is defined as "writing which is its own end, an utterance made because the soul is full of feeling, beauty, and truth, and wants to behold her own joy" (*WP*, 26). Prose is work; poetry is play. Bushnell extends his redefinition to include elements of prosody as well, specifically rhythm. When one writes in prose, i.e., for some ulterior motive "suggested by self-love," he is effectually "out of rhythm" with the universe, and "the music of the stars will not chime with him." However, "when he lets go his private want or end to play, then he is part of the great universe under God, and consciously one with it, and then he falls into the rhythmic dance of the worlds, giving utterance in beat and number, weaving and waving with those graces that circle the throne of all beauty, and chiming with the choirs of light in their universal, but, to the most of mankind, inaudible, hymn" (*WP*, 27).

In these terms, the popular American orator, though he often begins with an ulterior, partisan motive, may too become a poet. For "as he kindles with his theme and rises into inspired action . . . his cause is lifted out of the particular into the universal," so that "his advocacy, raised above the mere prose level, becomes a lofty, energetic improvising." He is sanctified and transfigured into "a free lyric in his own living person" (*WP*, 28–29). Here the existential distinction between labor and leisure upon which Bushnell's oration rests and the metaphysical distinction between work and play come together. For in the conversion of the orator we can begin to glimpse the fulfillment of the "prophecy" of the children and the kitten that opened the oration. In the person of the orator, American society finds the possibility of regeneration. Through him, partisan politics and the self-interest of the marketplace may be transfigured. The necessary element is religion, "for here alone does [the soul] finally escape from self, and come into the perfect life of play" (*WP*, 34). To dissolve the distinction between church and state, voluntary and involuntary language, material and spiritual progress, prosperity and virtue, labor and leisure, man must move from work to play. Bushnell closes with a vision of a "future age, yet to be revealed, which is to be distinguished from all others as the godly or godlike age,—an age not of universal education simply, or universal philanthropy, or external freedom, or political well-being, but a day of reciprocity and free intimacy between all souls and God" (*WP*, 35). This is his "christian commonwealth," a polity that brings together the twin traditions of political and Christian liberty.

In *Unconscious Influence*, Bushnell tried to suggest the power of an involuntary, nonverbal language; in *Work and Play*, he effectually redefines *voluntary* and *involuntary* and underscores the socially regenerative potential of verbal language. Publius had suggested that the ambiguity of political compromise could lead to the free play of virtue; Bushnell now suggests that the more language allows for play, the further society will progress spiritually. As it approaches a state of pure Christian love, he prophesies, there "shall arise a new body of literature, as much more gifted as the inspiration is purer and more intellectual." Religious poetry, the language of free play, is thus "the only real emancipator of man" (*WP*, 37). In light of all this, *Work and Play*, with its aesthetic of suggestion, can be seen as an attempt through language to bring its audience a bit closer to the fulfillment of the prophecy of the "christian commonwealth."

LIBERTY AND LOGOS

In the summer of 1848, when Bushnell delivered *Work and Play* before the Phi Beta Kappa graduates at Harvard, he was also in the midst of delivering, at the Yale, Harvard, and Andover seminaries, the series of discourses collected in 1849 as *God in Christ*. These two works present Bushnell in two distinct roles, as minister and as theologian. In *Work and Play*, his voice is pastoral and his aim was practical—to explain to lay graduates waiting to enter the marketplace or the political arena that the goals of their lives should be spiritual, as well as material. Here the minister draws together the two traditions of American liberty, imploring his audience not to forsake Christ for John Locke. In *God in Christ*, the pastoral voice is set aside and replaced by the scholarly, to address seminarians on the nature of the godhead. Although its purpose, too, was immediate—to end the denominational battles then raging in New England—it has none of the broad social implications of the other work.

Still, as their temporal proximity might suggest, *God in Christ* is informed by the same social vision that structures *Work and Play*. Indeed, in the "Preliminary Dissertation on Language" Bushnell draws what are perhaps the most fundamental connections between verbal language and political liberty in America.[22]

As with his earlier sermons and orations, the conceptual source of the "Preliminary Dissertation" is his initial perception as a Yale undergraduate of "the two-world range available to [him]," material and spiritual. Although all language operates with reference to the shared sensory experience of the material world, "language built on physical images is itself two stories high, and is, in fact, an outfit for a double range of uses."[23] In the first story, or "physical department" of language, words are used literally to signify "things" or "forms" of a tangible and recognizable universe; in the second story, or "intellectual department" of language, the same words are used figuratively to express the intangible realm of thought and spirit (*GC*, 24). In much of this, of course, Bushnell does not depart substantially from Locke and the Commonsense philosophers, who also find the origins of all words in sensory experience. But unlike the materialist philosophers, the theologian insists (with Coleridge and Emerson) upon the integrity of spiritual experience, though he does deny it a language of its own.[24] For him, all discourse that is not simply descriptive is understood "through the mediation of things," by analogy to the physical universe (*GC*, 21). Even when we say, for instance, that a theologian is involved *in* a controversy or that a regenerate soul resides *in* Christ, we understand the abstract preposition only by assuming that it means something like the physical condition of being *in* something, like a house. Up to this point, again, Locke would agree. However, whereas the philosopher would argue that the more abstract or figurative language gets, the less precise its meaning, the theologian would argue that abstract or figurative language has its own sort of precision and, used correctly, can succeed in expressing spiritual or intellectual matters. For "there is a vast analogy in things which prepares them, as forms, to be signs or figures of thoughts, and thus, bases or types of words" (*GC*, 22). He refers to the "vast analogy" with the Johannine term "Logos," explaining that "the outer world, which envelops our being, is itself language, the power of all language," written by "the universal author" and "EXPRESSED every where" (*GC*, 30).[25] Nevertheless, Bushnell admits, the intellectual department of language is never quite exact; it can suggest a nonliteral concept, but it cannot describe it.

Bushnell's immediate purpose in presenting language's "double range of uses" in *God in Christ* was to resolve the controversy then raging in New England over the true nature of the godhead. Both the Trinitarians and the Unitarians erred, he felt, in taking scriptural language literally. When the Bible speaks of a triune God or, in general, when it makes what seem to be illogical statements, the text must not be strained to yield logic or dogma. Rather, it must be read analogically, as suggesting spiritual truths, not as defining them.[26] But beyond the immediate purpose, Bushnell's explanation of the analogical or symbolic nature of all but the most basic descriptive statements and his grounding of such language in an analogical universe recalls man to his own spirituality, effectually locating him within the Logos of the universe. Man reaffirms God's sovereignty whenever he opens his mouth to speak, for had He not created the world as language, he would be unable to express himself. As Bushnell sees it, language, linking the Word to words, draws together heaven and earth, God and Man. Consider the implications: "Such a discovery, received in its true moment, were enough to make a thoughtful Christian stand in awe, even of his own words" (*GC*, 32). It were enough, too, to transform public discourse in America to engender the coming of the "christian commonwealth."

Bushnell's poetic approach to the Bible and the Trinity caused quite a stir in theological circles, and he was regularly attacked for espousing heretical views. This much could be expected; the Trinitarians and the Unitarians were entrenched in New England, and Bushnell was threatening the foundations of both positions. But he was also charged (in spite of his detailed linguistic formulations) with being vague and uncertain. The "Preliminary Dissertation" may thus be seen as an apologia with a double edge: it laid the theoretical grounds for *God in Christ*, and it served as a defense of his personal style. One day, he remarked to a friend, his critics would "give [him] credit for perspicuity instead of vagueness and uncertainty."[27] As the "Preliminary Dissertation" makes clear, Bushnell held that to be vague and uncertain was, in fact, to be perspicuous; although the overarching Logos effectually resolved the ontological rift between physical and spiritual universes, it did not, practically speaking, resolve the ambiguity inherent in all language. Those who demand clarity in language, from Hobbes and Locke to Hutcheson and Witherspoon, are only fooling themselves. For even literal signs "are never exact, being only names of genera." How much vaguer are intellectual terms, which only add their own ambiguities to this foundation of ambiguity. Consider the word *bitterness*, which, "taken physically, describes not a particular sensation common to all men," but has "an endless variety of significations, ranging between disgust and a positive relish of pleasure." Used figuratively, the word will "carry with it . . . associations so unlike, that it will be impossible to clothe it with the same precise import, as a word of sentiment." When we take into account the fact "that moral bitterness, in its generic sense, will not be a state or exercise of the same precise quality in [all] minds," the magnitude of the ambiguity of figurative language may be understood (*GC*, 44–45).

Two other factors add even more to this rudimentary ambiguity. The first involves the manner in which the meaning of figurative language is recovered. Bushnell reminds us that words "do not literally convey, or pass over a thought out of one mind into another." Rather, words "are only hints, or images, held up before the mind of another, to put *him* on generating or reproducing the same thought." The precision of this operation depends upon the degree to which the receiver's mind "has the same personal contents, or the generative power out of which to bring the thought required" (*GC*, 46). But since men's experiences necessarily differ, an exact transference of ideas is never accomplished. Second, because they convey meaning only through "the mediation of things," words necessarily "impute *form* to that which is really out of form." Intellectual language must be conceived only as a "kind of painting, in which the speaker, or the writer, leads on through a gallery of pictures or forms, while we attend him, catching at the thoughts suggested by his forms." To get at the true thoughts, we must "separate continually, and by a most delicate process of art, between the husks of the forms and the pure truths of thought presented in them." To a certain extent, we do this unconsciously, "and yet we do it imperfectly, often" (*GC*, 48–49).

The ambiguities of intellectual language suggest the limits of its use. Still, Bushnell argues, "words are given, not to imprison souls, but to express them," and the liberation achieved through language employs the very ambiguity that constrains it (*GC*, 50). Here lies the perspicuity of vagueness and uncertainty. We are enslaved by language only when we allow the forms it presents to determine the truths we try to recover from it. The "mere, uninspired, unfructifying logicker," who is satisfied "to live in definitions" substitutes words for truth (*GC*, 57). But a poet, "moving with a free motion, and tied to no one symbol," allows his readers to transcend the limitations of language (*GC*, 67). In his writing, "as form battles form, and one form neutralizes another, all the insufficiencies of words are filled out, the contraries liquidated, and the mind settles into a full and just apprehension of the pure spiritual truth." What Bushnell suggests is a poetics of contrariety, arguing that "we never come so near to a truly well rounded view of any truth as when it is offered paradoxically" (*GC*, 55). When a speaker or writer is most ambiguous, when he is "vague and uncertain," he is actually being most clear—and most free. Logic "imprisons"; poetry liberates. Bushnell employs here a rhetoric of liberty to explain the dynamics of language use, thus revealing the subtle ideological structure that underlies his theological text. Bushnell's rhetoric presents a strictly limited picture of man's freedom. In his analogical universe, language will always "represent . . . both [a] man's own liberty and the world in which he moves" (*GC*, 33). Although he exercises a certain freedom in choosing and formulating his utterances, what he says or writes is ultimately circumscribed by the Logos. Even when an individual, or an entire society, is wholly unaware of a word's etymology, the material origins of a word remain a constant "*latent presence*" that determines its meaning. For instance, because the word *congress* comes from the Latin *gressus*, or "the measured tread of dignity," it can never be used to signify the meetings of the undignified or low (unless, of course, ironically). The latent presence of *gressus* in *congress* causes it, "in spite of all revolutions and democratic levelings, to maintain its ancient aristocracy" (*GC*, 50–51). Linking political to linguistic conservatism, Bushnell constructs a model of man severely restricted by his situation in God's universe.

It is important to note that Bushnell does not mean to deny man's freedom of the will. On the contrary, in the midst of discussing the limits put on language by its inherent ambiguity and the latent presence of its material origin, he offers this example:

> Discussing the human will, for example, or the great question of liberty, the writer will be overpowered by the terms and predicates of language; which being mostly derived from the physical world, are charged, to the same extent, with a mechanical significance. And then we shall have a sophism, great or small, according to his capacity—a ponderous volume, it may be, of formulas, filled up, rolled about, inverted, crossed and twisted—a grand, stupendous, convoluted sophism—all a mere outward practice, however, on words and propositions, in which, as they contain a form of cause and effect in their own nature, it is easily made out that human liberty is the liberty of a scale-beam, turned by the heavier weights. Meantime, the question is only a question of consciousness, one in which the simple decision of consciousness is final;—to which, argument, whether good or bad, can really add nothing, from which nothing take. (*GC*, 62–63)

Again, logic leads to error because it denies the ambiguities of intellectual language. Freedom of the will is "a question of consciousness" and is thus not subject to the limiting laws of the material world, in this case, cause and effect. Neither can it be described by the physical department of language. Rather, the concept may only be approached analogically, and the argument against freedom of the will collapses. Bushnell answers "the great question of liberty" in the affirmative. Nevertheless, that freedom is not unlimited. For it follows from the concept of the Logos that when a man expresses his freedom, he is, in effect, acknowledging God's dominion over him at the same time. Even the liberation achieved by the poet through ambiguity and the multiplication of forms must be seen as a version of the liberation achieved by a Christian through accepting the yoke of Christ—freedom through submission to limits.[28]

To be sure, the ideology of the "Preliminary Dissertation" remains a "latent presence." Yet, given Bushnell's efforts over the decade to construct a link between language and liberty in America, to reorient American public discourse, the rhetoric he employs in *God in Christ* is significant. Over that period, he tried time and again to reestablish the position of spiritual life in the nation—and thus to reimagine the America of the founders—by opposing religious to political discourse, involuntary to voluntary society, play to work, poetry to prose. In *God in Christ*, Bushnell turns the matter on its head: all language, whether one knows it or not, partakes of the spirit of God. Man is left with two options: he may deny the spirituality of language and remain a slave to verbal forms, or he may become poet and accede to a true Christian liberty. The decade began for Bushnell with a strategy of divide and conquer. It ends with the promise of communion.

AMBIGUITIES AND GLITTERING GENERALITIES

Strictly speaking, the various sermons, orations, and lectures that Bushnell delivered during the 1840s do not constitute a systematic philosophy of language. His ideas were adapted and developed in response to specific and various historical occasions. From the campaign skirmishes of the Whigs and Democrats to the theological debates of the Unitarians and Trinitarians, his understanding of the different and often subtle ways language controls men's perceptions of the world and, indeed, the way they live their lives broadened and deepened. *God in Christ* is not so much a culmination of his thinking about language as it is another effort in an ongoing endeavor to establish the linguistic matrix of concrete social problems, to convert controversy, as it were, into contradiction.

Still, these works do cohere, if not as a philosophical system, then as an approach to cultural criticism, a Logos-centric approach deriving from the culture's dual heritage of liberty. On one hand, when Bushnell sees politics or economics in terms of language, he deflects criticism away from the institutional structure of American society. Partisan divisiveness and financial excesses result from bad talk, not from democracy and capitalism. To put America back on the right track, we need not alter the way we elect our government or do business; we must watch what we say. In effect, in urging social change, the minister recommends a change in rhetoric—a new campaign oratory, a revisionist historiography, a revitalized sermonics, and so on. In this manner, political and economic liberty is secured. On the other hand, Bushnell's strategy was not simply to maintain the hegemony of the American Way, but to inform the body politic with the spirit of Christ. The several dichotomies that structure the works, each issuing from the minister's initial "two-world" experience (church and state, voluntary and involuntary society, work and play, etc.), challenge the prominence of the spheres of activity by which the nation tends to define itself. His bifurcated worldview allows him to focus on the neglected spiritual sphere, both national and individual. Whether he calls for a resurgence of the ministerial voice, or a recognition of unconscious influence, or a literature of free play, his intention is to move away from those modes of expression which deny America its spiritual heritage and man his spiritual nature. If he could only "surround" his countrymen with a language that encouraged spirituality, he could make them "free indeed."

For Bushnell, however, the Civil War was a critical turning point on the road to the "christian commonwealth" and, accordingly, a test of his linguistic revisionism. The early difficulties of the Union armies caused many Americans to doubt the strident rhetoric of America's glorious destiny. After the setbacks suffered at the first battle of Bull Run, the Reverend Horace Bushnell, now retired from his parish, ascended once again into the pulpit of Hartford's North Church to inspirit his former parishioners and to rededicate them to the Union cause. *Reverses Needed* took as its text "If thou faint in the day of adversity, thy strength is small" (Proverbs 24:10). The substance of the sermon reflects, not only the minister's Puritan trait of finding in calamity a source of celebration, but the tenacity of his linguistic worldview. Like many others in the North, including Lincoln himself, Bushnell saw in the war the potential for a "new birth of freedom"; he found in it, too, a terrible confirmation of the failures of American public discourse.[29] In Lincoln's view, the Civil War tested whether "a new nation, conceived in liberty and dedicated to the proposition that all men are created equal . . . could long endure." Looking backward "fourscore and seven years," the president found solace in the rhetoric through which "our fathers brought forth" American independence. Bushnell's is a more critical account. He charges that the hostilities between North and South were the result of lacunae in the very rhetoric Lincoln celebrates: "Our Revolutionary fathers left us the legacy of this war," he claims, "in the ambiguities of thought and principle which they suffered in respect to the foundations of government itself" (*SIM*, 164).

In 1844, the minister had warned his parishioners that "the divorce of politics from conscience and religion . . . must infallibly end, if not arrested, in the total wreck of our institutions and liberties" (*PLG*, 17). Then he was concerned that Americans were more interested in political speeches than in sermons. By 1861, his attack extended beyond the emotional ballyhoo of political campaigns to the fundamental texts upon whose authority American government rested. Madison's ambiguities had come to haunt Bushnell, who was awakened to the difference between the ambiguities of poetic language and those of political expediency. The Declaration of Independence and the Constitution are only "forms of words," he charged, and exert authority only as we impart meaning to them. So it had been since the Revolution, when the exponents of two distinct American traditions, the Enlightenment and the Puritan, joined forces to forge them. Although the two factions found themselves "agreeing in forms of words[,] they were yet about as really not in agreement, and have in fact been struggling in the womb of it like Jacob and Esau from the first day until now" (*SIM*, 168). One group, represented by Jefferson (though it might just as easily have been Madison), "supposed . . . that a machine could be got up by the consent of the governed that would really oblige or bind their consent" (*SIM*, 166). This view, as Bushnell remarked of his own unregenerate vision, was not of two worlds but "of landscape only." With the coming of the Civil War, Jefferson's "glittering generalities" were discovered to be "specious fictions"—"about the shallowest, chaffiest fictions ever accepted by a people as the just account of their laws" (*SIM*, 167, 178, 172). They offered form without substance, the body politic without a soul. The second group, heirs of "our Hartford Hooker," believed that "God was to be the head of authority, and the rulers were to have their authority from him." For them, political language drew its binding force from Scripture, the phrase "consent of the governed" from the verse "Take you wise men, and understanding, and known among your tribes, and *I will make them rulers over you*" (*SIM*, 165). When the "forms of words" are informed by the Word, then the phrase becomes meaningful, and forms of government can exert authority.

In antebellum America, the ambiguities of political rhetoric allowed the South to claim the authority of a man-made compact and to secede from the Union. And since language, Bushnell felt, effectually brought about the war, language would ultimately have to bring about change. "It might not be amiss, at some fit time," he suggests, "to insert in the preamble of our Constitution a recognition of the fact that the authority of government in every form is derivable . . . only from God." At some fit time, but meanwhile these were "dark days and times of unspeakable trial" (*SIM*, 183). Now was not a time for words, but for action. Events could no longer be determined by opinion, but, tragically, by force.

"Adversity will be our strength, disappointments our arguments," until the true relation of language and liberty could be established in America. Then, Bushnell promised, they could build, "on eternal and right foundations, The Great Republic of the future ages" (*SIM*, 184).

CHAPTER SIX

Beyond Symbolism:
Philosophy of Language in
The Scarlet Letter

CRITICS have been telling us for some time that *The Scarlet Letter* is about language. The tradition begins with the New Critics, and the classic statement of the argument belongs to Charles Feidelson, who identified the romance as a quasi-tract in American symbolism, arguing that Hawthorne's "subject is not only the meaning of adultery, but also meaning in general; not only *what* the focal symbol [of the red *A*] means but also *how* it gains significance." Feidelson explained that "since the very focus of the book is a written sign," i.e., a single letter of the alphabet and so necessarily empty of meaning, Hawthorne is able to illustrate the complex way symbolic language—language freed from the arbitrary restraints of limited referentiality—can generate and accrue meaning by "circling interpretation through the minds of various characters." We carefully are never informed that the *A* stands for adultery because, through the course of the romance, it comes to mean many different things—Able and Angel explicitly, but also by implication Author, Authority, Adam's Fall, America—all these and more, an "inconclusive luxuriance of meaning" to reflect an irreducibly complex moral universe.[1]

Reiterated over the years, revised and revitalized by the current linguistic turn in literary studies, this reading has settled into a critical commonplace and has become as well a practical and effective pedagogic tool—so much so that it seems hardly necessary (or even worthwhile) to argue the *general* point of linguisticity any further. Clearly, language matters to *The Scarlet Letter*. Still, it is by no means clear how or why. What was once plain to Feidelson and his generation is no longer plain to us. More likely than not, for instance, recent rereadings characteristically tend to describe the linguisticity of *The Scarlet Letter* in negative terms: where Feidelson found a luxuriant plenitude of meaning, John Irwin (for example) finds a "constitutive uncertainty" and Millicent Bell, "the obliquity of signs."[2] David Van Leer has suggested that we might very well refer to Hawthorne's method as "antisymbolism," and Jonathan Arac, drawing upon de Man and Benjamin, has argued that we drop altogether the pretense of calling Hawthorne a symbolist and admit, once and for all, that Hawthorne is more accurately "an allegorist of uncanny power."[3]

To cast this critical shift as a radical departure would be to misconstrue the difference between Feidelson and his revisers. For whether they view Hawthorne's language from the vantage point of Cassirer and Richards or de Man and Derrida—whether they render symbols or hieroglyphs or allegories—they do fundamentally agree that *The Scarlet Letter* thematizes language by foregrounding and problematizing the relation between signs and their referents. Both positions assume, moreover, that Hawthorne's political aim is to free Hester, as it were, from the prison house of Puritan language, effectually underscoring his opposition to, or his discomfort with, the limitations inherent in the commonsense (and Commonsense) understanding that language can unproblematically render experience, that to label Hester an adulteress is to know her essence. So construed, very little distance remains between "luxuriant meaning" and "constitutive uncertainty," very little difference between saying the *A* means many things and that it means nothing at all. But neither should the interpretive shift be seen as a mere shift in critical sensibility, from modern to postmodern. Plainly, a variety of readings can be sustained by the text: from the prison door to the forest brook, from the town-beadle to little Pearl, from Hester's silence to Dimmesdale's dying confession (not to mention the ever-present *A*), the narrative itself seems to be held together by a chain of interpretive and communicative possibilities and uncertainties. The very fact that Hawthorne encourages, frustrates, and generally complicates attempts to uncover and generate meanings (both ours and those of his characters) argues for a broader view of the novel's linguisticity.

But what argues most strongly for a broader view is the suggestion at certain points in the narrative that a mode of communication exists beyond representation and interpretation, beyond symbolism and allegory. Most dramatically, the suggestion is embodied in Hawthorne's peculiar description of Dimmesdale's election sermon in chapter 22, perhaps the most significant example of public discourse in all of Hawthorne's fiction. The minister, we recall, had just returned from his emotionally liberating meeting with Hester in the forest, still "breathing the wild, free atmosphere of an unredeemed, unchristianized, lawless region."[4] The two had compacted to flee Boston, to escape the bondage of Chillingworth and "all these iron men and their opinions," and to search for a new life together in the safety of the Old World (*CE*, 1:197). Seven years' passion and remorse were set loose, and on the eve of the foremost event of his political career, Dimmesdale experiences "a revolution in the sphere of thought and feeling," leaving him to stumble about recklessly in a spiritual maze (*CE*, 1:217). Shocked at his own emotional state, the minister channels his feverish energy into the composition of the political sermon, his final official effort as a spiritual leader of the Puritan community. Yet we never hear a word of it. During its delivery we remain with Hester beside the scaffold, and instead of text, doctrine, and uses, we hear only the "indistinct, but varied, murmur and flow of the minister's very peculiar voice":

> Now she caught the low undertone, as of the wind sinking down to repose itself; then ascended with it, as it rose through progressive gradations of sweetness and power, until its volume seemed to envelop her with an atmosphere of awe and solemn grandeur. And yet, majestic as the voice sometimes became, there was for ever in it an essential character of plaintiveness. A loud or low expression of anguish—the whisper, or the shriek, as it might be conceived, of suffering humanity, that touched a sensibility in every bosom! At times this deep strain of pathos was all that could be heard, and scarcely heard, sighing amid a desolate silence. But even when the minister's voice grew high and commanding,—when it gushed irrepressively upward,—when it assumed its utmost breadth and power, so overfilling the church as to burst its way through the solid walls, and diffuse itself in the open air,—still, if the auditor listened intently, and for the purpose, he could detect the same cry of pain. What was it? The complaint of a human heart, sorrow-laden, perchance guilty, telling its secret, whether of guilt or sorrow, to the great heart of mankind; beseeching its sympathy or forgiveness,—at every moment,—in each accent,—and never in vain!

The thematic tensions of the novel are not resolved in the language of the sermon but in the linguisticity of the passage. Hawthorne deliberately fractures the experience of the sermon for his readers, filtering out its words through the meetinghouse walls in order to demonstrate dramatically that the meaning of a speech act encompasses more than the meaning of its words, that voice alone can carry significance. He tells us emphatically "that a listener, comprehending nothing of the language in which the preacher spoke, might still have been swayed to and fro by the mere tone and cadence" and have sensed the "passion and pathos, and emotions high or tender," as if the sounds themselves constituted a language of their own, a primal, inarticulate "tongue native to the human heart." Indeed, he goes so far as to insist that the "sermon had throughout a meaning . . . entirely apart from its indistinguishable words" and suggests, moreover, that "if more distinctly heard, [the words] might have been only a grosser medium, and have clogged the spiritual sense" (*CE*, 1:243–244).

Hawthorne's terminology here echoes, not the efforts of symbolists (from Humboldt through Coleridge to the Bushnell of *God in Christ*) to reestablish the connection between words and things, but the contentions of empiricists like Madison and Berkeley that meaning "is rendered dim and doubtful, by the cloudy medium through which it is communicated" and that "we need only draw the curtain of words, to behold the fairest tree of knowledge, whose fruit is excellent, and within the reach of our hand."[5] Words impede, rather than facilitate, communication. To be sure, Hawthorne's version of the empiricist argument (if I may extrapolate from the narrative) adds a new dimension to the critique. Whereas Madison and Berkeley argued, following Locke, that words are unavoidably inaccurate because they are inadequate to the very meaning they are attempting to convey, Hawthorne seems to be suggesting that words distort something else, an emotional, unverbalized supplement to the text, something akin to Thomas Reid's "natural language" of gesture, look, and tone of voice, or Bushnell's involuntary language of unconscious influence, or, most suggestively (and I will elaborate upon this below), Rousseau's prehistoric "cry of nature."[6] For the problem here is not of representation but of expression. Nor is it a matter of sincerity, as Commonsense philosophers like Hutcheson and Witherspoon would have it. Dimmesdale's words are not problematic because they fail to point to his ideas or because he did not mean what he said. Although there are, as we all know, innumerable instances of verbal ambiguity in *The Scarlet Letter* (Pearl's precocious pronouncements, for instance, or Dimmesdale's own feeble attempts at public confession), the text of the sermon is not ambiguous but wholly adequate to its message, which Hawthorne eventually summarizes in the following chapter. The problem is, rather, that the verbal message is only part of what the minister is trying (I use the term loosely) to communicate. Dimmesdale's sermon contains a double message—one public and political, the other personal and spiritual—in a double language, verbal and nonverbal, reflecting the minister's profoundly ambivalent feelings about the Puritans he serves and the woman he loves. What we have in this passage is neither symbolism nor antisymbolism, not the play of the signifier around some ambiguous, complex, or unapproachable signified, but Hawthorne's evocation of the signified itself, inarticulate but unambiguous, coincident with the words of the sermon but independent of them.

To read *The Scarlet Letter* in terms of a thematics of language grounded too firmly in the discourse on symbolism (and in the related critical distinction between symbol and allegory) is to obscure the significance of this passage for the romance itself, as well as for Hawthorne's developing philosophy of language. For, although he did not, like Bushnell, write a formal linguistic treatise, he clearly thought long and hard about questions of language, not only (to appropriate Matthiessen's distinction once more) about matters of style but also about the many and complex ways people communicate—and just as likely fail to communicate—with each other, both in the imaginative world of the romance and in the unimaginative world (Hawthorne felt) of nineteenth-century America. We see the salience of his linguistic thought throughout his career, in various authorial pronouncements about the nature of language, in his often peculiar descriptions of characters involved in (or deliberately removed from) speech situations, and in the celebrated intricacies of his style. For Hawthorne, as for Bushnell, ideas about the nature and function of language are inseparable from the way he thought about American society and about his role as a writer in that society. In this chapter, I will attempt to show that the way Hawthorne imagines language in his description of Dimmesdale's election sermon bears upon these broader concerns.

PRE-TEXTS FOR A PHILOSOPHY OF LANGUAGE

Just as Dimmesdale's election sermon may be said to emerge out of his ambivalent relation to Puritan society, so the complex linguisticity of Hawthorne's description of that sermon should be understood to have emerged from the author's ambivalent relation to Jacksonian society, a relation which was already being formed when, as a student at Bowdoin College, he rejected the more traditional professions for college men (law, medicine, the ministry) and first considered "becoming an Author and relying for support upon [his] pen" (*CE*, 15:139). Beneath the lighthearted tone of the letter in which he first tentatively presents his decision to his mother ("Indeed I think the illegibility of my handwriting is very authorlike") lay the anxiety of a young man with an economically uncertain future. The chorus of voices calling for the creation and support of a truly American literature (like the graduation address of his classmate Longfellow) are themselves testimony to the fact—or, more accurately, to the pervasive perception—that Americans had thus far produced, in Tocqueville's words, "properly speaking, no literature" and that they would not likely be able to produce one soon: Americans were simply too engrossed in practical pursuits to have time for more refined intellectual fare (*DIA*, 2:59). Even Emerson doubted that "any good book should be thrown out of our vortex of trade and politics."[7] Despite the personal encouragement of his friend Horatio Bridge and of his rhetoric professor Samuel P. Newman, he knew that the prospects of the fledgling American author were not promising: "Authors are always poor Devils, and therefore Satan may take them" (*CE*, 15:139). *American literature* must have seemed to him a veritable contradiction in terms.

To choose to become a professional writer in America—to throw off the yoke of British literary tyranny and to match pens with "the scribbling sons of John Bull"—Hawthorne had to face this cultural contradiction (*CE*, 15:139). The impact of the confrontation is felt throughout his writings, most clearly, perhaps, in the frantic ravings of Oberon, the law clerk and disappointed author in the early sketch "The Devil in Manuscript" (1835). Oberon resolves to burn his blotted manuscript tales of devils and witchcraft because, he explains, "they have drawn me aside from the beaten path of the world, and led me into a strange sort of solitude—a solitude in the midst of men—where nobody wishes for what I do, nor thinks or feels as I do."[8] He believes that he had sold his soul to the devil in setting aside his legal work to dabble in gothic fiction and that his damnation manifested itself in his alienation from the mainstream of American society, a felt loss of social selfhood. Soon, however, he reveals a less mysterious source for his emotional state—"nobody will publish them" (*T&S*, 331). In what amounts to a catalog of rejection notices, Hawthorne has Oberon give a fair account of the antebellum book trade. Among the seventeen publishers who had rejected his tales, one, pragmatically, "publishes nothing but school books"; another, blaming the glutted literary market, claims to have "five novels already under consideration"; a third, professing economic self-interest, "would not absolutely decline the agency, on [Oberon's] advancing half the cost of an edition, and giving bonds for the remainder, besides a high percentage to themselves, whether the book sells or not"; a fourth admits frankly "that no American publisher will meddle with an American work, seldom if by a known writer, and never if by a new one, unless at the writer's risk" (*T&S*, 331–332). Clearly, Hawthorne knew firsthand the priorities of the American publishing business and the consequences for an author in "a pecuniary society under democratic patronage."[9]

What is most significant about "The Devil in Manuscript," besides the biographical insight it provides, is the linguistic consequence Hawthorne imaginatively ascribes to the concrete conditions of authorship. The publishers had reduced his writing to a commodity, and Oberon, thrown back upon his verbal creations, comes himself to treat his manuscripts as mere things, signs without meaning, projecting his antipathy for the publishers onto the manuscripts themselves. His alienation from American society is thus mirrored in a commensurable alienation from the ink-blotted pages he had written. He begins to perceive an immense gap between the words as they appeared on paper and the thoughts and feelings he experienced while writing them. Words that had once seemed to him to embody "ideas . . . like precious stones" and "delicious stream[s] of thought" now seem like "nothing but a faded and indistinguishable surface" (*T&S*, 333–334). Under the weight of his failure, writing ceases to function for Oberon either as the embodiment of thought or as the expression of self.

The breakdown of language is, of course, a figment of the young writer's imagination: the narrator (his "intimate friend") realizes more rationally that the stories may not be masterpieces but recalls in them "passages of high imagination, deep pathos, original thoughts, and points of . . . varied excellence" (*T&S*, 334). Nevertheless, the perceived breakdown strains the very basic rhetorical assumption upon which Oberon and his contemporaries were trying to establish their careers, the assumption—common to the popular Commonsense rhetorics taught in American colleges during the period—that words can unproblematically represent thought.[10] In *A Practical System of Rhetoric*, for instance, Hawthorne's Bowdoin professor Samuel P. Newman devotes his entire first chapter to "thought as the foundation of good writing" and suggests that "many of the faults of *style* arise [first and foremost] from indistinctness in the *thoughts*, and an inability to discern their relations to each other" (italics mine).[11] Drawing heavily from influential Commonsense rhetoricians George Campbell and Hugh Blair, Newman does not (like Locke, say, or Madison in *Federalist* 37) see linguistic representation itself as a problem. To be sure, he admits "that words are but signs—that there is no natural connexion between them and the objects which they represent—and that the words of a language are changing," but he insists nevertheless that "each word in a language becomes the symbol of a particular object . . . by conventional agreement" and that, on the basis of that agreement alone, words can "'bring up to the mind subjects and thoughts which they are designed to represent'" (*PSR*, 119, 121, 118). Not all good thinkers are good writers, but writing is a skill that one can learn by following certain rules. "To use the English language skilfully," he writes, "the writer [simply] selects his words and composes his sentences, in a manner, which accurately and clearly conveys to those able to read this language, the thoughts existing in his own mind" (*PSR*, 117). It follows for Newman that differences in style between "two individuals [who] write on the same subject" necessarily reflect differences in "their peculiar modes of thinking—the extent of their knowledge—their tastes and their feeling." In short, we can know man's inner self through his writing: "The productions of the pen exhibit the characteristics of the mind" (*PSR*, 157).

Oberon ambivalently clings to these assumptions. After all, the ability to write well was supposed to be, in Newman's words, "an attainment, which amply repays all the effort that is here enjoined." And especially "in this land of free institutions," he who "holds an able pen . . . with honest and patriotic motives . . . may become a public benefactor" (*PSR*, 224). To be sure, Newman probably had in mind writing more like Oberon's legal documents than his witchcraft tales. Nevertheless, unpublished and disheartened, unable to reap the rewards Newman describes, Oberon grows more desperate and irrational, distorting the very principles that failed him. As the pages burn, he remarks that, not only were representations of thought being consumed in the fire, but "thought [itself], invisible and incorporeal" (*T&S*, 335). Writing, which was supposed to be an unproblematic mode of representing one's self to others, has forced Oberon away from others and back into himself. At his most desperate, as he watches his manuscript go up in flames, he briefly abandons his Commonsense assumptions and considers a way of emerging from his isolation. Before he realizes the extent of the conflagration, he hears from the street an increasing number of voices crying out "that terrible word," "Fire!"—a "universal cry" which then merges with the clanging of steeple bells. Finding a certain inarticulate eloquence in "their iron tongues"—in contrast to the imagined eloquence of his stories—he yearns to throw himself into "the multitude on the pavement below" and to "cry out in the loudest of the uproar, and mingle [his] spirit with the wildest of the confusion"—to end his seclusion by throwing himself violently (and thus merging his selfhood) into the mass of inarticulate, passionate humanity. Again, he considers this drastic measure only briefly, and when the frenzied author realizes that the flames which were consuming his tales had somehow spread, he abandons his self-obliterating scheme and offers the following comical conclusion, a grotesque parody of Commonsense theories of rhetoric: "Here I stand—a triumphant author! Huzza! Huzza! My brain has set the town on fire! Huzza!" (*T&S*, 336–337). Words, thoughts, and self are utterly and comically confused.

To the extent that "The Devil in Manuscript" is about language, it is about *writing*: it ascribes Oberon's emotional and linguistic breakdown to the commoditization of imaginative literature in American capitalist society and, in so doing, admits the possibility that, even on a theoretical level, the relation among a writer, his writing, and the ideas he means to represent may be more problematic than Hawthorne's teacher at Bowdoin was willing to admit. In "The Minister's Black Veil" (1836), Hawthorne adds a different dimension to his critique of language by focusing on speech, not writing, and by considering the possibility that, even without the limitations inherent in writing as a mode of communication (time, distance) and in a socioeconomic situation far simpler than Oberon's, we cannot simply put our thoughts and feelings into words.

Specifically, the impediments are psychological: Hawthorne has Reverend Hooper don a black veil to tell us symbolically that our ability to communicate with one another is severely limited because we are all spiritually isolated, humanly unable to express our innermost thoughts even to those we hold most dear. Only after death, Hooper says, will we be able to reveal the true nature of our souls to each other. Until then we remain separated from others by the deep-seated shame and fear we harbor. "I look around me," Hooper concludes on his deathbed, "and lo! on every visage a Black Veil" (T&S, 378, 384). I do not mean by this straightforward reading of Hooper's allegory to ignore the obvious narrative irony of the tale, that Hooper's vow sets him even further apart from his parishioners and (even more important) from his beloved Elizabeth, so that, for all his preaching about "secret sin, and those sad mysteries which we hide from our nearest and dearest, and would fain conceal from our consciousness, even forgetting that the Omniscient can detect them," he cannot "take away the veil from [his own words]" (T&S, 373, 378). To the contrary, I want to underscore this irony because through it Hawthorne complicates even further his critique of language. Besides cutting the minister off from his accustomed intimacy with his flock—however limited—Hawthorne suggests that the black veil "had the one desirable effect of making its wearer a very efficient clergyman." The enigmatic veil transforms a mild preacher of unremarkable talents into an imposing figure. He becomes "a man of awful power, over souls that were in agony for sin," and his many converts could attest to the curious blend of terror and sympathy that spoke to them "with every tremor of his melancholy voice" through "the aid of his mysterious emblem" (T&S, 381, 373, 381). His influence extends even to politics: when he delivered the annual election sermon before Governor Belcher, he "wrought so deep an impression, that the legislative measures of that year were characterized by all the gloom and piety of our earliest ancestral sway." The final irony of "The Minister's Black Veil" may very well be, not Hooper's tragic demise, but the fact that his extraordinary career is built upon an actual and emblematic concealment: he communicates best (if at great personal cost) by recognizing what words cannot do and by refusing to speak.

The reference to Belcher and the description of Hooper's "surprising conversions" locates "The Minister's Black Veil" during the period of the Great Awakening, a period marked by a thoroughgoing revolution in sermonic style.[12] Indeed, the change in Hooper's preaching, at least in a general way, recalls that revolution, and the uproar in Hooper's community recalls the intense, prolonged debates which pitted rationalist "Old Lights" like Charles Chauncy against pietist "New Lights" like Jonathan Edwards. According to Chauncy, briefly, preaching had to be rational to be effective: "unless the *reasonable nature* is suitably wro't upon, the *understanding* enlightned, the *judgment* convinc'd, the *will* perswaded, and the *mind* intirely changed," a preacher's efforts were worthless. He interpreted Paul's strictures against "the forwardness of those that had the *gift* of *tongues* to speak in languages which others did not understand" to mean that the passionate, figurative language of the revivalists only obscured the meaning of religious truth.[13] But Edwards countered, "Our people do not so much need to have their heads stored, as to have their hearts touched." He argued that powerfully figurative language and an "exceeding affectionate" mode of preaching "shall tend very much to set divine and eternal things in a right view, and to give the hearers such ideas and apprehensions of them as are agreeable to truth, and such impressions on their hearts, as are answerable to the real nature of things."[14] For Edwards, preaching had to be affective to be effective.

If Hawthorne wants us to recall the fire and brimstone of sermons like Edwards's *Sinners in the Hands of an Angry God* and the harvests of souls reaped by enthusiast preachers like George Whitefield and Gilbert Tennent, he also wants us to recognize the difference between the fictional Hooper and his historical colleagues. He is careful to point out that Hooper's preaching did not dramatically change after he put on the veil and, in fact, deliberately directs the reader away from Hooper's language and style altogether. Hooper's first veiled sermon, we are told, was "marked by the same characteristics of style and manner, as the general series of his pulpit oratory" (*T&S*, 373). "There was nothing terrible in what Mr. Hooper said," he writes, certainly "no violence." Indeed, "there was no other apparent cause" for Hooper's effectiveness than the veil itself (*T&S*, 381). Let me emphasize that the veil does not simply add a metaphorical dimension to Hooper's sermons. The difference between Hooper's veil and, say, Edwards's famous spider is its decidedly nonverbal nature: Edwards explains to his audience that God "holds you over the pit of hell, much as one holds a spider, or some other loathsome insect over the fire"; Hooper does not verbalize the sermon's message until the deathbed scene.[15] If Hawthorne tells us that "a subtle power was breathed into Hooper's words" as a result of his donning the veil, he does so only to underscore the fundamental inadequacy of language: the veil empowers the words but does not allow us to see through them (*T&S*, 373). The veil adds to the sermon a message that is understood—when it is understood—viscerally. Hawthorne (through Hooper) insists upon the material veil itself as a metaphor for secret sin, and not upon a verbal evocation of the veil, as if to tell us that even striking imagery and an emotional delivery would not have the expressive or evocative power necessary to convert souls. Had he been able to speak and unburden himself, one wonders, would the words have been as effective? What seems to be necessary, according to Hawthorne's narrative logic, is precisely the ineluctable "ambiguity of sin or sorrow which enveloped the poor minister," the suggestion but ultimate (tragic) suppression of his innermost thoughts and feelings (*T&S*, 380).

"The Minister's Black Veil" imagines a world markedly different from that of "The Devil in Manuscript"—a world unencumbered by the socioeconomic constraints of Jacksonian America and where preaching can be effectual. Clearly it is important that Hooper is a preacher and Oberon a writer, but it would be difficult to say that, for Hawthorne, speech per se succeeds where writing does not. Neither writer nor preacher has an easy time of things: Oberon goes mad, Hooper dies alone. Words fail both. Clearly, too, cultural environment is significant, but in neither of these tales does Hawthorne imagine a mode of public discourse that can actually bring people together. Hawthorne cannot rest with a simple understanding of language. Words cannot simply represent thought. Each work presents verbal communication as the complex interplay of self, society, and language and displays the author's heightened sensitivity to what words cannot (or do not) do. In particular, for whatever reason—whether impeded by socioeconomic factors or inhibited by psychological ones—language in these works emphatically does not bring people together. In fact, in each case, an attempt at public discourse results in increased isolation. And while, at the same time, we can see alternative modes of communication (nonverbal, passionate, symbolic) emerging in the narratives as dramatic counterpoints to the failures of words, these modes clearly carry for Hawthorne their own very serious risks.

LOVE LETTERS AND LANGUAGE THEORY

To add yet another dimension to Hawthorne's developing "philosophy" of language, let me turn at this point away from his published works to his private correspondence, in particular, to the *Love Letters* (as they were called when they were first "privately printed" in 1907) that he wrote to Sophia Peabody.[16] I want to focus here on the beginnings of that correspondence, the series of letters he wrote to his future wife between the years 1839 and 1841. These were critical years for Hawthorne, albeit not his most creative. In 1839 he received his first political appointment, as measurer at the Boston Custom-House. That same year he became engaged to Sophia. So the author was thrust into the marketplace and had his first glimpse of the machinery of American politics at the same time as he began to enjoy his first sustained adult emotional relationship. For their author, the letters to Sophia mediate between these two spheres of his existence, between his private and his public lives, and they constitute the best record we have of what he thought and felt during these crucial years. But they are not a complete record: Hawthorne did not tell Sophia everything. Most important, although he constantly complains to her about his job, he does not tell her very much about it.[17] He chooses rather to use the love letters as a refuge from the Custom-House, to keep his two lives completely separate. He conceived of the letters as an alternative mode of discourse, a way of cultivating the intimacy he had achieved with Sophia, and his Custom-House experience seemed completely antithetical to that discourse. The Custom-House was "the most ungenial place in the whole world to write a love-letter in," he explained, an "'earthy cavern' . . . surrounded by all those brawling slang-whangers . . . those miserable men who [never] received a letter which uttered a single word of love and faith—which addressed itself in any manner to the soul" (CE, 15:354, 430). He even toyed with keeping two separate journals: one "of all my doings and sufferings, my whole external life, from the time I awake at dawn, till I close my eyes at night"; the other "of my inward life throughout the self-same day—my fits of pleasant thought, and those likewise which are shadowed by passing clouds—the yearnings of my heart toward my Dove—my pictures of what we are to enjoy together" (CE, 15:395). The love letters are the closest we come to that second journal. But, try as he may, Hawthorne was led to conclude that even these quintessentially private letters could tell very little, in a direct way, about his "inward life."[18]

Hawthorne often apologized for his letter writing. He was "not an epistolarian by nature" (CE, 15:389). He only wrote letters when "compelled by an internal or external necessity," and he did not, except in certain instances, take much care with them. By his own admission, in short, he was "not a good letter-writer" (CE, 15:522). Yet between his declarations of love for Sophia and his complaints about working for the government, Hawthorne thought a lot about letter writing. Indeed, much of the correspondence concerns the correspondence itself. So much depended upon the "blessed art of writing" (CE, 15:442). The letters were "no small portion of [his] spiritual food," "the sunshine of [his] life" (CE, 15:291, 296). In his letters, he could refer to himself and Sophia as husband and wife; he could even deny that they were separate persons ("Has not each of us a right to use the first person singular," he writes, "when speaking on behalf of our united being?")—as if language could bridge the distance between Boston and Salem, break down the barriers between them, and reorder their circumstances (CE, 15:355). He even develops something of a letter fetish: he yearns for the arrival of each new epistle and agonizes over the inefficiencies of the post office; he pores over them again and again; he keeps them near his heart; he kisses them; he seems attracted to the sheer physical presence of the letters, as if they were Sophia, "as if she had stolen into my chamber," he writes, "and made me sensible of her presence" (*CE*, 15:354). We certainly need to allow for romantic hyperbole here: after all, Hawthorne's epistolarian effusions stand side by side with "half a page of nonsense about Sophie Hawthorne's nose" (*CE*, 15:379). We need to allow as well for literary convention. In *La Nouvelle Héloïse*, Rousseau's popular and quintessential epistolary novel of separated lovers, which Hawthorne first read in 1829, the hero Saint-Preux writes to the heroine Julie:

> Do not be surprised [. . .] if your letters which describe you so well sometimes have the same effect as your presence on your idolatrous lover. Rereading them, I lose my reason, my head strays in continual delirium, a devouring flame consumes me, my blood takes fire and boils over, a frenzy causes me to tremble. I imagine I see you, touch you, press you to my breast . . . adored object, enchanting girl, source of delight and voluptuousness, seeing you, how can one not see the angelic companions created for the blessed? . . . ah come! . . . I feel her . . . she vanishes, and I embrace only a shadow . . . [19]

Moreover, Hawthorne (like Saint-Preux) more frequently and calmly considers the letters as the representation of ideas or of emotions: like Oberon, following Newman and the Commonsense rhetoricians, he seems to believe that words written with a particular intent can be understood as such and can accurately reflect or communicate the disposition of the writer. Still, I think we need to take seriously even Hawthorne's flirtation with this notion—the ability of written language to create or at least to represent a longed-for reality—as a manifestation of his continuing struggle (if ultimately a failed one) to locate and to harness the power of the written word.

Rousseau was the quintessential theorist of love letter writing, and a brief look at his novel will help to clarify the broader implications of Hawthorne's remarks. In Rousseau's second preface to the novel, "A Dialogue between a Man of Letters and M. J. J. Rousseau on the Subject of Romances," the author explains that the effectiveness of a love letter depends not upon the correctness or brilliance of the language but upon the honesty of the emotion. "Read a love letter written by someone in his study," he writes, and "it will be merely a short-lived, sterile emotion which will leave you only words to remember it by." But read "a letter that love has truly dictated," and it "will be [so] loosely written, verbose, drawn out to great lengths, disorderly, [and] repetitious," that "you don't remember any words, or turns of phrase," but "you feel your soul touched; you feel moved without understanding why."[20] The connection between words and emotions is more oblique than between words and thoughts: for Rousseau, language best expresses emotion by its reckless extravagance, by its very failure, in other words, to represent it accurately.

Hawthorne, too, sees the incommensurability of words and emotions, though he does not compensate through exuberance. More often than not, the letters cannot bear the emotional weight he places upon them. Language fails him: sometimes because his love seems too great ("Oh belovedest," he writes, "no words can tell how thirsty my spirit is for thine" [*CE*, 15:511]); sometimes because the political and economic atmosphere of the Custom-House is deadening ("Let me plead this in excuse for my dullness and mistiness," he explains, "the difficulty of pouring one's self out in a soul-written letter, amid the distractions of business and society" [*CE*, 15:462]); and sometimes—and I think most significantly—because words are inherently and hopelessly inadequate to effect the intimacy for which Hawthorne longed. The Hawthorne we find in the *Love Letters* is a writer still struggling with the limitations of his medium, coming again to realize what in his fiction he already seemed to know, that though he may strain to communicate, his words only confirm and compound his sense of separation. "This striving to talk on paper does but remove you farther from me," he writes (*CE*, 15:384). "Most glad would he be to think that there would never, henceforth, be occasion for his addressing a letter to thee. For would not that imply that thou wouldst always hereafter be close to his bosom?" (*CE*, 15:522). He distinguishes between "writing," with its constant and necessary reminders of distance and absence, and the communion of speech, which he terms "living words" (*CE*, 15:444). Speech confirms presence—Sophia's presence, to be precise. Writing suffers from its essential materiality and from circumstance: Hawthorne complains of his "iron pen," of "greasy" paper, of his "uncouth scribble," of the inept postmaster—of all "the impediments of this mode of utterance" that prevent him and Sophia from communicating to each other (*CE*, 15:321, 506, 435, 397). But Hawthorne's speculations extend beyond letter writing, and he develops a bifurcated view of writing in general. The radical disjunction between the intellectual or spiritual signified and the material signifier is painfully clear to him: "My Dove, there were a good many things that I meant to have written in this letter; but . . . the soul of my thought has not readily assumed the earthly garments of language" (*CE*, 15:305–306). "Imagine all that I cannot write" (*CE*, 15:328).

Like Rousseau, Hawthorne considers speech a privileged mode of communication. In his *Essay on the Origin of Languages*, Rousseau argues that writing may encourage exactitude but only at the expense of the expressiveness of speech. "In writing," he explains, "one is forced to use all the words according to their conventional meaning. But in speaking, one varies the meanings by varying one's tone of voice, determining them as one pleases." Indeed, "these tones of voice . . . penetrate to the very depths of the heart, carrying there the emotions they wring from us, forcing us in spite of ourselves to feel what we hear."[21] Hawthorne even more emphatically distinguishes between words and tone of voice. "I cannot do without thy voice," he tells Sophia, "thou knowest not what a sweet influence it has upon me, *even apart from* the honied wisdom which thou utterest. If thou shouldst talk in an unknown tongue, I should listen with infinite satisfaction, and be much edified in spirit at least, if not in intellect. When thou speakest to me, there is mingled with those *earthly words*, which are mortal inventions, a far *diviner language*, which thy soul utters and my soul understands" (*CE*, 15:491–492; italics mine). Not only does Hawthorne see speech in terms of two modes of language—one earthly and verbal, the other spiritual and unconscious—but he clearly warns against mixing modes: "I have felt, a thousand times, that words may be a thick and darksome veil of mystery between the soul and the truth which it seeks. Wretched were we, indeed, if we had no better means of Communicating ourselves, no fairer garb in which to array our *essential* selves, than these poor rags and tatters of Babel" (*CE*, 15:462; italics mine). Verbal language *is* effective, but only in its sphere, "explaining outward acts, and all sorts of external things," like social relations. But the soul must "explain itself in its own way"—silently. Or, at least, without words. "I wish there was something in the intellectual world analogous to the Daguerrotype (is that the name of it?) in the visible," he writes, "something which should print our deepest, and subtlest, and delicatest thoughts and feelings, as minutely and accurately as the above- mentioned instrument paints the various aspects of Nature" (*CE*, 15:384). He speculates that after death, "when we shall be endowed with our spiritual bodies, . . . they will be so constituted, that we may send thoughts and feelings any distance, in no time at all, and transfuse them warm and fresh into the consciousness of those whom we love" (*CE*, 15:294). But "content[ing] ourselves to be earthly creatures," he proposes to Sophia four modes by which to "hold communion of spirit." In ascending order: "by letters (dipping our pens as deep as may be into our hearts)[;] by heartfelt words, when they can be audible; by glances—through which medium spirits do really seem to talk in their own language—and by holy kisses, which I do think have something supernatural in them" (*CE*, 15:295). From writing to silence (and beyond). It is in the context of these speculations about language that Hawthorne expresses his weariness and suspicion of public discourse in general—of "caucus" and "stump" speeches, of Father Taylor's sermons, of "Mr. Emerson's lectures," and of Margaret Fuller's conversations: "And what wilt thou do to-day, persecuted little Dove," he writes, "when thy abiding-place will be a Babel of talkers? Would that Miss Margaret Fuller might lose her tongue!—or my Dove her ears, and so be left wholly to her husband's golden silence" (CE, 15:382, 450, 431, 382–383, 511).

The Tower of Babel story—a recurring point of reference in debates over the origin of language—becomes in the *Love Letters* a trope for the inefficiency of verbal communication. Hawthorne's pun on the word *Babel*—"rags and tatters of Babel," "Babel of talkers"—is part of a playful but significant revision of the biblical myth of the origins of linguistic diversity: man's fall was not into languages but into language. "When man arrives at his highest perfection," Hawthorne suggests, "he will again be dumb!—for I suppose he was dumb at the Creation, and must perform an entire circle to return to that blessed state" (CE, 15:512). Only when a man achieves a certain degree of intimacy, as Hawthorne has with Sophia, an intimacy above the material world and outside the artificial structures of society, then the blessed state may be approached: "Dearest wife, I truly think that we could dispense with audible speech, and yet never feel the want of an interpreter between our spirits. We have soared together into a region where we talk together in a language that can have no earthly echo. Articulate words are a harsh clamor and dissonance" (CE, 15:511–512). Still, Hawthorne keeps writing—what else could he do under the circumstances?—and he continues to apologize for the letters, hoping Sophia will be able to read, as it were, between the lines.

As part of a continuing critique of language, the *Love Letters* both reaffirm Hawthorne's earlier skepticism—that language cannot represent our "essential selves"—and go beyond it in several significant ways. First of all, they add a sociological distinction not apparent in either "The Devil in Manuscript" or "The Minister's Black Veil" (but crucial to *The Scarlet Letter*): Hawthorne suggests that communication may be possible in the private realm which may not be possible in the public. Second, they posit a mode of nonverbal communication that may, in the private realm at least, overcome the inadequacies of representational language to effect a bridge between individuals who have achieved a certain profound intimacy—at no apparent cost to selfhood. Significantly, this mode has nothing to do with symbolism or verbal ambiguity. The distinctions Hawthorne makes in the *Love Letters* are not between figurative and logical language, poetry and prose, tale and sketch, romance and novel, but between words and silence. However important these distinctions may be, the *Love Letters* give no indication that any sort of verbal language is less than inadequate.

A PHILOSOPHY OF SELF-WRITING

The reflections upon language that pervade the *Love Letters* clearly ad-umbrate the linguisticity in Hawthorne's description of Dimmesdale's election sermon. Both texts distinguish between voice and speech, both bemoan the inadequacy of words, both speculate about the efficacy of intimate, nonverbal discourse. But in the *Love Letters*, these notions are postulated within the framework of a larger, fundamental conceptual distinction between public and private realms—a distinction that gener-ally parallels Bushnell's distinction between work and play: whatever success Hawthorne has in communicating his "essential self" to his fiancée is predicated not only upon the intimate relationship already ex-isting between them but also upon his ability to remove himself (whether physically or emotionally) from the influence of the Boston Custom-House. Dimmesdale's sermon, inasmuch as it is grounded in this fundamental distinction, draws its dramatic power from the extent to which Dimmesdale is able to explode the categories of public and private, from his capacity to express his essential self in a communal ser-mon, to effect intimacy in the marketplace.

To make our way from the linguistic theory of the *Love Letters* to the linguistic imagining of *The Scarlet Letter*, we must make our way, as it were, through "The Custom-House." For in significant ways, the two Custom-House experiences mirror each other. In the *Love Letters* he complains about the "slang-whangers"; in "The Custom-House" he disparages the intercourse—or lack of it—between the elderly officers: the Whig Collector's "tremor of a voice, which, in long-past days, had been wont to bellow through a speaking-trumpet, hoarsely enough to frighten Boreas himself to silence"; the permanent Inspector's "voice and laugh . . . [which] came strutting out of his lungs, like the crow of a cock, or the blast of a clarion" but reflected "no power of thought, no depth of feeling, no troublesome sensibilities"; the "old sea-stories, and mouldy jokes, that had grown to be pass-words and countersigns among them"; and "the frozen witticisms . . . [which] came bubbling with laughter from their lips." Little substantive communication seemed to be going on. Indeed, Hawthorne describes the Collector sitting "amid the rustle of papers, the administering of oaths, the discussion of busi-ness, and the casual talk of the office; all which sounds and circum-stances seemed but indistinctly to impress his senses, and hardly to make their way into his inner sphere of contemplation" (*CE*, 1:20). In light of these observations, the fact that Hawthorne makes sure to remark that his own "medium of vocal communication with other parts of the edi-fice" was a "tin pipe" which "ascend[ed] through the ceiling" of his office seems especially meaningful (*CE*, 1:7–8). Neither Custom-House was the place for anything but superficial, boundary-maintaining conversation.

Similarly, in both Custom-Houses, Hawthorne's ability to write is curtailed. He cannot write (or read) love letters in Boston; he cannot write romances in Salem. The only "lettered intercourse" available to him in Salem was with "a junior clerk . . . who, it was whispered, occasionally covered a sheet of Uncle Sam's letter paper with what, (at the distance of a few yards,) looked very much like poetry" (*CE*, 1:27). "So little adapted is the atmosphere of a Custom-House to the delicate harvest of fancy and sensibility," he explains in the sketch, "that, had I remained there through ten Presidencies yet to come, I doubt whether the tale of 'The Scarlet Letter' would ever have been brought before the public eye" (*CE*, 1:34). Indeed, Hawthorne's sense of the imaginative discordance between the world of the Custom-House and that of *The Scarlet Letter* was readily noted by the early reviewers of *The Scarlet Letter*, who remarked upon the striking differences in style between the romance and the sketch. The utopian George Ripley, for instance, contrasted the romance's "gorgeous web of enchantment" to the "piquant daguerreotype" and the "graphic delineation" of the sketch. Anne W. Abbot noted the author's "wizard power over language" in the romance but could detect in the sketch "expressions which savor somewhat strongly of his late unpoetical associations."[22] Hawthorne himself indicates a precise, if tacit, understanding of the social determinants of language—an understanding remarkably similar to those which inform Bushnell's *Work and Play*—by calling "The Custom-House" a "sketch of official life" and *The Scarlet Letter* "a tale of human frailty and sorrow" (*CE*, 1:1, 48). The correlation he builds between genre and theme implies a similar and parallel correlation between modes of language and realms of social interaction that echoes the discourse of the *Love Letters*. When he addressed himself to the world of government and commerce, he employed a language that was adapted to that world's practical, mundane concerns. But when he dealt with matters of the heart and spirit, whose world existed beyond the sphere of the marketplace, his language became less direct, more (to use Whitman's term) "elliptical." In short, "official life" could appropriately be "sketched," but "human frailty and sorrow" had necessarily to be "told." The fact that both modes were written did not seem to enter into the formulation.

For Hawthorne, sketch and romance (he would later formulate an equivalent distinction between novel and romance) use different modes of language to address what he felt were discontinuous aspects of American experience. Like Bushnell, he felt that the two sociolinguistic realms ought to reinforce each other. But he perceived with Tocqueville that practical pursuits dominated American life and sustained only practical modes of discourse and that other aspects of experience (spiritual, emotional, aesthetic) were denigrated or ignored. In this way, the stylistic disparity between the sketch and the romance reiterates the ambivalence of the literary nationalists. What Longfellow glibly passed over in his youthful optimism, what frustrated Oberon a decade later, Hawthorne still remarks upon bitterly: he contrasts "the comfortable livelihood" that the Custom-House clerks earned by "worthless scratchings of the pen" to the meager rewards bestowed upon the writers of an American literature "filled, not with the dullness of official formalities, but with the thought of inventive brains and the rich effusion of deep hearts" (*CE*, 1:28). There is something about political and commercial America that cannot or will not sustain an American literature. Hawthorne must turn his back on the Custom-House if he is to write *The Scarlet Letter*.

But we underestimate the psychic pressures exerted by America's political ideology if we see Hawthorne simply dismissing American politics and economics—the world of the Custom-House—in favor of the values of art and imagination. The sketch *is* indeed an attack on political and commercial America, but the terms of the attack are those of Jacksonian political rhetoric. Hawthorne's well-known complaint, that his tenure at the Custom-House had sapped his creativity, is part of a larger argument that reveals the complex nature of Hawthorne's complicity in the American ideology. Observing his own imaginative enervation and the lethargy of his fellow customs officers, Hawthorne "was led to conclusions in reference to the effect of public office on the character, not very favorable to the mode of life in question," for, "while he leans on the mighty arm of the Republic, [a man's] own proper strength departs from him," and his soul loses "its sturdy force, its courage and constancy, its truth, its self-reliance, and all that gives the emphasis to manly [American] character" (*CE*, 1:38–39). I add the adjective *American* here to emphasize that Hawthorne was not proposing a viable alternative to the American way of life. Rather, he criticizes the system of political patronage best known as "the spoils system" because it betrays American ideals. Better "to struggle amid a struggling world," better "to dig gold in California," than "to be made happy, at monthly intervals, with a little pile of glittering coin out of his Uncle's pocket" (*CE*, 1:38–39). In these terms Hawthorne characterizes his co-workers by "that lack of energy that distinguishes the occupants of alms-houses, and all other human beings who depend for subsistence on charity, on monopolized labor, or any thing else but their own independent exertions" (*CE*, 1:7). In these terms, too, he answers the charges of his Puritan ancestors: "A writer of storybooks! What kind of a business in life,—

what mode of glorifying God, or being serviceable to mankind in his day and generation,—may that be?" Included among the "strong traits of [Puritan] nature" that "have intertwined themselves" with Hawthorne's are those which led him to rejoice at his departure from the spoils system (which he was to rejoin readily enough in 1853), not to an isolated life of the mind, but to the world of American individualism (*CE*, 1:10). His return to the profession of authorship involved both a revaluation of the function of literature and a return to the "true" America of the Puritan ethic.

My point is that Hawthorne did not simply propose the life of the imagination as an alternative to life in the marketplace but the profession of authorship as a participation in the life in the marketplace, as if the obstacles placed before Oberon had effectually been removed, as if it were now possible "to open an intercourse with the world" (*T&S*, 1152). It is in light of this that we must understand the peculiar opening paragraph of "The Custom-House." Although the sketch is clearly the most overtly political of his writings before the campaign biography of Franklin Pierce appeared in 1852, the ostensive subject of the opening paragraph is not politics per se but literary decorum: Hawthorne apologizes for intruding upon the reader with so much talk about himself and ponders the propriety of autobiographical discourse. The apologia is clearly disingenuous. The sketch was, in its day, the stuff of scandal—so clearly recognized as a piece of political revenge upon the local Whig establishment which had removed him from office in 1848 that Hawthorne felt the need to add a preface to the second edition disclaiming (equivocally, to be sure) all malevolent intentions.[23] Furthermore, we learn from the sketch virtually nothing of a private nature about the author: what we do learn is either Hathorne family history—and thus a matter of national historical record—or pure fiction. The passage needs to be read, rather, as a deliberate attempt to establish autobiography as the theoretical starting point of his political critique, to bridge the gap between self and society. As we have seen, one of the major themes to be developed in the sketch is the effect of public office on the self (especially upon the writing self), in particular the spiritual debilitation that attends the careers of political appointees. The opening paragraph prepares the ground for the ensuing exploration of this theme by discussing the constraints placed upon the expression of selfhood in a democratic-liberal society, i.e., a society founded upon individual rights and the limits placed upon them. It offers, in other words, a philosophy of self-writing for America.

"It is a little remarkable," the passage begins, "that—though disinclined to talk overmuch of myself and my affairs at the fireside, and to my personal friends—an autobiographical impulse should ... have taken possession of me, in addressing the public" (*CE*, 1:3). Hawthorne's surprise at his impulsive breach of social decorum—he describes it soon afterward as a violent "seiz[ing] the public by the button"—bespeaks, on one hand, a political culture in which the realms of public and private are clearly differentiated and marked by the restriction of certain types of "talk" to one or the other realm: "talking of myself" to the fireside, talking of impersonal matters to more public forums. On the other hand, it assumes a natural (i.e., antisocial and unconscious) desire to transgress the sociolinguistic boundaries and to assert one's self verbally in public. For Hawthorne, the politics of autobiography is defined by the opposition of these forces: he imagines autobiography as a potentially disruptive, if not subversive, political force in a society constituted by the constraints (and liberties) of the social contract. Hawthorne's profession of "native reserve" only complicates further the opposition of these forces: he can say in public what he cannot (or will not) say even in private. The transgression thus represents not so much the complete dissolution of sociolinguistic categories (making the private public, à la Rousseau's *Confessions*) as an ironic inversion that sustains the very categories being transgressed. Hawthorne seems to be pulled in opposite directions. The goal of the passage is to arrive at a *political* resolution of the conflict, to delineate (in the closing words of the paragraph) the "extent" to which, and the "limits" within which, "an author . . . may be autobiographical, without violating either the reader's *rights* or his own" (*CE*, 1:4; italics mine).

As the paragraph continues, it becomes clear that the opening sentence syntactically obscures certain crucial distinctions: what seems at first a "remarkable" perversion of linguistic propriety is soon explained to be a manifestation of a general and fundamental truth about the way authors relate to their readers. "The truth seems to be," Hawthorne suggests, "that, when he casts his leaves forth upon the wind, the author addresses, not the many who will fling aside his volume, or never take it up, but the few who will understand him, better than most of his schoolmates and lifemates" (*CE*, 1:3). Needless to say, authors do not cast their leaves to the wind, but neither do they seize the public by the button. Hawthorne's two figures contravene each other: the button seizing represents in exaggerated form the physical closeness of an interlocutor; the written page, thrown to the wind, signifies the unbridgeable distance between author and reader. The juxtaposition of incompatible figures problematizes the initial differentiation of public and private discourse. Literary discourse can be satisfactorily categorized as neither: the conditions of its creation and reception—the distance between author and reader marked by the printed page—complicate and confuse the differentiation of realms. Both author and reader are alone, one in the moment of composition, the other during the activity of reading. The author addresses the reader only in abstraction; the reader knows the author only through his words. Yet Hawthorne suggests that because literary discourse is by definition impersonal, it may very well allow (or seem to allow) for a more intimate relation with an unknown, absent reader than even fireside chats with family and friends. The initial inversion needs to be reformulated: Hawthorne can *write* and publish what he cannot even *speak* in private. One might think that to represent literary production as talking would be to transform a complex socioeconomic process (which by its very nature distances the producer from the consumer) into a more personal one, to achieve a sort of intimacy by presuming intimacy. Yet Hawthorne's impulsive behavior confirms for him the profound if paradoxical truth that writing (its status within the business of publishing still obscured, to be sure) may actually communicate more presence than speech and that, in more political terms, it may even effectually break down the artificial barriers that separate us and allow us to form more intimate bonds than the bonds of family and friendship.

Still, for Hawthorne, writing cannot wholly transcend its status as public discourse, and the brief incursion of the private into the domain of the public ultimately breaks down. He cannot condone the liberties taken by those authors who "indulge themselves in such confidential depths of revelation as could fittingly be addressed, only and exclusively, to the one heart and mind of perfect sympathy; as if the printed book, thrown at large on the wide world, were certain to find out the divided segment of the writer's own nature, and complete his circle of existence by bringing him into communion with it" (*CE*, 1:3–4). In the very act of rejecting such self-indulgence, Hawthorne acknowledges that such sympathetic communion is possible, even desirable. But he retreats nevertheless to the security of more formal social relations. To "speak all," he writes, would not be "decorous." At this point in the passage Hawthorne abandons his fable of authorship and refers once again (this time more emphatically) to writing as speaking—as if the illusion of physical presence were enough to restore the boundaries between individual selves. In fact, Hawthorne's return to speech represents a mode of compromise, an attempt to secure some middle ground for autobiographical discourse between silence and self-revelation, between isolation and communion. Because "thoughts are frozen and utterance benumbed, unless the *speaker* stand in some *true* relation with his audience," the author is advised to "*imagine* that a friend, a kind and apprehensive though not the closest friend, is listening to our talk" (*CE*, 1:4; italics mine). The weight placed upon the adjective "true" is ironically undercut by the noun "speaker" and the verb "imagine." Writing, after all, only simulates presence: it is enough to "thaw" his "native reserve" and thus free him to "prate of the circumstances that lie around us, and even of ourself," but it also allows him to "keep the inmost Me"—the realm of the inexpressible—"behind its veil." Writing about one's self, according to this passage, is an equivocal activity. Like Hooper's veil, it can reveal because it can also conceal. It can draw individuals closer because it keeps them separate. In short, Hawthorne's philosophy of self-writing asserts that rights must be respected despite the fact that societies are not built solely upon rights.

So construed, the opening paragraph of "The Custom-House" sets out the complex politico-linguistic considerations that will concern him, not only in the sketch, but in the romance as well. It prepares us for a sort of intimacy the sketch deliberately does not deliver. It sets up distinctions that it wants to but cannot break down. But the world of *The Scarlet Letter* is an imaginative alternative to the world of "The Custom-House," offering linguistic possibilities that the sketch cannot countenance. Dimmesdale's sermon effectually answers the challenge of Hawthorne's introduction: it gives an example of public discourse that at the very same time communicates the minister's "inmost Me." After establishing the limits for a nineteenth-century author (and these are very complex indeed) Hawthorne takes us back to the very origins of American society, to a time when the personal and public were not considered separate spheres, when, in fact, "iniquity [was] dragged out into the sunshine" and made to reveal itself in the marketplace (*CE*, 1:54). *The Scarlet Letter* revaluates the conceptual foundations of American social organization: Dimmesdale's passionate plea, in "a tongue native to the human heart," breaks through, not only the walls of the Puritan meetinghouse, but of the Custom-House as well.

THE SCARLET LETTER AND THE "CRY OF NATURE"

"Man is born free, and everywhere he is in chains" (*BPW*, 141). Given Rousseau's pervasive influence on post-Enlightenment social and political thought, the profound irony with which he begins *On the Social Contract* may be said as well to inform *The Scarlet Letter*, to authorize, in fact, the fundamental, symbolic opposition of the prison and the wild rosebush with which Hawthorne begins his "tale of human frailty and sorrow" (*CE*, 1:48). The polarization and valuation of these elements echo the Rousseauian inversion of Hobbes: society does not save savage man from the state of nature; it corrupts him. Thus, the prison, "the black flower of civilized society," is associated with crime, ugliness, and decay, while the rosebush produces "delicate gems" and is the "token that the deep heart of Nature could pity and be kind" (*CE*, 1:48). The symbolic tableau generates the clash of moral oppositions that necessarily (if not simply) structure the romance—nature versus civilization, passion versus authority, freedom versus repression, emotion versus reason, self versus society—and issue in the double language of Dimmesdale's election sermon. To explain more clearly both the political and the intellectual-historical significance of the critique of language that may be said to underlie, and to link together, the opening paragraph of "The Custom-House" and the description of Dimmesdale's election sermon, I will need at this point to turn to the language philosophy of Jean-Jacques Rousseau.[24]

Significantly, Rousseau's initial contribution to the Enlightenment discourse on language appeared as part of the political anthropology of his *Discourse on the Origins and Foundations of Inequality among Men* (1755). For, like Hobbes, Locke, and (in particular) Condillac before him, Rousseau understood the origin of language in social (rather than divine) terms. But because he believed that man's rise from the state of nature into a state of society was actually a decline into inequality, corruption, and oppression, he could not leave the social origin of language as an unchallenged premise. Because language and society presuppose each other, language becomes implicated in the misery that attends man's rise. He therefore makes much of man's prelinguistic state, when, living happily and alone in the state of nature, man had no language and no need of one. Moreover, Rousseau deliberately obscures and problematizes the prehistorical development of savage man into civilized man—between an isolated being who merely perceives and feels and one who, living among others, reasons, reflects, and speaks—arguing that, man's ability to fulfill his needs being wholly sufficient in the state of nature, "thousands of centuries would have been necessary to develop successively in the human mind the operations [like speech] of which it was capable" (*BPW*, 48). Discussions of the origin of language must, he argues, begin in paradox: without language, man's rise into a state of society is simply inconceivable, yet the steps leading to its formation itself are equally inconceivable. Indeed, Rousseau proceeds in his argument only by "disregard[ing] for a moment the immense space that there must have been between the pure state of nature and the need for languages," and he leaves unanswered the question, "Which was the more necessary: an already formed society for the invention of languages, or an already invented language for the establishment of society?" (*BPW*, 49, 51). His digressive remarks on the origin of language enter the exposition at the very point of greatest obscurity, serving rhetorically as a perceptible barrier between the two states, reinforcing their fundamental differences.

Because of the paradox written into the study of language's origin, because of the unimaginable gulf between man in the state of nature and man in the state of society, the rhetorical burden placed upon the description of "man's first language" becomes immense. Rousseau responds with a sentence whose structure performatively recapitulates the theoretical and unbridgeable gulf by suspending predication until the full implications of the subject are elaborated and the full effect of the unimaginable adjective "first" is felt: "man's first language, the most universal, the most energetic [i.e., forceful, emphatic] and the only language he needed before it was necessary to persuade men assembled together, is the cry of nature" (BPW, 49). Before the history of perfectibility begins, before the implications of man's inherent freedom are worked out, man's "language" is already perfect in many ways: it is the *most* universal (immediately understood by all, before the separation of men into nations and languages); it is the *most* energetic (not reliant upon reflection or leisure but proceeding immediately from man at his most healthy and vigorous); it is the *only* one he needs (wholly sufficient because, in a presocial state, his needs are few and easily satisfied). The "cry of nature" is pure expressivity, unmediated by design or reflection, virtually unmotivated because nearly instinctual, "elicited [i.e., wrenched, *arraché*] only by a kind of instinct in pressing circumstances, to beg for help in great dangers, or for relief of violent ills," a language in name only because it bears little resemblance to the rational systems of signs that constitute languages as we know them. Rousseau's term, "the cry of nature," while recalling Condillac on the origin of language, echoes more immediately Rousseau's own insistence in the preface to the Discourse that natural law consists exclusively of "two principles that are prior to reason" and which are spoken "directly by the voice of nature": the first, self-love, "makes us ardently interested in our well-being and our self-preservation," and the second, pity, "inspires in us a natural repugnance to seeing any sentient being, especially our fellow man, perish or suffer" (BPW, 35). The "cry of nature" follows the "voice of nature": it is motivated by self-love and elicits pity; it unites men in a presocial, prerational bond that, if only temporary, is powerful and pure.

Language as it later developed, coincident with the development of reason and the formation of primitive societies, represents a falling away from the radical identification possible through this preverbal language. "Reason," Rousseau argues, "is what engenders egocentrism, and reflection strengthens it. Reason is what turns man in upon himself . . . [and] what isolates him and what moves him to say in secret, at the sight of a suffering man, 'Perish if you will; I am safe and sound'" (BPW, 54). The great irony at the heart of Rousseau's reflections on language in the Discourse on Inequality is that the moment man chooses to associate with other men and develops the ability to speak to them at will, he drastically delimits his power to communicate and, in effect, declares his fundamental isolation from them. Verbal language is necessarily self-reflective, assertive of boundaries and, hence, of social selfhood. When Rousseau describes the "cry of nature" as "the only language [men] needed before it was necessary to persuade men assembled together," he is preparing the ground for the well-known assertion that opens part 2 of the *Discourse*: "The first person who, having enclosed a plot of land, took it into his head to say *this is mine* and found people simple enough to believe him, was the true founder of civil society" (*BPW*, 60). Inequality is a direct effect of property rights, and property rights are an assertion of language.

The polemical thrust of Rousseau's rhetoric in the *Discourse on Inequality* requires him to drive a wedge between society and nature and, hence, between linguistic and prelinguistic man. His narrative is strictly linear: one epoch ends, another begins. And although he allows some vestiges of man's presocial state into the narrative at certain points (i.e., man's emotional identification with characters in a drama) and implies that the corrupt nature of society may be ameliorated (primarily in the dedication to Geneva), the distinction he builds is otherwise clear and uncomplicated.[25] It should be noted that, of course, Rousseau is no naive primitivist. For all the dramatic quasi-nostalgia of the *Discourse of Inequality*, he clearly understands the "remarkable change in man" not only as irrevocable but as desirable (*BPW*, 150). In *On the Social Contract*, he explains, "Although in this [social] state he deprives himself of several of the advantages belonging to him in the state of nature, he regains such great ones." In politico-economic terms, he summarizes man's rise from the state of nature in terms of "credits and debits": "What man loses through the social contract is his *natural liberty* and an unlimited right to everything that tempts him and that he can acquire. What he gains is *civil liberty* and the proprietary ownership of all he possesses." In more psychological terms: "His faculties are exercised and developed, his ideas are broadened, his feelings are ennobled, his entire soul is elevated to such a height that, *if the abuse of this new condition did not often lower his status to beneath the level he left*, he ought constantly to bless the happy moment that pulled him away from it forever and which transformed him from a stupid, limited animal into an intelligent being and a man" (*BPW*, 151; italics mine). But only *if*: both the political blueprints of *On the Social Contract* and, just as significant, the nostalgic rhetoric of the *Discourse on Inequality* are generated, as it were, by the subjunctive clause I have underscored.

The plaintive undertone of Dimmesdale's sermon should be understood as the intellectual-historical offspring of Rousseau's "cry of nature." But not in any simple way. On one hand, it is a passionate, spontaneous, and inarticulate expression of suffering, and it elicits a sympathetic response that is equally spontaneous, passionate, and inarticulate, not only from Hester, but from the entire congregation. ("His hearers could not rest," Hawthorne writes, "until they had told one another of what each knew better than he could tell or hear" [*CE*, 1:248].) Furthermore, Dimmesdale's involuntary, primitive cry transcends the limits of political community as it "so overfill[s] the church as to burst its way through the solid walls, and diffuse itself in the open air," linking Dimmesdale emotionally not only to Hester, with whom we begin the passage, but, as Hawthorne's prose swells in its rhapsodic description and encourages a certain narrative disorientation, to "the great heart of mankind" (*CE*, 1:243). On the other hand, it is clearly not the cry of a savage man but of a highly civilized and rational man pushed past the brink of reason and reflection. Although *The Scarlet Letter* returns to national origins, it presumes man in a civilized state. Hence, the second sentence of the romance: "The founders of a new colony, whatever Utopia of human virtue and happiness they might originally project, have invariably recognized it among their earliest practical necessities to allot a portion of the virgin soil as a cemetery, and another portion as the site of a prison" (*CE*, 1:47). Dimmesdale's cry is only a vestige of Man's primitive state: it comes only as an undertone to an orthodox political sermon, and, for all its apparent power, the impact of the sermon's text itself on the Puritan community remains undiminished. Indeed, the cry seems ironically to underscore the political message of the text for the Puritan audience.

Moreover, we distort the romance—and the sermon's significance within it—if we see its moral oppositions purely in Rousseauian or post-Enlightenment terms. For Hawthorne asks us to place the introductory tableau in two different intellectual historical contexts. If the prison and the rosebush recapitulate Rousseau's opposition of society (civil liberty) and nature (natural liberty), they are also symbolic renderings of the concept of liberty articulated by John Winthrop in his well-known speech before the General Court in Boston in 1846, in the midst of the period covered by the action in the romance. Winthrop, we may recall, had also posited a "twofold liberty—natural . . . and civil or federal." Simply considered, the rosebush recalls natural liberty, which accords man an unlimited scope to "do what he lists" but, considering their postlapsarian, unregenerate state, ultimately "makes men grow more evil, and in time to be worse than brute beasts" and therefore threatens society's peace, stability, and security. The prison recalls civil liberty, which, to the contrary, prepares men for associated life by freeing them from the contingencies of their "wild" natural state. Civil liberty is the liberty of men and women under "the covenant between God and man, in the moral law, and the politic covenants and constitutions, amongst men themselves," and it is "maintained and exercised in a way of subjection to authority."[26]

We might say that Hawthorne engages Rousseauian philosophy in *The Scarlet Letter* by invoking the Puritans and that the narrative is generated through a clash not of particular values (passion versus authority, say, or nature versus society), but more precisely through the interpenetration of value systems that share fundamental concepts and terms but valorize them differently.[27] The dramatic conflicts that engage us in *The Scarlet Letter* and culminate in the election day sermon are enactments of the conceptual differences between Winthrop and Rousseau. Historically, as Hawthorne knew, the Puritan errand was based on mutuality, a correspondence of wills even more encompassing than that designated by Rousseau's "general will." As Winthrop explained on board the *Arbella*, the saints were to "be knitt together in this worke as one man," which meant for them that the "ligaments" which bound them together were to be both contractual and spiritual, the body politic one with the body of Christ. Theoretically, the Puritan system fails when the correspondence breaks down, when wills collide, when contracts are not supported by "ligaments . . . of love."[28] In his "little speech on liberty," Winthrop defended his social vision with an analogy that reveals the multileveled integrated structure of Puritan society and bears strikingly upon the plot of *The Scarlet Letter*:

> The woman's own choice makes such a man her husband; yet being so chosen, he is her lord, and she is to be subject to him, yet in a way of liberty, not of bondage; and a true wife accounts her subjection her honor and freedom, and would not think her condition safe and free, but in her subjection to her husband's authority. Such is the liberty of the church under the authority of Christ, her king and husband; his yoke is so easy and sweet to her as a bride's ornaments; and if through frowardness or wantonness, etc., she shake it off, at any time, she is at no rest in her spirit until she take it up again; and whether her lord smiles upon her, and embraceth her in his arms, or whether he frowns, or rebukes, or smites her, she apprehends the sweetness of his love in all, and is refreshed, supported, and instructed by every such dispensation of his authority over her.[29]

Winthrop conceived of society as a series of analogous relationships—political, ecclesiastical, marital—all characterized by a voluntary submission of will; authority could then be seen as a manifestation of love, and acquiescence to authority, as an exercise of freedom. He *assumes* that once a contract is entered into voluntarily, it will be sustained by "ligaments of love." But Hester Prynne could not love the husband she voluntarily married. Her "frowardness and wantonness" arose because she was subject to Roger Chillingworth, not in a way of liberty, but of bondage. Their relationship was solely contractual. With the failure of civil liberty to define her emotional life, she opted for the contingencies of natural liberty and the potential for emotional fulfillment. With her husband absent, perhaps dead, she abjured her legal marriage for a relationship that "had a consecration of its own" (CE, 1:195).

Seen through the lens of Rousseauian thought, the tragedy of Hester Prynne and Arthur Dimmesdale adumbrates the decline of the Puritan polity and the rise of a more equitable social order, when "the whole relation between man and woman [would be established] on a surer ground of mutual happiness" (CE, 1:263). Not that minister and parishioner are to be seen as innocent victims of Puritan repression; their crime was a serious one, even from a Rousseauian perspective. (La Nouvelle Héloïse, we should recall, frowns upon adultery as an affront to virtue, and, more generally, the Discourse on Political Economy and On the Social Contract make clear that the individual will should be subject to the "general will.") But while both Winthrop and Rousseau would have seen Hester's and Dimmesdale's adultery as an unwarranted act of natural liberty, Winthrop would have seen the act as a sign of personal depravity, and Rousseau would have seen its emergence as both emblematic and symptomatic of the limitations of Puritan social thought, as the failure of Puritan liberty to allow for the "mesh of good and evil" in their hearts (CE, 1:64; italics mine). The story of The Scarlet Letter, we should recall, occurs during that transitional age, as Hawthorne describes it, "in which the human intellect, newly emancipated, had taken a more active and a wider range than for many centuries before," and Hester herself is a Rousseauian figure, imagining how "the whole system of society [was] to be torn down, and built up anew" (CE, 1:164, 165). But this is only part of the story Hawthorne would write. As much as he sympathizes with Hester, he does not exonerate her or emancipate her. As much as he is drawn intellectually to Rousseau, he cannot abandon Winthrop. And not simply because among the Puritan traits intertwined with his was the belief in human depravity. Rather, he was fascinated by the Puritan attempt to conflate private and public, the state of an individual's soul with the state of the colony. He was drawn in particular to the mode of resocialization adopted by the Puritans by which "iniquity is searched out, and punished in the sight of rulers and people" (CE, 1:62). As the title indicates, the romance is about this process of resocialization, about how the scarlet letter goes about doing its office. The Rousseauian conflict between private passion and public responsibility, between natural and civil liberty, is generated and sustained in terms of Winthrop's utopian vision. Implicitly understanding this, Hester suggests to Dimmesdale that a shift in geography, either to the emptiness of the wilderness or to the obscurity of the Old World, would relieve the tensions of their ordeals; the shift would also alleviate the dramatic tension that gives power to the narrative.

Hawthorne wants to cultivate this tension both thematically and stylistically, both by sustaining the political conflict between Hester and Dimmesdale on one hand and the Puritan community on the other and by accentuating the generic difference between political history and human drama. The narrative ramifications first become apparent when Hester Prynne crosses the threshold of the prison to take her place upon the scaffold in the marketplace. Rather than be led to her public ignominy by the town beadle, who "prefigured and represented in his aspect the whole dismal severity of the Puritanic code of law," Hester "repel[s] him, by an action marked with natural dignity and force of character, and step[s] into the open air, as if by her own free-will" (CE, 1:52). In this scene, Hawthorne converts into narrative the complex categories introduced in the opening tableau: Hester exerts her natural liberty in the face of the civil liberty of the Puritan community. However, the author adds a crucial ambiguity to the scene by holding back on the voluntary nature of Hester's action: "*as if* by her own free-will." At this point in Hawthorne's narrative, political history and human drama meet; from this point on the story of Hester's public penance coincides with the story of her private torment and inner rebellion. Had she been allowed an unambiguous exertion of free will, her tale would have been of political interest only: "she might have come down to us in history, hand in hand with Anne Hutchinson, as the foundress of a religious sect" (CE, 1:165). Instead, Hawthorne complicates the reader's understanding of her conflict with the community by suggesting that more than politics is at play.

Like Bushnell (and, mutatis mutandis, Winthrop), Hawthorne knew that a political community should be bound together not only by social compact but by other, less explicable "ligaments." Matters of citizenship and residency are complicated in Hawthorne's romance by half-understood, barely perceived motives: guilt, love, sorrow. When he explains Hester's motives for remaining in Boston, he notes immediately that she was "kept by no restrictive clause of her condemnation." Other, more potent forces were at work. Stronger than the will to free herself from the circumscribed life before her was "a fatality, a feeling so irresistible and inevitable that it has the force of doom, which almost invariably compels human beings to linger around and haunt, ghost-like, the spot where some great and marked event has given the color to their lifetime." Surely, too, it was her love for Dimmesdale, "with whom she deemed herself connected in a union, that, unrecognized on earth, would bring them together before the bar of final judgment, and make that their marriage altar." In either case, Hester's free will—the philosophical foundation of all political theories of individual liberty and social compact from Locke and Rousseau to Jefferson and Madison, and ostensibly such a strong feature of her makeup—is severely undercut, not by Puritan intolerance, but by the forces of human nature. Hester was born free, and now the psychological "chain that bound her was of iron links, and galling to her inmost soul, but could never be broken" (CE, 1:79–80).

"Histories," Bushnell wrote, "make little account of the power men exert insensibly over each other." In Hawthorne's reimagining of American history, such "unconscious influence" is found to be of extraordinary significance. The generic doubleness of *The Scarlet Letter* promotes a synthetic view of history and society, one that accounts for both the "voluntary" and "involuntary" experience of its characters. In effect, the romance sustains two plots: one, centering on a social ritual consciously devised by the Puritans to deal with Hester's adultery, and another, constituting a "drama of guilt and sorrow" that defies the efforts of the ritual to circumscribe her experience (CE, 1:253).[30] As the romance approaches its denouement, first and most dramatically during Dimmesdale's election-day performance and then on Hester's conciliatory return to Boston, the two plots are drawn together to form a social drama with crucial implications for both the fictive world of seventeenth-century Boston and the world of Hawthorne's nineteenth-century audience.

In the Puritan plot, Hester and Dimmesdale are called upon to perform opposite but equivalent functions in the maintenance of the Puritan Way. As a minister, Dimmesdale is expected to reinforce the theological foundation of the Puritan polity by partaking in the initial stage of Hester's ordeal of resocialization on the scaffold in the marketplace. For her part, Hester is asked to confirm Puritan authority by performing the reciprocal function of becoming resocialized. The development of the plot had been well mapped out: in "a land where iniquity is dragged out into the sunshine," a deviant is isolated, defined in terms of the social structure, and thereby brought under control—either by removal (exile, execution) or by reaggregation (penance, repentance). The scarlet letter, like the pillory and the stocks, was an "effectual . . . agent in the promotion of good citizenship" in two ways: it cleared the path for Hester's reentry into the community by specifying the outward terms of her penance, and it also served as a continuing ritual of consensus for the community, as Hester is transformed into "a living sermon against sin" (CE, 1:55, 63). Through the limiting and defining powers of language, the Puritans hoped to convert a potential threat to the New England

Way into an affirmation of their errand. Indeed, the Puritan ritual of resocialization depicted in *The Scarlet Letter* employs a mode of language akin to Winthrop's in his "little speech on liberty": like natural and civil liberty, Hester and the Puritan community form a binary opposition—inscribed by the magistrates in the scarlet *A*—which strictly defines the Puritan enterprise and restricts the activities of those who participate in it.

What I call the second plot of *The Scarlet Letter* is strictly speaking neither subplot nor parallel plot, for it transpires, as it were, *within* the Puritan plot. It too begins on the scaffold in the marketplace on the day of Hester's ignominy. Hester's social isolation from the community of saints produces a metaphysical alienation: the scarlet letter "had the effect of a spell, taking her out of the ordinary relations with humanity, and inclosing her in a sphere by herself" (*CE*, 1:54). Although she continues to play a role in society, both economically (as a seamstress) and ritually (as "the general symbol at which the preacher and the moralist might point"), "there was nothing that made her feel as if she belonged to it" (*CE*, 1:79, 84). Hawthorne describes her as a ghost who hovers "apart from mortal interests, yet close beside them" (*CE*, 1:84). It is important to remark, however, that Hester Prynne is not Walter Mitty; she does not escape into a dream world of her own. The formal separation of Hester's political from her spiritual presence points rather to the fullness and coherence of her experience but forces the reader to perceive as separate the second plot of the romance: her ghostlike relationship with the people of Boston, her private relationship with Pearl, her covert relationships with Dimmesdale and Chillingworth, and from a different perspective, the sufferings of the young minister and the physician's attempts to enslave his soul—all of which have little to do with the mechanics of socialization, except to underscore its shortcomings.

Significantly, Hester realizes that she "communicated with the common nature by other organs and senses than the rest of human kind" (*CE*, 1:84). The doubleness of Hester's experience does not issue in the bifurcation of word and voice that characterizes Dimmesdale's sermon, but it does make her fluent in a different sort of nonverbal language, one that threatens to dissolve the distinctions characteristic of Puritan thought by giving her "a sympathetic knowledge of the hidden sin in other hearts" (*CE*, 1:86). The duplicity she discovers confuses her, frightens her, but it also explodes for her the notion of visible sanctity and clears the way for her attack on Puritan society. She could detect beneath "the form of [an] earthly saint" a sinfulness like her own. She could see behind "the sanctified frown of some [coldhearted] matron" that a "mystic sisterhood" joined them (*CE*, 1:87). The crucial, functional difference between Hester's newfound language and the language of the Puritan community surfaces at critical junctures in the text, when, as it were, the plots intersect. Consider, for instance, Hester's encounter with Governor Bellingham over the custody of her child, Pearl. Bellingham's plan to separate mother and daughter rests on the opposition of saint and sinner that structures and defines the lives of the Puritans in the romance: it was "not unreasonably argued" by those "of authority and influence" that the interests of Pearl, and by implication those of the community as well, were not well served "by trusting an immortal soul . . . to the guidance of one who hath stumbled and fallen, amid the pitfalls of this world" (*CE*, 1:100, 110). Accordingly, the Puritan magistrates and ministers "judge warily" of Pearl's "Christian nurture" by testing how well she has learned her catechism, or in other words, how well she has assimilated the language of the community (*CE*, 1:111). But Hester, privy to a hidden world the Puritans refuse to acknowledge, argues for a broader view of Christian nurture, one that centers, not on the exclusion of the scarlet letter from Pearl's experience, but on its pivotal position in a complex process of moral growth, for both Pearl and herself. The nurture she champions is based, not on the inculcation of moral precepts that repeat, in a sense, Winthrop's definition of liberty, but on the engendering of a full and coherent experience of joy and sorrow, of love, hate, guilt, and remorse, which Winthrop's scheme—even as it seeks to join spiritual and political, private and public—denies or delimits.

When Hester does battle with Bellingham in this scene, the radical implications of her challenge are as yet unclear to her. Her opposition is resolute and passionate, but her defense is articulated in the language of her opponents. Whereas "she felt that she possessed indefeasible rights against the world," she could only argue that Pearl was "the scarlet letter, only capable of being loved, and so endowed with a million-fold the power of retribution for [her] sin" (*CE*, 1:112–113). Eventually, however, she sees the scarlet letter for what it is—a language, a structure, an arbitrary device for arranging society. She moves "from passion and feeling, to thought" and "assume[s] a freedom of speculation" that leads her to reject the "iron framework of reasoning" that so far had determined the outward course of her life (*CE*, 1:164, 162). She could then look back on her crime and rethink its significance. When she meets Dimmesdale in the forest (a makeshift state of nature), she can dismiss the Puritan definition of liberty and formulate her own: "What we did had a consecration of its own." She can justify her declaration of independence in terms of a new (Rousseauian) standard of judgment: "We *felt* it so!" And she knows that all that is needed to demolish one structure and to build another is an act of language, a verbal compact: "We said so to each other!" (*CE*, 1:195). Her experience of nonverbal communication leads her to substitute one social contract for another.

Hester is thus a formidable American heroine: "The tendency of her fate and fortunes had been to set her free" (*CE*, 1:199). But, again, Hawthorne does not allow Hester's revolutionary repudiation of the Puritan covenant to resolve the generic and thematic tensions of the romance. In the closing scenes, Hawthorne holds back on the liberating energies released by his heroine, shifting his primary focus from Hester to Dimmesdale, who, unlike her, "had never gone through an experience calculated to lead him beyond the scope of generally received laws" (*CE*, 1:200). With natural liberty potent within him but held tightly in check by the civil liberty that governed his life, the minister keeps the generic and thematic tensions of the romance alive.

Which brings us back to Dimmesdale's election sermon. It is clear that Hawthorne fully recognized the ritualistic importance of the sermon for the Puritan community, that it was the supreme example of the language which defined Puritan life, the justification of their communal existence, the authority that ultimately gave meaning to Hester's *A*. So it is certainly significant that he treats the delivery of the sermon as a point of coalescence for all the radical forces that, throughout the romance, had been threatening the very foundation of Puritan society and, from a different perspective, as a distillation of the thematic tensions— between passion and authority, between personal liberty and social responsibility, between Rousseau and Winthrop—that had thus far sustained the narrative. And it is all the more significant that he defers his synopsis of Dimmesdale's text—"the relation between the Deity and the communities of mankind, with a special reference to the New England which they were here planting in the wilderness"—for his description of the minister's voice. For in so doing, he establishes the sermon as both a reaffirmation and a challenge to the New England Way. It reinforces the values and design of the theocracy, envisioning "a high and glorious destiny for the newly gathered people of the Lord," but it also suggests, at a deeper emotional level, the tragedy of a man whose sorrow stems from the flaws and limitations of that system (*CE*, 1:249). Like the historical election sermons of the Puritan colony, Dimmesdale's jeremiad combines celebration and lamentation. For the Cottons, the Danforths, and the Mathers, of course, the lamentation itself was a mode of celebration: only God's chosen could merit such adversity. For Dimmesdale, however, the lamentation undercuts the opposition of saint and sinner that forms the marrow of Puritan theology and the basis of their corporate self-image. The sympathy it unconsciously elicits bespeaks a wholly different foundation for social cohesion, more natural and more powerful, if transitory and unworkable. Still, the two messages do not cancel each other out: the undertone informs the prophecy and, in effect, demands an expansion of the audience's faculties of apprehension, allowing them to accept and to hold in suspension the contradictory communications of their minister, if only for the moment.

The events that follow merely recapitulate the double message of the sermon in social-symbolic terms. When Dimmesdale bares his breast upon the scaffold, he reinforces the Puritan corporate self-image by accepting for himself the terms by which the community had defined Hester and at the same time destroys the authority of those terms by arguing, in effect, that saint and sinner may in fact be one and the same. But the revelation is so variously interpreted that its meaning seems lost among the interpretations. Again, when Hester later returns to Boston and, "of her own free will," resumes the scarlet letter, she draws together in that one action natural and civil liberty, transforming society's scorn and her own rebelliousness into a mutual recognition of "human frailty and sorrow" and the tragic limitations of social structure. But hers is an act of compromise and deferral. She assumes a marginal position in her society—as comforter and counselor to those who, like herself, harbor sorrows that society will not address. To be sure, she does not become a Puritan apologist; she still believes that something more is needed "to establish the whole relation between man and woman on a surer ground of mutual happiness," to ensure that contractual and affectional "ligaments" coincide. But that cannot be achieved by secession and repudiation; it must wait for "some brighter period, when the world should have grown ripe for it, in Heaven's own time" (*CE*, 1:263).

As heirs of the Puritans, Hawthorne's readers stood at that "brighter period"—or so it was widely held. Yet *The Scarlet Letter* offers a heritage that at once supports and undercuts such patriotic assumptions. It creates a legend of national importance, one that works toward a resolution of the problem of liberty, of maintaining self-government by governing the self. The generic doubleness of the romance opens up a whole realm of experience abandoned (so the argument ran) by the materialists of mid-nineteenth-century America, and the linguistic doubleness of Dimmesdale's sermon suggests a mode of discourse that stems from a dissolution of the boundaries between self-assertion and social control, an alternative to conventional language, momentary and epiphanic to be sure, but imaginatively forceful nonetheless.

Let me conclude by underscoring two points. First, Hawthorne did not, as I explained earlier, propose the life of the imagination as an alternative to the life of the marketplace. But neither did he want to recapitulate the "prevalent modes of thinking" (to use Longfellow's phrase) in America.

He recognized that it "was a folly, with the materiality of this daily life pressing so intrusively upon [him], to attempt to fling [him]self back into another age; or to insist on creating the semblance of a world out of airy matter, when, at every moment, the impalpable beauty of [his] soap-bubble was broken by the rude contact of some actual circumstance" (*CE*, 1:37). Yet he felt that, ideally, he should have been able to combine the two worlds, "to diffuse thought and imagination through the opaque substance of to-day, and thus to make it a bright transparency; to spiritualize the burden that began to weigh so heavily; to seek, resolutely, the true and indestructible value that lay hidden in the petty and wearisome incidents, and ordinary characters, with which [he] was . . . conversant." He felt that a "better book than [he should] ever write was there." His definition of the field of romance as "a neutral territory, somewhere between the real world and fairy-land, where the Actual and the Imaginary may meet, and each imbue itself with the nature of the other" speaks to the conciliatory tendencies of his poetics (*CE*, 1:36). Still, he felt that the "better book" could not be written in nineteenth-century America. The writing of historical romance was a strategy of expedience: it required a retreat from individualistic, practical, acquisitive American society and thus bespoke the divorce of spiritual from political America, of private from public, of self from society. At best, this was a partial achievement for an American writer. Perhaps "at some brighter period, when the world should have grown ripe for it" (to borrow Hawthorne's phrase), the need for historical romance would vanish, and the "better book" could be written. For Hawthorne in 1850, that goal could only be approximated.

Second, the question of language is a philosophical question for Hawthorne only insofar as it is a narrative question, only insofar as it participates in, indeed, as it constitutes the social and political life of the novel. *The Scarlet Letter* may be more correctly said to embody attempts to discover and communicate meanings—to explore the possibilities of language as a human activity—than to champion a particular mode of representation. So construed, moreover, the political implications of the novel's linguisticity may be seen to be much broader and more complex than prior readings suggest. Hawthorne does not want so much to "free" Hester as to complicate our notions of the ways communities are—and ought to be—constituted by language. By the very act of creating a fictional world acutely and self-consciously alive to meaning, Hawthorne inscribes the philosophy of language into his narrative and reformulates the conceptual origins of civil society: he returns us to seventeenth-century Boston in order to revaluate the nation's Puritan origins as linguistic origins. *The Scarlet Letter* is about language inasmuch as it is about America.

From Logocracy to Renaissance

I WILL BRING this study to a close by returning to the twin assertions with which Matthiessen defined and delimited his method and scope in *American Renaissance*: first, that his five writers "felt that it was incumbent upon their generation to give fulfilment to the potentialities freed by the Revolution, to provide a culture commensurate with America's political opportunity": and, second, that we can learn much about the period when we observe these writers "discovering the fresh resources of words" (*AR*, xv, 30). Although my intention has been to challenge the authority of Matthiessen's canon and the literary-historical assumptions that sustain it, I have not sought to dispute these assertions in any fundamental way. It has been my contention, rather, that what is true about Emerson, Thoreau, Hawthorne, Melville, and Whitman is also true about numerous other writers, including (but not limited to) Webster, Longfellow, Madison, and Bushnell. Each felt in his own generation and in his own sphere the obligation to Revolutionize American culture, and each felt that the key to the fulfillment of American potential had something to do with the nature and function of language. In short, I argue that the very criteria Matthiessen used to build the canon can also be used to explode it.

Matthiessen's literary history begins theoretically in the political and ideological upheavals of the Revolution and ends between 1850 and 1855 in "one extraordinarily concentrated moment of expression" (*AR*, vii). It is a story of promise and delayed fulfillment, of political birth and cultural new birth or coming of age (Matthiessen uses both analogies, intending, I think, to conflate the gradual inevitability of one with the revolutionary suddenness of the other) some threescore and ten years later. The interval is characterized (implicitly, for Matthiessen writes next to nothing about it) by uncertainty about both the meaning of America and the power of language. *American Renaissance* assumes a vital connection between art and politics, understands one to lie potentially in the other, but, at the same time, subordinates politics to aesthetics in such a way as effectually to deny to political expression—indeed, to anything but great works of literature—an imaginative or functional integrity of its own. *The American Scholar* was not only America's *intellectual* declaration of independence, for instance, but its declaration of *true* independence. When Emerson discovered (through Coleridge and the Germans) the mystery of language, he discovered the real America.

The story I have tried to tell here is different in several ways. First of all, although it too begins with the Revolution, it does not assume the quasi-biblical narrative framework of promise and fulfillment but treats it as a myth inscribed in the works of the writers themselves. Each of my six writers imagined an America different from the America he knew, and his writing—whenever and whatever he wrote—is a manifestation of his desire to realize his vision. Webster felt his *Grammatical Institute* would complete the Revolution; Whitman felt the same of his "Real Grammar" and "Real Dictionary." Madison believed the ratification of the Constitution would secure the political gains of 1775–1783; Bushnell believed its rewriting would restore and Christianize the Union. The historical mythos of *American Renaissance* is clearly written into the literature itself from the very moment of the Revolution and, in fact, forms its imaginative core. In my story, no one vision of America is privileged over another: Webster's nation of pure-blooded Saxon yeomen, Madison's miraculous convention, Longfellow's pastoral village, Bushnell's "christian commonwealth," Hawthorne's Puritan Boston, Whitman's city of virile young men—all are equally fictional and thus equally "American," if differently so and if more or less politically palatable. The implication of this point of view is, of course, that *American* has no particular, transcendent meaning but is a rhetorical construct whose very essence is its polyvalence, its ambiguity, its susceptibility to differing interpretations.

In this history, it follows, no form or individual work of literature is privileged over another. Longfellow may have distinguished between polite and practical literature, Bushnell between poetry and prose, Hawthorne between ghost stories and legal documents, but their rhetorical distinctions, aspects of the myth of American promise and fulfillment, should not be ours. *The Federalist* is no less an imaginative achievement than *Leaves of Grass*. Perhaps we may as literary historians legitimately and usefully distinguish among genres—novels, poems, plays, essays, histories—but to distinguish masterpieces according to a particular standard of taste is arbitrarily (that is, ideologically) to limit the scope of literary study and to obscure the broader cultural and historical significance of the works labeled as masterpieces. Certainly we have come a long way in this regard since Matthiessen wrote *American Renaissance*, as the rise of early American literary study alone evidences. But we still write books about "American literature" and draw conclusions about it (and about America) without looking beyond the "major" works and "major" authors, so the caveat bears repeating. There is no one "American" literary tradition just as there is no one "America." American literary history should embody the diversity and inclusiveness of "America" itself. The story I have tried to tell here is about some of the different ways Americans imagined language between the Revolution and the Civil War, and one of the morals of the story is that the ways "major" authors (here Whitman and Hawthorne) imagined language are not necessarily more "American"—or more complex—than the ways other authors did.

Finally, no one theory of language is seen as more valid—more "literary" or more "American"—than another, Coleridge no more than Locke. What I have tried to show—in my introductory review of American literary and linguistic historiography and in the individual chapters that follow—is that a wide variety of discourses were available to American writers from the Revolution to the Civil War (and I cannot claim to have covered them all) and that they entered into these several discourses in different ways and for different purposes. Symbolism may very well have been, as Feidelson claimed, a "pervasive presence," but it was not so exclusively—even among the figures he chose to study. Bushnell, Hawthorne, and Whitman certainly shared an interest in the idea of symbolism as well as in the artistic possibilities afforded by symbolic language, but they were also drawn to other aspects of the study of language—to the origin of language, comparative philology, grammar, sociolinguistics—with important consequences for their work. What draws my six writers together is that they imagined language within an American context, as part of a larger imagining of the culture at large. Some treated language as a cultural product, some as cultural process, but all as a way of realizing the promise of "America."

We can thus take the early-republican observation of the fictional traveler Mustapha Rub-a-dub Keli Khan in *Salmagundi* that America is "a pure unadulterated LOGOCRACY or *government of words*" as a countervailing literary-historical principle of organization in opposition to Matthiessen's notion of an American Renaissance. To move as I do in each of my two parts from the 1780s to the 1850s is not to suggest that American literary history is defined by a teleological movement *from* Logocracy *to* Renaissance but that we should proceed intellectually from the one to the other, that our understanding of "major" antebellum writers, particularly in terms of the linguisticity of their writings, should be conditioned by our understanding of the broader culture in which they are embedded. Not that by moving from Webster to Whitman or Madison to Hawthorne we are going from background to foreground but that by introducing each of the earlier writers (along with the respective "minor" or "nonliterary" writer that follows him) in all his rhetorical and intellectual complexity, we are forced to view each of the more familiar writers—and the course of American literary history—differently. The linguisticity of the American Renaissance needs to be seen as only one of the ways language was imagined in post-Revolutionary America.

Notes

Preface

1. See, e.g., Jane Tompkins, *Sensational Designs: The Cultural Work of American Fiction, 1790–1860* (New York: Oxford University Press, 1985). Chapter 6 is entitled "The Other American Renaissance" (pp. 147–185). Tompkins's subject is sentimental fiction; I have expanded the meaning of her term. A good introduction to the recent efforts to reform the canon is the series of "Extra" articles highlighted in *American Literature*, including: Annette Kolodny, "The Integrity of Memory: Creating a New Literary History of the United States," 57 (1985): 291–307; William Spengemann, "American Things/Literary Things: The Problem of American Literary History," 57 (1985): 456–481; Emory Elliott, "New Literary History: Past and Present," 57 (1985): 611–621; Sacvan Bercovitch, "America as Canon and Context: Literary History in a Time of Dissensus," 58 (1986): 99–107. See also Bercovitch, "The Problem of Ideology in American Literary History," *Critical Inquiry* 12 (1986): 631–653; and the various essays collected in Bercovitch, ed., *Reconstructing American Literary History* (Cambridge: Harvard University Press, 1986).

2. In referring to the diversity of works on the subject with the general term "the study of language," I follow Hans Aarsleff, *From Locke to Saussure: Essays on the Study of Language and Intellectual History* (Minneapolis: University of Minnesota Press, 1982), p. 4.

3. See J. Hillis Miller, *The Linguistic Moment: From Wordsworth to Stevens* (Princeton: Princeton University Press, 1985) as an example of the sort of criticism that argues a metacritical rather than a historical thesis, relying on theories of language contemporaneous with the critic rather than with the writers. Miller explains that his book is about "moments of suspension within the texts of poems . . . when they reflect or comment on their own medium" and that each "linguistic moment" manifests "a breaking of the illusion that language is a transparent medium of meaning" (p. xiv).

4. Tzvetan Todorov, "Language and Literature," in *The Structuralist Controversy: The Languages of Criticism and the Sciences of Man*, ed. Richard Macksey and Eugenio Donato (Baltimore: Johns Hopkins University Press, 1972), pp. 126–127.

5. Terry Eagleton, *Literary Theory: An Introduction* (Minneapolis: University of Minnesota Press, 1983), p. 97.

6. I do not mean to belittle the importance of the "linguistic turn" of modern philosophy, which is as well known as the literature is immense. But its subject, especially in the case of the Anglo-American school, is language in the abstract and not the interpretation of particular texts. For overviews of the Anglo-American school, see Richard Rorty, ed., *The Linguistic Turn: Recent Essays in Philosophical Method* (Chicago: University of Chicago Press, 1970); and J. R. Searle, ed., *The Philosophy of Language* (New York: Oxford University Press,

1971). The central texts of the post-Saussurean school include: Jacques Derrida, *Of Grammatology*, trans. Gayatri Spivak (Baltimore: Johns Hopkins University Press); and Michel Foucault, *The Archaeology of Knowledge*, trans. A. M. Sheridan Smith (New York: Pantheon, 1972). For an introduction to the German school of Hermeneutics, see Kurt Mueller-Vollmer, ed., *The Hermeneutics Reader* (New York: Continuum, 1985). Of more immediate importance to this study are those scholarly works which attempt to introduce the linguistic turn of the philosophers to the practice of intellectual history, and these scholars often invoke the sensitivity of the literary critic to language as a model for their efforts. See, e.g.: Quentin Skinner, "Meaning and Understanding in the History of Ideas," *Studies in the Philosophy of History* 8 (1969): 3–53, and "Conventions and the Understanding of Speech Acts," *The Philosophical Quarterly* 20 (1970): 118–38; J.G.A. Pocock, "Languages and Their Implications: The Transformation of the Study of Political Thought," in *Politics, Language and Time: Essays in Political Thought and History* (New York: Atheneum, 1971), pp. 3–103, and "The Reconstruction of Discourse: Towards a Historiography of Political Thought," *MLN* 96 (1981): 959–980; Martin Jay, "Should Intellectual History Take a Linguistic Turn? Reflections on the Habermas-Gadamer Debate," in *Modern European Intellectual History: Reappraisals and New Perspectives*, ed. Dominick LaCapra and Steven L. Kaplan (Ithaca: Cornell University Press, 1982), pp. 86–110; Dominick LaCapra, *Rethinking Intellectual History: Texts Contexts, Language* (Ithaca: Cornell University Press, 1983); Christopher Norris, *The Deconstructive Turn: Essays in the Rhetoric of Philosophy* (London: Methuen, 1984); and Carroll Smith-Rosenberg, "Writing History: Language, Class, and Gender," in *Feminist Studies/Critical Studies*, ed. Teresa De Lauretis (Bloomington: Indiana University Press, 1986), pp. 31–54.

7. Roman Jakobson, "Linguistics and Poetics," in *Language in Literature*, ed. Krystyna Pomorska and Stephen Rudy (Cambridge: Harvard University Press, 1987), p. 70.

Introduction
The Study of Language and the American Renaissance

1. The sketch of American literary historiography that follows owes much to Richard Ruland, *The Rediscovery of American Literature: Premises of Critical Taste, 1900–1940* (Cambridge: Harvard University Press, 1967); Russell J. Reising, *The Unusable Past: Theory and the Study of American Literature* (New York: Methuen, 1986); and Bercovitch, "The Problem of Ideology in American Literary History."

2. F. O. Matthiessen, *American Renaissance: Art and Expression in the Age of Emerson and Whitman* (New York: Oxford University Press, 1941; reprint, 1972), p. xi. Hereafter, *AR*. Matthiessen has received considerable scholarly attention in his own right. See: William E. Cain, *F. O. Matthiessen and the Politics of Criticism* (Madison: University of Wisconsin Press, 1988); Jonathan Arac, "F. O. Matthiessen: Authorizing an American Renaissance," in *The American Renaissance Reconsidered*, ed. Walter Benn Michaels and Donald E. Pease (Baltimore: Johns Hopkins University Press, 1985), pp. 90–112; Frederick C. Stern, *F. O. Matthiessen, Christian Socialist as Critic* (Chapel Hill: University of North

Carolina Press, 1981); and Giles Gunn, *F. O. Matthiessen: The Critical Achievement* (Seattie: University of Washington Press, 1975).

3. Gérard Genette, "Valéry and the Poetics of Language," in *Textual Strategies: Perspectives in Post-Structuralist Criticism*, ed. Josué V. Harari (Ithaca: Cornell University Press, 1979), pp. 359–373.

4. It is interesting to note that Arthur A. Ekirch, in a survey of American intellectual historiography, lists Matthiessen as an intellectual historian with an interest in "literary and philosophical ideas" and "the New Criticism of the literary scholars of the 1940's and 1950's." See Ekirch, *American Intellectual History: The Development of the Discipline*, American Historical Association Pamphlets, no. 102 (Richmond, Va.: William Bird Press, 1973), p. 33.

5. Charles Feidelson, Jr., *Symbolism and American Literature* (Chicago: University of Chicago Press, 1953), p. 1. Hereafter, *SAL*. On Feidelson and the influence of his work, see Barbara Foley, "From New Criticism to Deconstruction: The Example of Charles Feidelson's *Symbolism and American Literature*," *American Quarterly* 36 (1984): 44–64; Kenneth Dauber, "Criticism of American Literature," *Diacritics* 7 (1977): 56–57; Gary Lee Stonum, "Undoing American Literary History," *Diacritics* 11 (1981): 3–5; and Reising, *The Unusable Past*, pp. 173–187.

6. John T. Irwin, *American Hieroglyphics: The Symbol of the Hieroglyph in the American Renaissance* (New Haven: Yale University Press, 1980). Hereafter, *AH*.

7. See Lionel Trilling, "Manner, Morals, and the Novel," in *The Liberal Imagination: Essays on Literature and Society* (New York: Doubleday, 1950), and Richard Chase, *The American Novel and Its Tradition* (New York: Doubleday, 1957). For an overview of this tradition, see Reising, *The Unusable Past*, pp. 92–162.

8. Richard Poirier, *A World Elsewhere: The Place of Style in American Literature* (New York: Oxford University Press, 1966). Hereafter, *AWE*. Michael Davitt Bell, *The Development of American Romance: The Sacrifice of Relation* (Chicago: University of Chicago Press, 1981). Hereafter, *DAR*.

9. Of all the books I review in this essay, only Poirier's goes beyond the Civil War and makes claims for American literature in general. I have included Poirier here because he begins during the period I am focusing upon, conceiving of it as the seedbed of the stylistic tendencies that, he feels, define American writing.

10. The following few paragraphs draw some ideas and phrases from previous remarks about *The Development of American Romance* in my "Critical Myths and Historical Realities; or, How American Was the American Renaissance?" *Review* 5 (1983): 35–38.

11. Michael West, "Charles Kraitsir's Influence on Thoreau's Theory of Language," *ESQ: A Journal of the American Renaissance* 20 (1973): 262–274; "Scatology and Eschatology: The Heroic Dimensions of Thoreau's Wordplay," *PMLA* 89 (1974): 1043–1064; "*Walden*'s Dirty Language: Thoreau and Walter Whiter's Geocentric Etymological Theories," *Harvard Library Bulletin* 22 (1975): 117–128. Several other contemporaneous articles addressed Thoreau's philological interests as well: Gordon V. Boudreau, "Thoreau and Richard C. Trench: Conjectures on the Pickerel Passage of *Walden*," *ESQ* 20 (1974): 117–124; Richard H. Dillman, "The Psychological Rhetoric of *Walden*," *ESQ* 25

(1979): 79–91; and Philip F. Gura, "Henry Thoreau and the Wisdom of Words," *New England Quarterly* 52 (1979): 38–54.

12. An important nonliterary work published about this time was Donald A. Crosby, *Horace Bushnell's Philosophy of Language in the Context of Other Nineteenth-Century Philosophies of Language* (The Hague: Mouton, 1975). It should also be noted here that historical interest in the study of language was growing in academic circles in general at this time, brought about in part by the publication in translation of Michel Foucault's *Les mots et les choses* in 1970 and of Jacques Derrida's *De la grammatologie* in 1974. Other works on the study of language published around this time include: Murray Cohen, *Sensible Words: Linguistic Practice in England, 1640–1785* (Baltimore: Johns Hopkins University Press, 1977); James H. Stam, *Inquiries into the Origins of Language: The Fate of a Question* (New York: Harper and Row, 1976); Stephen K. Land, *From Signs to Propositions: The Concept of Form in Eighteenth-Century Semantic Theory* (London: Longman, 1974); and (somewhat earlier) Hans Aarsleff, *The Study of Language in England, 1780–1860* (Princeton: Princeton University Press, 1967).

13. Philip F. Gura, *The Wisdom of Words: Language, Theology, and Literature in the New England Renaissance* (Middletown, Conn.: Wesleyan University Press, 1981). Hereafter, *WOW*.

14. Gura cites M. H. Abrams's *Natural Supernaturalism: Tradition and Revolution in Romantic Literature* (New York: W. W. Norton, 1971) as the inspiration for asserting the religious origins of American Romantic discourse.

15. It is difficult to see how Bushnell can be considered a transitional figure for the writers of the American Renaissance, except in theoretical terms. By the time his major works on language appeared (*God in Christ* in 1849 and *Christ in Theology* in 1851), Emerson, Hawthorne, and Melville already had well-developed styles.

16. Noah Webster is mentioned only once by Matthiessen, in the same paragraph as H. L. Mencken (*AR*, 644).

17. Quoted in Horace Traubel, "Foreword" to Walt Whitman, *An American Primer* (Boston, 1904; reprint, San Francisco: City Lights Books, 1970), pp. [viii–ix].

18. H. L. Mencken, *The American Language: An Inquiry into the Development of English in the United States* (New York: Knopf, 1919). Mencken kept enlarging and revising his work over the next several decades. References in this essay are taken from the fourth edition (New York: Knopf, 1936; reprint, 1937). Hereafter, *AL*.

19. On the scholarly impact of *The American Language*, see Raven I. McDavid, Jr., "The Impact of Mencken on American Linguistics," in *Critical Essays on H. L. Mencken*, ed. Douglas C. Stenerson (Boston: G. K. Hall, 1987), pp. 149–156. On the role of *The American Language* in Mencken's own "Battle of the Books," see W.H.A. Williams, *H. L. Mencken* (Boston: Twayne Publishers, 1977), pp. 67–82. On Mencken's style in relation to *The American Language*, see Alistair Cooke, "Mencken and the English Language," in *On Mencken*, ed. John Dorsey (New York: Knopf, 1980), pp. 84–113.

20. George Philip Krapp, *The English Language in America*, 2 vols. (New York: Ungar, 1925), 1:v. Hereafter, *ELA*.

21. Curiously—and ironically—Whitman's use of the word "saloons" in this passage is sanitized and gallicized in Mencken's *The American Language* to read "salons" but is maintained as "saloons" when quoted in Krapp's *The English Language in America*. See Whitman, *An American Primer*, ed. Horace Traubel (1904; reprint, San Francisco: City Lights Books, 1970), p. 2.

22. The important work of Allen Walker Read in the thirties divides itself between the history of American English and the history of its study. On the history of the language, see "The Comments of British Travelers on Early American Terms Relating to Agriculture," *Agricultural History* (July 1933): 99–109; "The Scope of the American Dictionary," *American Speech* (October 1933): 10–20; "Bilingualism in the Middle Colonies, 1725–1775," *American Speech* 12 (1937): 93–99; and "The Assimilation of the Speech of British Immigrants in Colonial America," *JEGP* 37 (1938): 70–79. On the study of language, see "The Philological Society of New York, 1788," *American Speech* 9 (1934): 131–136; "Noah Webster as a Euphemist," *Dialect Notes* 6 (1934): 385–391; "American Projects for an Academy to Regulate Speech," *PMLA* 51 (1936): 1141–1179; and "Edward Everett's Attitude towards American English," *New England Quarterly* 12 (1934): 112–129. His "British Recognition of American Speech in the Eighteenth Century," *Dialect Notes* 6 (1933): 313–334, has a foot in each camp.

23. See, e.g., Albert H. Marckwardt, *American English* (New York: Oxford University Press, 1958; 2d ed., rev. J. L. Dillard, 1980); and J. L. Dillard, *Toward a Social History of American English* (Berlin: Mouton, 1985). For a selection of the new work on American English, see J. L. Dillard, ed., *Perspectives on American English* (The Hague: Mouton, 1980). Noah Webster is not even indexed in any of these works. The exception that proves the rule is Charlton Laird, *Language in America* (New York: World Publishing, 1970). Laird gives substantial space to Webster and his "cracker-barrel lexicography," but his conclusion underscores the clear change in methodology: "Noah Webster had great influence upon American lexicography, but he probably had less influence than is normally assumed. In fact, he probably had less influence than Goold Brown, and Brown had less influence than his despised rival, Samuel Kirkham. Brown taught the teachers of oral language, but Kirkham and his multitudes of cheap little books taught the users of oral English. He told them what to do; they probably did not do it much, but no doubt they tried to. In language no man counts for much" (p. 308).

24. It should be noted that as early as 1927, Leon Howard was projecting "a historical study which I shall make at some future date concerning American English and the attitude toward it both in this country and abroad during the period roughly bounded by the wars of the Revolution and of 1812" ("A Historical Note on American English," *American Speech* 2 [1927]: 499 n.3). See also his "Towards a Historical Aspect of American Speech Consciousness," *American Speech* 5 (1930): 301–305. As far as I know, the study was never completed.

25. Dennis E. Baron, *Grammar and Good Taste: Reforming the American Language* (New Haven: Yale University Press, 1982), p. 3. Hereafter, *GGT*.

26. On the rhetoric of the jeremiad, see Perry Miller, *The New England Mind: From Colony to Province* (Cambridge: Harvard University Press, 1953;

reprint, Boston: Beacon Press, 1961), and Sacvan Bercovitch, *The American Jeremiad* (Madison: University of Wisconsin Press, 1978). Miller and Bercovitch differ on the relationship between the jeremiad and American culture, Miller seeing the genre as a mode of guilt displacement, and Bercovitch, as a ritual of consensus. Baron's understanding of the literature of language reform is closer to Miller's.

27. David Simpson, *The Politics of American English, 1776–1850* (New York: Oxford University Press, 1986), p. 3. Hereafter, *PAE*.

28. John Adams to the President of Congress, 5 September 1780, in *Works*, ed. Charles Francis Adams (Boston: Little, Brown, 1850–1856), 7:250. The letter is reprinted in Mitford McLeod Mathews, ed., *Beginnings of American English: Essays and Comments* (Chicago: University of Chicago Press, 1931; reprint, 1963), pp. 41–43, with the following comment: "The following letter, which is given in full, needs no comment to make its meaning clear" (p. 41).

29. Adams, *Works*, 7:249–250.

30. On Adams's letter, see Baron, *GGT*, pp. 17–18, and Simpson, *PAE*, pp. 29–32. On the efforts to establish a language academy in the United States, see Read, "American Projects for an Academy to Regulate Speech"; Shirley Brice Heath, "A National Language Academy? Debate in the New Nation," *Linguistics: An International Review* 189 (1977): 9–43; and Marina Camboni, "The Voice of Columbia: Aspects of the Debate over the English and/or American Language, 1743–1800," *Revue française d'études américaines* 12 (1987): 107–118.

31. John Quincy Adams, *Lectures on Rhetoric and Oratory*, 2 vols. (Cambridge, Mass., 1810), 1:30–31; Washington Irving, William Irving, and James K. Paulding, *Salmagundi; or, The Whim-Whams and Opinions of Launcelot Longstaff, Esq., and Others*, in *The Complete Works of Washington Irving* (Boston: Twayne Publishers, 1977), 6:142–143.

Chapter One
"*NOW* is the Time, and *This* is the Country"

1. H. L. Mencken uses the verb "invent" in the opening line of *The American Language* (*AL*, 3): "The first American colonists had perforce to *invent* Americanisms." But the process by which words like *maize, canoe,* and *bluff* came into the language is—and Mencken himself would clearly agree—less accurately characterized by invention than by borrowing and adaptation.

2. For an account of Webster's speller, its history, and its influence, see E. Jennifer Monaghan, *A Common Heritage: Noah Webster's Blue-Back Speller* (Hamden, Conn.: Archon Books, 1983). For historical and critical accounts of the dictionary of 1828, see Charles Swann, "Noah Webster: The Language of Politics/The Politics of Language," *Essays in Poetics* 13 (1988): 41–81; Eva Mae Burkett, *American Dictionaries of the English Language before 1861* (Metuchen, N.J.: Scarecrow Press, 1979), pp. 113–257; Joseph Harold Friend, *The Development of American Lexicography, 1798–1864* (The Hague: Mouton, 1967); and Krapp, *ELA*, 1:351–377.

3. Benjamin T. Spencer, *The Quest for Nationality: An American Literary*

Campaign (Syracuse, N.Y.: Syracuse University Press, 1957), pp. 27–28; italics mine. For his account of the early national period, see pp. 25–72. Although *Quest* is a history of ideas, "concerned rather with literary intention than result," Spencer explicitly aligns his study with other, complementary works, like Matthiessen's *American Renaissance*, which provide "a reckoning of the *full* achievement of the American imagination" (vii, italics mine). Spencer's quotation from Webster is found in "To John Canfield, 6 January 1783," in *Letters of Noah Webster*, ed. Harry Warfel (New York: Library Publishers, 1953), p. 4. Hereafter, *LNW*.

4. See Harry R. Warfel, *Noah Webster: Schoolmaster to America* (New York: Macmillan, 1936); and Ervin C. Shoemaker, *Noah Webster: Pioneer of Learning* (New York: Columbia University Press, 1936). More recent works in the same tradition include: John S. Morgan, *Noah Webster* (New York: Mason/Charter, 1975); and Bruce Southard, "Noah Webster: America's Forgotten Linguist," *American Speech* 54 (1979): 12–22. Both Mencken's and Krapp's renderings of Webster, though very different, fall into this group.

5. Richard J. Moss, *Noah Webster* (Boston: Twayne Publishers, 1984), preface and p. 92. The current revaluation of Webster began with the work of Richard M. Rollins. See his "Words as Social Control: Noah Webster and the Creation of the American Dictionary," *American Quarterly* 28 (1976): 415–430, as well as *The Long Journey of Noah Webster* (Philadelphia: University of Pennsylvania Press, 1980). See also Joseph J. Ellis, *After the Revolution: Profiles of Early American Culture* (New York: W. W. Norton, 1979), pp. 161–212; Baron, *GGT*, pp. 41–67; Brian Weinstein, "Noah Webster and the Diffusion of Linguistic Innovations for Political Purposes," *International Journal of the Sociology of Language* 38 (1982): 85–108; V. P. Bynack, "Noah Webster's Linguistic Thought and the Idea of an American National Culture," *Journal of the History of Ideas* 45 (1984): 99–114; Simpson, *PAE*, pp. 52–90; and Marina Camboni, "The Voice of Columbia: Aspects of the Debate over the English and/or American Language, 1743–1800," *Revue française d'études américaines* 12 (1987): 113–116.

6. The rise of early American studies has provided us with new ways to consider both the continuities and discontinuities perceivable in our literary history and has given new integrity to the literature produced before the American Renaissance—indeed, has helped redefine what we mean, and recover what our earliest writers meant, by *literature*. The most important revaluations of the literature of the early republic include: Emory Elliott, *Revolutionary Writers: Literature and Authority in the New Republic, 1725–1810* (New York: Oxford University Press, 1982); Jay Fliegelman, *Prodigals and Pilgrims: The American Revolution against Patriarchal Authority, 1750–1800* (Cambridge: Cambridge University Press, 1982); Robert A. Ferguson, *Law and Letters in American Culture* (Cambridge: Harvard University Press, 1984); Cathy N. Davidson, *Revolution and the Word: The Rise of the Novel in America* (New York: Oxford University Press, 1986); William L. Hedges, "Toward a Theory of American Literature, 1765–1800," *Early American Literature* 6 (1972): 26–38, and "The Myth of the Republic and the Theory of American Literature," *Prospects* 4 (1979): 101–120. On the literariness of the nonbelletristic writings of the Revolutionary

period, see Robert A. Ferguson, "'We Hold These Truths': Strategies of Control in the Literature of the Founders," in *Reconstructing American Literary History*, ed. Sacvan Bercovitch (Cambridge: Harvard University Press, 1986), pp. 1–28.

7. The only attempt to consider Webster as a writer that I know of, besides that of Simpson in *Politics of American English*, was written by biographer Richard M. Rollins. See his "The Three Faces of Noah Webster," in *The Autobiographies of Noah Webster: From the Letters and Essays, Memoir, and Diary*, ed. Rollins (Columbia: University of South Carolina Press, 1989), pp. 1–64.

8. It should be noted that in his "Memoir of Noah Webster, LL.D.," Webster emplots his life in terms of his publications and their impact upon the public. The memoir may be found in Rollins, *The Autobiographies of Noah Webster*, pp. 127–186.

9. It might be well to recall that, as John Adams remembered it, Thomas Jefferson was chosen to draft the Declaration of Independence in part because he "brought with him a reputation for literature" (quoted in *The Works of Thomas Jefferson*, ed. Paul Leicester Ford [New York: G. P. Putnam's Sons, 1904], 1:29 n. 3). For a brief description of the eighteenth-century notion of literature, see Terry Eagleton, *Literary Theory: An Introduction* (Minneapolis: University of Minnesota Press, 1983), pp. 17–18. For a brief historical essay on the changing meanings of *literature*, see Raymond Williams, *Keywords: A Vocabulary of Culture and Society* (New York: Oxford University Press, 1976), pp. 150–154. See also Eagleton, *Literary Theory*, pp. 1–16.

10. Noah Webster, *A Collection of Papers on Political, Literary, and Moral Subjects* (New York, 1843; reprint, New York: Burt Franklin, 1968), p. 173; Webster, *An American Dictionary of the English Language*, 2 vols. (New Haven and New York, 1828), 1:preface [n.p.].

11. Webster, *A Grammatical Institute of the English Language, Part I* (Hartford, 1783), p. 14. Hereafter, *GI*; *LNW*, p. 4.

12. See Sterling A. Leonard, *The Doctrine of Correctness in English Usage, 1700–1800*, University of Wisconsin Studies in Language and Literature, no. 25 (1929; reprint, New York: Russell & Russell, 1962); and Murray Cohen, *Sensible Words: Linguistic Practice in England, 1640–1785* (Baltimore: John Hopkins University Press, 1977), pp. 78–136, for the intellectual background of Webster's ideas.

13. Although Webster does remove the final *k* from *musick, publick*, etc., what were to be his best-known orthographic reforms were not yet instituted: he retains, for instance, the *re* in *centre* and *theatre* and the *our* in *honour* and *favour*. In fact, he argues against the "inclination in some writers to alter the spelling of words, by expunging the superfluous letters" and reasons that those who wish to drop the *u* in *honour* and *favour* "have dropped the wrong letter—they have omitted the letter that is sounded and retained one that is silent; for the words are pronounced *onur, favur*." He argues that "to attempt a progressive change is idle; it will keep the language in perpetual fluctuation without an effectual amendment. And to attempt a total change at once, is equally idle and extravagant, as it would render the language unintelligible. We may better labour to speak our language with propriety and elegance, as we have it, than to attempt

a reformation without advantage or probability of success" (*GI*, 11–12n). Webster would drastically change his mind in the *Dissertations*.

14. For Webster's responses to Dilworth's Ghost, see *LNW*, pp. 9–36. See also Monaghan, *A Common Heritage*, pp. 47–51.

15. For accounts of Webster's reforms, see Monaghan, *A Common Heritage*, pp. 34–46; and Shoemaker, *Noah Webster: Pioneer of Learning*, pp. 70–75.

16. Barlow to Webster, 31 August 1782, in *Notes on the Life of Noah Webster*, comp. Emily Ellsworth Fowler Ford, ed. Emily Ellsworth Ford Skeel, 2 vols. (New York· Privately printed, 1912), 1:55; Timothy Pickering to his wife, 31 October 1783, in Ford, *Notes*, 1:96; Elizur Goodrich to Webster, 29 September 1783, quoted in Monaghan, *A Common Heritage*, pp. 42, 40. On the extent of Webster's innovations in the *Grammatical Institute*, see Monaghan, *A Common Heritage*, chap. 2, esp. pp. 36–37; and Shoemaker, *Noah Webster: Pioneer of Learning*, pp. 64–113.

17. Dilworth is rejected outright in the second part of the *Grammatical Institute* because his grammar "is not constructed upon the principles of the English language." But Webster turns instead to other authoritative works: Robert Lowth, *A Short Introduction to English Grammar* (1763); John Ash, *Grammatical Institutes; or, An Easy Introduction to Dr. Lowth's English Grammar* (1763); and James Buchanan, *A Regular English Syntax* (1766).

18. Buckminster to Webster, 17 November 1783, in Ford, *Notes*, 1:62–63.

19. Thomas Dilworth, *A New Guide to the English Tongue*, 13th ed. (London, 1751; reprint, Leeds, England: The Scolar Press, 1967), p. iii. The *New Guide* was first published in 1740. Hereafter, *NG*.

20. For instance:

8. Divine Providence disposes all Things most wisely; not only in what concerns the World in general, but every one of us in particular: So that in what Condition soever he puts us, we may assure ourselves that it is best for us, since He chuses it, who cannot err. (*NG*, 128)

17. It is a commendable Thing for a Boy to apply his Mind to the Study of good Letters; they will be always useful to him; they will procure him the Favour and Love of good Men, which those that are wise value more than Riches and Pleasure. (*NG*, 129)

25. Obedience comprehendeth the whole Duty of a Man, both towards God, his Neighbour, and himself; we should therefore let it be engraven on our Hearts, that we may be useful in the Common-Wealth, and loyal to our Prince. (*NG*, 130)

On *King* GEORGE

Long may the King *Great Britain*'s Scepter sway,
While all his Subjects peaceably obey:
And when God's Providence shall him remove
From these below, to highest Realms above;
To his own Race, may he the Crown resign,
For ever to continue in that Line. (*NG*, 136)

21. For instance:

Q. What is *Grammar*?
A. Grammar *is the Science of Letters, or the Art of Writing and Speaking properly and syntactically.*

According to John Barrell, the question-and-answer form was "frequently adopted" by eighteenth-century grammarians. See Barrell, "The Language Properly So-Called: The Authority of Common Usage," in *English Literature in History, 1730–1780: An Equal, Wide Survey* (London: Hutchinson, 1983), p. 141.

22. See Barrell, *English Literature*, pp. 110–175. See also Olivia Smith, *The Politics of Language, 1791–1819* (Oxford: Clarendon Press, 1984), pp. 1–33.

23. The text of the preface is printed in italics, and emphasized words are printed in roman type. I have reversed the system here.

24. For instance (*NG*, iv):

It has been a general and true Observation, that with the Reformation of these Realms, *Ignorance* has gradually vanished at the Increase of *Learning* amongst us, who take the Word of God for a *Lantern to our Feet, and a Light to our Paths.* Thus,
They who grop'd their Way to Virtue and Knowledge in the Days of Darkness and implicit Zeal, were taught little more than to mumble over a few Prayers by Heart, and never called upon to read, much less permitted to enquire into the Truth of what they professed. But,
Since etc.

25. On the Puritans and language, see William Haller, *The Rise of Puritanism* (New York: Columbia University Press, 1938; reprint, Philadelphia: University of Pennsylvania Press, 1972), pp. 128–172; Perry Miller, *The New England Mind: The Seventeenth Century* (New York: Macmillan, 1939; reprint, Boston: Beacon Press, 1961), pp. 331–362; and Larzer Ziff, *Puritanism in America: New Culture in a New World* (New York: Viking, 1973), pp. 3–15.

26. For instance (*GI*, 108):

Is it true that you have heard good news?
It is true indeed.
Do you believe what you have heard?
I am very certain, it is true.
I think I may rely on your word.
I would not tell a lie for all America.
Will you drink a dish of tea?
Sir, I am much obliged to you; I chuse not to drink any.
What! do not chuse to drink any?
No, Sir, I am not fond of it.
Perhaps you like coffee better.
No Sir. I like chocolate.
At what o'clock shall you prefer it?
Just at what hour you please.

27. See Warfel, *Noah Webster: Schoolmaster to America*, p. 43; Ellis, *After the Revolution*, p. 169; Rollins, *Long Journey*, p. 21. Webster included an excerpt from *The Crisis* in part 3 of the *Grammatical Institute*. He was "Introduced to Mr. T. Paine, Common Sense" on 27 February 1786 (Ford, *Notes*, 1:151). Webster's rejection of Paine later in life as "an Englishman of low birth" who "debased himself by infidelity and licentious principles" only underscores the extent of the influence Paine must have had on the young man of letters (Webster, *History of the United States* [New Haven, 1832], quoted in Moss, *Noah Webster*, pp. 38–39). On the uniqueness of Paine's style among Revolutionary writers, see Bernard Bailyn, *"Common Sense,"* in Library of Congress Symposia on the American Revolution, *Fundamental Testaments of the American Revolution* (Washington, D.C.: Library of Congress Publications, 1973), pp. 7–23; and Eric Foner, *Tom Paine and Revolutionary America* (New York: Oxford University Press, 1976), pp. 71–106. See also: Jack P. Greene, "Paine, America, and the 'Modernization' of Political Consciousness," *Political Science Quarterly* 93 (1978): 73–92; J. Rodney Fulcher, *"Common Sense* vs. *Plain Truth*: Political Propaganda and Civil Society," *The Southern Quarterly* 15 (1976): 57–74; and Stephen Fender, "Thomas Paine," in *American Literature in Context I, 1620–1830* (London: Methuen, 1983), pp. 81–96. Other examinations of Paine's style focus on post-Revolutionary works, in particular *Rights of Man*, including: Smith, *Politics of Language*, pp. 35–67; and James T. Boulton, *The Language of Politics in the Age of Wilkes and Burke* (London: Routledge & Kegan Paul, 1963), pp. 134–150. On the possible influence of Webster's writings on Paine's later works, see Smith, *Politics of Language*, pp. 40–41.

28. Thomas Paine, *The Writings of Thomas Paine*, ed. Moncure Daniel Conway, 4 vols. (New York: Putnam's, 1894), 1:84–85. Hereafter, *WTP*.

29. For a less politically tendentious account of these aspects of British grammatical history, see Cohen, *Sensible Words*, esp. pp. 88–96. See also Barrell, *English Literature*, pp. 119–126.

30. I deal in this section with what I take to be the two general senses of the word used by Webster throughout his public and private writings. As for Webster's own definitions of the word: in *A Compendious Dictionary of the English Language* (New Haven, 1806), he includes, "one's own, peculiar, fit, just, plain." In *An American Dictionary of the English Language* (New Haven, 1828), he lists, "1. Peculiar; naturally or essentially belonging to a person or thing; not common. 2. Particularly suited to. 3. One's own. 4. Noting an individual. . . . 5. Fit; suitable; adapted; accommodated. 6. Correct; just; as a *proper* word; a *proper* expression. 7. Not figurative. 8. Well formed; handsome. 9. Tall; lusty; handsome with bulk. 10. In *vulgar language*, very; as *proper* good; *proper* sweet." (I have omitted Webster's examples.) See also the entries in Johnson's *Dictionary*, and Thomas Sheridan's *A General Dictionary of the English Language* (London, 1780), as well as the *OED*, for possible meanings available to Webster.

31. Alexis de Tocqueville, *Democracy in America*, trans. Henry Reeve, rev. Francis Bowen, ed. Phillips Bradley, 2 vols. (New York: Vintage Books, 1945), 2:68. Hereafter, *DIA*.

32. Tocqueville's most immediate models for the general notion of cultural

relativity were, most significantly in terms of the relation of politics to culture, Montesquieu's *The Spirit of Laws* (1748), as well as Madame de Stael's *Literature Considered in Its Relation to Social Institutions* and, perhaps less philosophically than stylistically, her *On Germany* (1810). But Montesquieu does not talk about language, and de Stael's remarks on the differences between French and German are rather superficial and wholly apolitical. (See *Germany*, trans. O. W. Wight [New York, 1859], 1:90–93.) Condillac, in contrast, presents a clear theoretical model of the relation of language to politics, and I use it here to help explain Tocqueville and to compare him to Webster. On Montesquieu's theory of "esprit general," see David Wallace Carrithers, "Introduction" to Montesquieu, *The Spirit of Laws: A Compendium of the First English Edition*, ed. Carrithers (Berkeley: University of California Press, 1977), pp. 23–30. On Tocqueville's relation to Montesquieu, see Melvin Richter, "The Uses of Theory: Tocqueville's Adaptation of Montesquieu," in *Essays in Theory and History: An Approach to the Social Sciences*, ed. Richter (Cambridge: Harvard University Press, 1970), pp. 74–103. On the general intellectual background of Tocqueville's thought and on his methodology, see Gita May, "Tocqueville and the Enlightenment Legacy," in *Reconsidering Tocqueville's Democracy in America*, ed. Abraham S. Eisenstadt (New Brunswick, N.J.: Rutgers University Press, 1988), pp. 25–42; James T. Schleifer, "Tocqueville as Historian: Philosophy and Methodology in the *Democracy*," in Eisenstadt, *Reconsidering Tocqueville*, pp. 146–167; Whitney Pope, *Alexis de Tocqueville: His Social and Political Theory* (Beverly Hills: Sage Publications, 1986), pp. 27–76; Francois Furet, "The Intellectual Origins of Tocqueville's Thought," *The Tocqueville Review/La Revue Tocqueville* 7 (1985–1986): 117–129; James Ceaser, "Alexis de Tocqueville on Political Science, Political Culture, and the Role of the Intellectual," *The American Political Science Review* 79 (1985): 656–672; and Schleifer, *The Making of Tocqueville's Democracy in America* (Chapel Hill: The University of North Carolina Press, 1980). On the idea of linguistic relativity in eighteenth-century thought, see David Morse, *Perspectives on Romanticism: A Transformational Analysis* (London: Macmillan, 1981), pp. 1–33; Lia Formigari, "Language and Society in the Late Eighteenth Century," *Journal of the History of Ideas* 35 (1974): 275–292; and, especially on its development in Germany, Roger Langham Brown, *Wilhelm von Humboldt's Conception of Linguistic Relativity* (The Hague: Mouton, 1967), pp. 69–84. On Condillac's importance in the development and dissemination of this idea, see Hans Aarsleff, "The Tradition of Condillac: The Problem of the Origin of Language in the Eighteenth Century and the Debate in the Berlin Academy before Herder," in *From Locke to Saussure: Essays on the Study of Language and Intellectual History* (Minneapolis: University of Minnesota Press, 1982), pp. 146–209. Aarsleff's argument is that the German/Herderian tradition has its roots in French/Condillacian thought. It seems to me that Tocqueville's more ideological sense of cultural relativity is clearly in the French, rather than the German, tradition.

33. Etienne Bonnot de Condillac, *An Essay on the Origin of Human Knowledge* trans. Thomas Nugent (London, 1756; reprint, Gainesville, Fla.: Scholar's Facsimiles & Reprints, 1971), pp. 298, 284. For general accounts of Condillac's theory of language, see Isabel F. Knight, *The Geometric Spirit: The Abbé de Condillac and the French Enlightenment* (New Haven: Yale University Press, 1968),

pp. 144–175, 192–197; and Ellen McNiven Hine, *A Critical Study of Condillac's Traité des Systèmes* (The Hague: Martinus Nijhoff Publishers, 1979), pp. 183–205.

34. Consider also Tocqueville's comments on literature several chapters before his remarks on language: "I should say more than I mean if I were to assert that the literature of a nation is always subordinate to its social state and its political constitution. I am aware that, independently of these causes, there are several others which confer certain characteristics on literary productions; but these appear to me to be the chief. The relations that exist between the social and the political condition of a people and the genius of its authors are always numerous; whoever knows the one is never completely ignorant of the other" (*DIA*, 2:63). The classic attack on Tocqueville's deductive methodology is George Wilson Pierson, *Tocqueville and Beaumont in America* (New York: Oxford University Press, 1938), pp. 758–760.

35. Webster to Timothy Pickering, 10 August 1786, in Ford, *Notes*, 1:163. The entry in his diary for 10 October reads, "Read Abbe de Cadillac [*sic*]; at club at Mr. Appleton's."

36. Webster, "On the Education of Youth in America" (1788), in *A Collection of Essays and Fugitiv Writings* (Boston, 1790; reprint, Delmar, N.Y.: Scholars' Facsimiles and Reprints, 1977), p. 3.

37. Condillac, *Essay*, pp. 289, 286, 291, 294.

38. Webster, *Dissertations on the English Language* (Boston, 1789; reprint, Menston, England: The Scolar Press, 1967), p. 406. Hereafter, *DEL*. Although he will admit that one variable may affect another, especially that national character provides the energy for government, each of the three needs to be settled separately. Consider one of his best-known calls for cultural independence: "Americans, unshackle your minds, and act like independent beings. You have been children long enough, subject to the control, and subservient to the interest of a haughty parent. You have now . . . an empire to raise and support by your exertions, and a national character to establish and extend by your wisdom and virtues" ("On the Education of Youth," p. 36).

39. Democracy will, for Webster, affect the language spoken by Americans, but not in the way Condillac suggests. Consider, for instance, this assertion from the introduction to his *Compendious Dictionary of the English Language* (1806): "From the changes in civil policy, manners, arts of life, and other circumstances attending the settlement of English colonies in America, most of the language of heraldry, hawking, hunting, and especially that of the old feudal and hierarchical establishments of England will become utterly extinct in this country; much of it already forms a part of the neglected rubbish of antiquity" (quoted in *On Being American: Selected Writings, 1783–1828*, ed. Homer D. Babbidge, Jr. (New York: Praeger, 1967), p. 134.

40. The definitions are from the *American Dictionary* of 1828. In 1808, Webster called for an "*Association of American Patriots* for the purpose of forming a *National Character*, asserting the *rights*, securing the *interests*, & maintaining the *honor*, the *dignity*, & the *Independence* of the *United States*" (Webster Papers, New York Public Library). Clearly, the italicized words were inextricably related in Webster's mind.

41. Condillac, *Essay*, pp. 286, 287.

42. Condillac uses the term "analogy" to refer either to a mode of reasoning or to the relation between phrases and expressions, i.e., semantic and stylistic units. Webster, like other linguists, uses the term to refer to regular grammatical and vocal patterns. For example: "If we examine the structure of any language, we shall find a certain principle of analogy running through the whole. We shall find in English that similar combinations of letters have usually the same pronunciation; and that words, having the same terminating syllable, generally have the accent at the same distance from that termination. These principles of analogy were not the result of design—they must have been the result of accident, or that tendency which all men feel towards uniformity" (*DEL*, 27). See Sterling Andrus Leonard, *The Doctrine of Correctness in English Usage, 1700–1800* (New York: Russell & Russell, 1962).

43. Condillac, *Essay*, p. 297. The passage is quoted in *DEL*, pp. 30–31.

44. Johann David Michaelis, *A Dissertation on the Influence of Opinions on Language and of Language on Opinions* (1760; trans., London, 1769), p. 78. The quotation is found in *DEL*, pp. 166–167. On Michaelis, see James O'Flaherty, *The Quarrel of Reason with Itself: Essays on Hamann, Michaelis, Lessing, Nietzsche* (Columbia, S.C.: Camden House, 1988), pp. 163–174.

45. Michaelis, *Dissertation*, pp. 1–3. The discussion of names for the "Supreme Being" is on pp. 4–5, 19–20. In 1788, Webster published a brief article that borrows its title and many of its ideas from Michaelis's *Dissertation*. (The article is reprinted in Webster, *A Collection of Essays and Fugitiv Writings*, pp. 222–228.) Here Webster's concern, like Michaelis's, is etymology, not pronunciation or grammar. But here, too, Webster distorts his source. Webster's point is that "the *mere use of words* has led nations into error, and still continues the delusion" and that etymological investigations "may assist us in correcting our ideas" (pp. 222, 228). Michaelis does assert that "much good is contained in etymology" but is generally more circumspect and allows that etymological research might also lead to error: "What I perceive in every etymology is, that, in such and such a nation, some body has thought thus or thus; but to know whether his thoughts be right or wrong requires a particular inquiry, which has nothing to do with etymology" (Michaelis, *Dissertation*, pp. 12, 13–14).

46. On Webster and Federalism, see *Sketches of American Policy* (Hartford, 1785); and *An Examination into the Leading Principles of the Federal Constitution* (Philadelphia, 1787). On Webster and "Federal English," see Baron, *GGI*, pp. 41–67.

47. Michaelis, *Dissertation*, p. 3.

48. Much has been made of Webster's obsession with Tooke's *Diversions of Purley* and its continuing influence on his philological work. See, for instance, Charlton Laird, "Diversions of *The Diversions of Purley* in the New World," *Rendezvous* 1 (1966): 1–11; and Simpson, *PAE*, pp. 81–90.

49. John Horne Tooke, *Epea Pteroenta, or the Diversions of Purley* (London, 1860), pp. 6, 151. The first volume appeared in 1786. See Hans Aarsleff, *The Study of Language in England, 1780–1860* (Princeton: Princeton University Press, 1967), pp. 44–72.

50. On the politics of Tooke's philology, see Smith, *Politics of Language*, pp. 110–153.

51. On the political and religious role of the Anglo-Saxon myth in British history, see Hugh A. MacDougall, *Racial Myth in English History: Trojans, Teutons, and Anglo-Saxons* (Hanover, N.H.: University Press of New England, 1982), esp. pp. 31–86. The impact of the myth on nineteenth-century, post-Tookean philology may be found on pp. 119–124.

Chapter Two
"A Fine Ambiguity"

1. William Dean Howells, "The Art of Longfellow," in *Longfellow among His Contemporaries*, ed. Kenneth Walter Cameron (Hartford, Conn.: Transcendental Books, 1978), pp. 352, 354. Hereafter, *LAC*. The article was originally published in the *North American Review* 184, no. 610 (March 1907): 472–485. For an overview of Howells's opinion of Longfellow, see Edward Wagenknecht, "Longfellow and Howells," in *Henry W. Longfellow Reconsidered: A Symposium*, ed. J. Chesley Mathews (Hartford, Conn.: Transcendental Books, 1970), pp. 52–57.

2. Quoted in Wagenknecht, "Longfellow and Howells," p. 54.

3. Ibid., p. 55.

4. Steven Allaback, "Longfellow Now," in *Papers Presented at the Longfellow Commemorative Conference, April 1–3, 1982* (Washington: U.S. Government Printing Office, 1982), p. 112.

5. Jane Tompkins, *Sensational Designs: The Cultural Work of American Fiction, 1790–1860* (New York: Oxford University Press, 1985), p. 34. Lawrence Buell's paperback edition of Longfellow's poetry (Henry Wadsworth Longfellow, *Selected Poems*, ed. Lawrence Buell [New York: Penguin Books, 1988]) may be said to be the most recent effort at revival. His introduction (pp. vii–xxxii), an excellent general overview of Longfellow and his poetry, nevertheless relies upon the sorts of explanations and apologies I have sketched in this paragraph. The ultimate influence this new edition has upon the poet's reputation remains, of course, to be seen.

6. Henry James, *William Wetmore Story and His Friends* (1903; reprint, New York: Grove Press, n.d.), pp. 312–313.

7. Quoted in Wagenknecht, "Longfellow and Howells," p. 55.

8. Newton Arvin, *Longfellow: His Life and Work* (Boston: Little, Brown, 1963), p. 22. See pp. 22–23 for a discussion of James's comments.

9. To Stephen Longfellow, 13 March 1824, in *The Letters of Henry Wadsworth Longfellow*, ed. Andrew Hilen, 4 vols. (Cambridge: Harvard University Press, 1966), p. 83. Hereafter, *LHWL*. Longfellow's relationship with his father is summarized, and the correspondence quoted at length, in Lawrance Thompson, *Young Longfellow (1807–1843)* (New York: Macmillan, 1938), pp. 55–61.

10. Quoted in Thompson, *Young Longfellow*, p. 59.

11. Henry Wadsworth Longfellow, "Our Native Writers," in *The Native Muse: Theories of American Literature*, ed. Richard Ruland (New York: Dutton, 1972), p. 237. Hereafter, *ONW*.

12. [Henry Wadsworth Longfellow], "The Literary Spirit of Our Country,"

United States Literary Gazette, 1 April 1825, 27–28, 25. The essay was one of a series published under the rubric "The Lay Monastery" and pseudonymously signed, "The Lay Monk."

13. My definitions of *polite* are taken from the *Oxford English Dictionary* and are contemporaneous with Longfellow.

14. Longfellow, "The Literary Spirit of Our Country," 25, 26. On Commonsense associationism in American literary thought, see Benjamin Spencer, *The Quest for Nationality: An American Literary Campaign* (Syracuse, N.Y.: Syracuse University Press, 1957), esp. pp. 68–70; Terence Martin, *The Instructed Vision: Scottish Common Sense Philosophy and the Origins of American Fiction* (Bloomington: Indiana University Press, 1961), pp. 109–11; and Emory Elliott, *Revolutionary Writers: Literature and Authority in the New Republic* (New York: Oxford University Press, 1986), pp. 31–33.

15. Longfellow, "The Literary Spirit of Our Country," 24.

16. See Montesquieu, *The Spirit of Laws*, trans. Thomas Nugent, 2 vols. (New York: Hafner Publishing Company, 1949), esp. 1:221–270.

17. William Wordsworth, *The Poems*, ed. John O. Hayden (Harmondsworth: Penguin Books, 1977), 1:455, 568. The phrases are taken from "Michael, A Pastoral Poem" and "The world is too much with us . . ." respectively.

18. It should be noted that in "The Literary Spirit of Our Country" Longfellow considers nothing but natural scenery as the source of national literary spirit.

19. His own remarkable linguistic abilities for the most part yet untapped, the young Longfellow had written of the polyglot Jones, "Eight Languages he was critically versed in—eight more he read with a dictionary and there were still twelve more which he had studied less perfectly, but which were not wholly unknown to him; making in all twenty eight languages to which he had given his attention. I have somewhere seen or heard the observation, that as many languages as a person acquired, so many times was he a man. Mr. Jones was equal to about sixteen men, according to that observation" (*LHWL*, 1:104).

20. Sir William Jones was, of course, a crucial figure in the rise of comparative philology, but it was not this aspect of his work that seems to have attracted Longfellow. On Jones and the "new philology," see Hans Aarsleff, *The Study of Language in England, 1780–1860* (Princeton: Princeton University Press, 1967), pp. 115–161. For the influence of philosophers I do not consider in this chapter, see Robert Stafford Ward, "The Influence of Vico upon Longfellow," *ESQ* 58 (1970): 57–62; and John Griffith, "Longfellow and Herder and the Sense of History," *Texas Studies in Language and Literature* 13 (1971–1972): 249–265.

21. These include: *Elements of French Grammar* (Portland, 1830), a translation of a grammar by C. F. L'Homond; *Syllabus de la grammaire italienne* (Boston, 1832), written by Longfellow in French; *Manuel de proverbes dramatiques* (Portland, 1830); *Novelas españolas* (Portland, 1830); *Cours de langue française* (Boston, 1832); and *Saggi de' novellieri italiani d' ogni secolo* (Boston, 1832). The last four were edited by Longfellow.

22. See Longfellow, Notebook, No. 1, pp. 135–138, and "History of Modern Languages," n.p. (MSS, Houghton Library, Harvard University). Both are lecture notes, the first from 1830, the second, from 1844. In the second, he clearly planned to speak about "The origin of Language" in an "Introductory

Lecture." In the second, too, Longfellow refers to "Note=book N⁰· 1," and we may infer that his introductory lectures regularly included remarks on this issue.

23. Longfellow, Notebook, No. 1, p. 18.

24. James Harris, *Hermes: or, A Philosophical Inquiry concerning Language and Universal Grammar* (London, 1751; reprint, Menston, England: The Scolar Press, 1968), pp. 423–424. Longfellow quotes from p. 407.

25. Longfellow, Notebook, No. 1, pp. 63–65.

26. The *North American Review* articles include: "Origin and Progress of the French Language," 32 (1831): 277–317; "Spanish Devotional and Moral Poetry," 34 (1832): 277–315; "History of the Italian Language and Dialects," 35 (1832): 283–342; "Spanish Language and Literature," 36 (1833): 316–344; "Old English Romances," 37 (1837): 374–419; "Anglo-Saxon Literature," 47 (1838): 90–134; and "The French Language in England," 51 (1840): 285–308. This list does not include Longfellow's best-known *North American Review* article, "Defence of Poetry," which I will discuss at length below.

27. See Carl L. Johnson, "Longfellow's Studies in France," in *Henry W. Longfellow Reconsidered: A Symposium*, ed. J. Chesley Mathews (Hartford, Conn.: Transcendental Books, 1970), pp. 44–45. The translation I am using is by Thomas Roscoe, published as J.C.L. Simonde di Sismondi, *Historical View of the Literature of the South of Europe*, 2 vols. (London: Henry G. Bohn, 1846). Hereafter, *LSE*. Longfellow himself refers to this translation, as well as to the French original. On the American vogue of Sismondi, see Howard Mumford Jones, *The Theory of American Literature* (Ithaca: Cornell University Press, 1965), pp. 61–63.

28. Henry Wadsworth Longfellow, *Origin and Growth of the Languages of Southern Europe and of Their Literature*, ed. George T. Little (Brunswick, Maine: Bowdoin College Library, 1907), p. 9. Hereafter, *OGL*.

29. See Augustus William Schlegel, *A Course of Lectures on Dramatic Art and Literature*, trans. John Black (London: Henry G. Bohn, 1846), pp. 23–28. Longfellow met Schlegel in Bonn. See Arvin, *Longfellow*, p. 33.

30. See Alexander Pope, "A Discourse on Pastoral Poetry," in *Poetry and Prose of Alexander Pope*, ed. Aubrey Williams (Boston: Houghton Mifflin, 1969), pp. 3–7.

31. Let me note here that I use the term *pastoral* in the broad (Leo) Marxian sense of the term rather than in the more restricted, classical sense of poetry about shepherds. See Leo Marx, *The Machine in the Garden: Technology and the Pastoral Ideal in America* (New York: Oxford University Press, 1964), and, more recently, "Pastoralism in America," in *Ideology and Classic American Literature*, ed. Sacvan Bercovitch and Myra Jehlen (Cambridge: Cambridge University Press, 1986), pp. 36–69. See also Lawrence Buell, "American Pastoral Ideology Reappraised," *American Literary History* 1 (1989): 1–29.

32. Longfellow, "Defence of Poetry," *The North American Review* 34 (1832): 56. Hereafter, *DOP*.

33. Sir Philip Sidney, *The Defence of Poesy*, in *Sir Philip Sidney: Selected Prose and Poetry*, ed. Robert Kimbrough, 2d ed. (Madison: University of Wisconsin Press, 1983), p. 103. The passage Longfellow quotes on p. 58 of his "Defence" may be found on pp. 156–158 of Sidney's *Defence*.

34. William Charvat, *The Profession of Authorship in America, 1800–1870*

(Columbus: Ohio State University Press, 1968), p. 292. On Longfellow in particular, see pp. 100–167.

35. Sidney, too, refers to "certain Goths, of whom it is written that, having in the spoil of a famous city taken a fair library," forbade its burning, arguing, "while they are busy about those toys, we shall with more leisure conquer their countries." But Sidney puts this in the category of "the ordinary doctrine of ignorance" and dismisses it because it "is generally against all learning, as well as poetry." See *The Defence of Poesy*, p. 139.

36. Ibid., pp. 135, 140.

37. For instance, "Yet the true glory of a nation . . . consists not in what nature has given to the body, but in what nature and education have given to the mind:—not in the world around us, but in the world within us:—not in the circumstances of fortune, but in the attributes of the soul:—not in the corruptible, transitory, and perishable forms of matter, but in the incorruptible, the permanent, the imperishable mind" (*DOP*, 59). For other examples, see my preceding paragraph.

38. See Percy Bysshe Shelley, "A Defence of Poetry," in *Shelley: Selected Poetry, Prose, and Letters*, ed. A.S.B. Glover (London: The Nonesuch Press, 1951), p. 1055. Shelley's "Defence" was written in 1821 but was not published until 1840.

39. The designation is from James Russell Lowell's review of *Kavanagh* in the *North American Review*. It is quoted in the introduction to Henry W. Longfellow, *Kavanagh, a Tale*, ed. Jean Downey (New Haven: College and University Press, 1965), p. 14. Hereafter, *KAT*.

40. On Matthews and Young America, see Perry Miller, *The Raven and the Whale: The War of Words and Wits in the Era of Poe and Melville* (New York: Harcourt, Brace, & World, 1956). On *Kavanagh* as a satire on Matthews, see pp. 251–252.

41. See, e.g., Arvin, *Longfellow*, p. 127.

42. In his journal entry for 6 January 1847, Longfellow formulates an early version of Churchill's second argument in just these terms: "Much is said now-a-days of a national literature. Does it mean anything? Such a literature is the expression of national character. We have, or shall have, a composite one, embracing French, Spanish, Irish, English, Scotch, and German peculiarities. Whoever has within himself most of these is our truly national writer. In other words, *whoever is most universal is also most national.*" See Samuel Longfellow, ed., *Life of Henry Wadsworth Longfellow*, 3 vols. (Boston: Houghton, Mifflin and Company, 1891), 2:73–74 (italics mine). The *Life* is included in the standard edition of Longfellow's works as vols. 13–15.

Chapter Three
"A Tongue According"

1. Horace Traubel, "Foreword" to Walt Whitman, *An American Primer*, ed. Traubel (Boston: Small, Maynard & Company, 1904; reprint, San Francisco: City Lights Books, 1970), pp. [viii–xi]. Traubel's foreword is reprinted in a footnote to the transcription of Whitman's manuscript of the primer in Walt Whitman, *Daybooks and Notebooks*, 3 vols., ed. William White (New York: New

York University Press, 1978), 3:728–729n. All further references to the *Primer* will be to this later edition and will be noted in the text, along with other writings in this volume, as *D&N*. Throughout this chapter, Whitman's manuscript corrections (strikeouts and other marks) will be silently deleted, unless otherwise noted. Traubel reports that the title *An American Primer* was Whitman's "adopted headline," though it appears only as a jotting on p. 86 of the manuscript. White prefers "The Primer of Words, for American Young, Men, and Women, for Literats, Orators, Teachers, Musicians, Judges Presidents, &c."— which Traubel found "among Whitman's memoranda" and reproduced in facsimile in his edition. Nevertheless, I refer to the work throughout by the better-known title, *An American Primer*.

2. See James Perrin Warren, "Dating Whitman's Language Studies," *Walt Whitman Quarterly Review* 1 (1983): 1–7.

3. Malcolm Cowley, ed., *Walt Whitman's Leaves of Grass: The First (1855) Edition* (New York: Viking Press, 1959), p. 28. Hereafter, *LOG*.

4. Walt Whitman, *Notebooks and Unpublished Prose Manuscripts*, ed. Edward F. Grier, 6 vols. (New York: New York University Press, 1984), 5:1622–1623. Hereafter, *NUM*.

5. Whitman scholarship is not lacking for commentary on his language and study of language, but most critics are concerned either, like Mencken, with the poet's use of, and contributions to, American English or, like Matthiessen, with the linguistic theories that underlie his poetry. See Sherry G. Southard, "Whitman and Language: An Annotated Bibliography," *Walt Whitman Quarterly Review* 2 (1984): 31–49. Of particular importance are C. Carroll Hollis, *Language and Style in "Leaves of Grass"* (Baton Rouge: Louisiana State University Press, 1985), and, most recently, James Perrin Warren, *Walt Whitman's Language Experiment* (University Park: Pennsylvania State University Press, 1990).

6. See C. Carroll Hollis, "Whitman and William Swinton: A Co-operative Friendship," *American Literature* 30 (1959): 425–449. On the rise of nineteenth-century linguistics, see Holger Pedersen, *The Discovery of Language: Linguistic Science in the Nineteenth Century* (Bloomington: Indiana University Press, 1962), and R. H. Robbins, *A Short History of Linguistics*, 2d ed. (London: Longman, 1979), pp. 133–197.

7. In the 1856 edition of *Leaves of Grass*, Whitman removed his earlier prose preface and included many of its passages in various poems. His passage on language appears, with changes, in "Poem of Many in One":

> Language using controls the rest;
> Wonderful is language!
> Wondrous the English language, language of live men,
> Language of ensemble, powerful language of resistance,
> Language of a proud and melancholy stock, and of all who aspire,
> Language of growth, faith, self-esteem, rudeness, justice, friendliness,
>   amplitude, prudence, decision, exactitude, courage,
> Language to well-nigh express the inexpressible,
> Language for the modern, language for America.

See Walt Whitman, *Leaves of Grass: Facsimile of the 1856 Edition*, introd., Gay Wilson Allen (n.p.: Norwood Editions, 1976), p. 191.

8. See Baron, *GGT*, pp. 119–168. On this period of Whitman's life, see Gay Wilson Allen, *The Solitary Singer: A Critical Biography of Walt Whitman* (New York: Grove Press, 1955), pp. 25–40, and Justin Kaplan, *Walt Whitman: A Life* (New York: Simon and Schuster, 1980), pp. 82–94.

9. On Murray's *Grammar*, see Baron, *GGT*, pp. 142–150. I will comment further on Whitman's relation to Murray below.

10. See Michael Rowan Dressman, "Walt Whitman's Plans for the Perfect Dictionary," *Studies in the American Renaissance: 1979*, ed. Joel Myerson (Boston: Twayne, 1979), pp. 457–74, and James Perrin Warren, "The 'Real Grammar': Deverbal Style in 'Song of Myself,'" *American Literature* 56 (1984): 1–16. Baron briefly considers Whitman's place in the reformist tradition in *GGT*, pp. 115–116.

11. "America's Mightiest Inheritance" is reprinted with introduction and notes in Walt Whitman, *New York Dissected: A Sheaf of Recently Discovered Newspaper Articles by the Author of Leaves of Grass*, ed. Emory Holloway and Ralph Adimari (New York: Rufus Rockwell Wilson, 1936), pp. 49–65. Hereafter, *NYD*. "Our Language and Literature" may be found in *D&N*, 3:809–811. An edited version, with critical comments, may be found in C. Carroll Hollis, "Whitman and the American Idiom," *Quarterly Journal of Speech* 43 (1957): 408–420. (The essay itself appears on pp. 419–420. The rest of the article deals with other aspects of Whitman's "Words" notebook.)

12. See John E. Bernbrock, S.J., "Walt Whitman and Anglo-Saxonism" (Ph.D. diss., University of North Carolina, Chapel Hill, 1961), pp. 27–30, 40–52. All references will be to the second edition of the *Hand-book*, with the altered title, *A Hand-book of the Engrafted Words of the English Language* (New York: D. Appleton and Company, 1854). This edition is identical to the first.

13. The composite nature of the English language was a significant aspect of its study well before the advent of comparative and historical linguistics, indeed, well before Tooke and Webster, though the elements of its composition were somewhat differently perceived. See, for example, John Free, *An Essay towards an History of the English Tongue* (London, 1749; reprint, Menston, England: The Scolar Press, 1968), and V. J. Peyton, *The History of the English Language* (London, 1771; reprint, Menston England: The Scolar Press, 1970).

14. Whitman similarly dates the 1860 edition of *Leaves of Grass*, "Year 85 of The States."

15. See James H. Stam, *Inquiries into the Origin of Language: The Fate of a Question* (New York: Harper and Row, 1976), pp. 97ff.

16. Wilhelm von Humboldt, *Humanist without Portfolio*, trans. and ed. Marianne Cowan (Detroit: Wayne State University Press, 1963), p. 274.

17. M. Schele de Vere, *Outlines of Comparative Philology* (New York: G. P. Putnam & Co., 1853), pp. 22–23. For more on Whitman and Schele de Vere, see Hollis, "Whitman and William Swinton"; James Perrin Warren, "Walt Whitman's Language and Style" (Ph.D. diss., Yale University, 1982), pp. 1–48; and Warren, "Organic Language Theory in the American Renaissance," in *Papers in the History of Linguistics*, ed. Hans Aarsleff et al. (Amsterdam: John Benjamins, 1987), pp. 513–521.

18. Compare Whitman's argument here to Bunsen's: "Religion and language show, more than any other organic activity of man, the preponderating

activity of the *sensus communis*. Neither word nor rite suggested by an individual would otherwise be intelligible, and capable of being received or practised, as integrally their own, by a community. The composition of works of art or of science shows, on the contrary, a prevalence of the individual factor; but the artist and man of science know that their most individual works are expressions of a common perception, and therefore independent of self." Bunsen, *Outlines of the Philosophy of Universal History, Applied to Language and Religion*, 2 vols. (London: Longman, Brown, Green, and Longmans, 1854), 1:37.

19. *A Hand-book of the Engrafted Words of the English Language*, p. 21.

20. Ibid., p. iv.

21. William Swinton [and Walt Whitman], *Rambles among Words: Their Poetry, History, and Wisdom* (New York: Charles Scribner, 1859), pp. 288–289. On Whitman's collaborative efforts, see Hollis, "Whitman and William Swinton," and James Perrin Warren, "Whitman as Ghostwriter: The Case of *Rambles among Words*," *Walt Whitman Quarterly Review* 2 (1984): 22–30.

22. Max Müller, quoted in Bunsen, *Outlines*, p. 486. Whitman's transcription may be found in *D&N*, 3:691–692.

23. Whitman adds an "Appendant for Working-People, Young Men and Women, and for Boys and Girls," comprising of some brief remarks on pronunciation and a list of predominantly French words "much needed in English." The relation of this appendix to the main body of the article and Whitman's notion of "waiting" should be apparent. I will discuss the most significant issues raised in the appendix in the following section on *An American Primer*. It should be noted, however, that Whitman's introduction of new French words, which repeats in the penultimate chapter of *Rambles among Words*, flies in the face of the *Hand-book*'s characterizing the "practice of using French words and phrases in English speech" as being "in bad taste" (p. 28).

24. Lindley Murray, *An English Grammar: Comprehending the Principles and Rules of the Language*, 3d ed., 2 vols. (York: Longman, 1816), 1:520.

25. John Witherspoon, "The Druid," in *The Beginnings of American English: Essays and Comments*, ed. Mitford McLeod Mathews (Chicago: University of Chicago Press, 1931; reprint, 1963), p. 17. On this issue, see Mencken, *AL*, pp. 3–89.

26. John Pickering, *A Vocabulary or Collection of Words and Phrases Which Have Been Supposed to be Peculiar to the United States of America* (Boston: Cummings and Hillard, 1816; reprint, New York: Burt Franklin Reprints, 1974), p. 11. Pickering's introductory essay may also be found in Mathews, *The Beginnings of American English*, pp. 64–77. Whitman included two clippings on Pickering in his "Words" notebook. See *D&N*, 3:687–688, 724.

27. Noah Webster, *Letter to the Honorable John Pickering* (Boston: West and Richardson, 1817; reprint, New York: Burt Franklin, 1974), pp. 45, 10–11, 7, 45. In his *Dissertations*, Webster had argued that English had reached a state of perfection between the reigns of Elizabeth and Anne. There Webster was talking about grammatical structure and analogy; here about vocabulary.

28. Whitman, *Leaves of Grass: Facsimile of the 1856 Edition*, p. 348.

29. Ralph Waldo Emerson, *Nature*, in *Selected Writings of Emerson*, ed. Donald McQuade (New York: Modern Library, 1981), p. 17. Italics mine.

30. Ibid.

31. John Adams to the President of Congress, 5 September 1780, in *Works*, ed. Charles Francis Adams (Boston: Little, Brown, 1850–1856), 7:249.

32. Swinton [and Whitman], *Rambles among Words*, p. 287.

Chapter Four
Consensus through Ambiguity

1. John Adams to the President of Congress, 5 September 1780, in *Works*, ed. Charles Francis Adams (Boston: Little, Brown, 1850–1856), 7:250.

2. Thomas Jefferson to Edward Carrington, 16 January 1787, in Jefferson, *Writings*, ed. Merrill D. Peterson (New York: Library of America, 1984), p. 880.

3. Jefferson to Carrington, p. 880; James Madison, *Letters and Other Writings*, 4 vols. (Philadelphia, 1865–1867), 3:441; Fisher Ames, "The Dangers of American Liberty," in *Works of Fisher Ames*, ed. Seth Ames, 2 vols. (New York, 1854), reprint, 2:356–357.

4. Alexander Hamilton, James Madison, and John Jay, *The Federalist Papers*, ed. Garry Wills (New York: Bantam Books, 1982), p. 2. All subsequent references to this text will be cited by essay and page number in the text. The importance of language and language theory to early American politics is most thoroughly examined in Thomas Gustafson, *Representative Words: Politics, Literature and the American Language, 1776–1865* (Cambridge University Press, forthcoming). For varying perspectives on the centrality of language, see also: Cynthia Jordan, "'Old Words' in 'New Circumstances': Language and Leadership in Post-Revolutionary America," *American Quarterly* 40 (1988): 491–513, and *Second Stories: The Politics of Language, Form, and Gender in Early American Fictions* (Chapel Hill: University of North Carolina Press, 1989), esp. pp. 1–26; Michael Warner, "Textuality and Legitimacy in the Printed Constitution," *Proceedings of the American Antiquarian Society* 97 (1987): 59–84; Baron, *GGT*, pp. 7–40; and Simpson, *PAE*, pp. 29–51.

5. John Witherspoon, "The Druid," in *The Beginnings of American English: Essays and Comments*, ed. Mitford McLeod Mathews (Chicago: University of Chicago Press, 1931; reprint, 1963), p. 16.

6. Thomas Jefferson to John Waldo, 16 August 1813, in Jefferson, *Writings*, pp. 1295, 1299. See also Jefferson's letter to John Adams, 15 August 1820, pp. 1442–1443.

7. Washington, quoted in Clinton Rossiter, "Introduction" to *The Federalist Papers* (New York: New American Library, 1961), pp. vii–viii; Jefferson, *Writings*, p. 479.

8. Rossiter, "Introduction" to *The Federalist Papers*, p. vii.

9. Adrienne Koch, "Philosopher-Statesmen of the Republic," in *Literary History of the United States*, ed. Robert E. Spiller, et al., 3d ed. (New York: Macmillan, 1963), 1:146–149. Lone voices on the style of *The Federalist*'s writers are: Louis C. Schaedler, "James Madison, Literary Craftsman," *William and Mary Quarterly*, 3d ser., 3 (1946): 515–533; Bower Aly, *The Rhetoric of Alexander Hamilton* (New York: Russell & Russell, 1965); and, most recently, Albert Furtwangler, *The Authority of Publius: A Reading of the Federalist Papers* (Ith-

aca: Cornell University Press, 1984). For a general approach to reading the literature of the founders somewhat different from the one I develop here, see Robert A. Ferguson, "'We Hold These Truths': Strategies of Control in the Literature of the Founders," in *Reconstructing American Literary History*, ed. Sacvan Bercovitch (Cambridge: Harvard University Press, 1986), pp. 1–28. See also his "Ideology and the Framing of the Constitution," *Early American Literature* 22 (1987): 157–165.

10. David F. Epstein, *The Political Theory of the Federalist* (Chicago: University of Chicago Press, 1984), p. 3; Charles A. Beard, *An Economic Interpretation of the Constitution* (New York, 1913); Robert A. Dahl, *A Preface to Democratic Theory* (Chicago: The University of Chicago Press, 1956), pp. 4–33; Furtwangler, *The Authority of Publius*, p. 32; Garry Wills, *Explaining America: The Federalist* (New York: Doubleday, 1981), p. xxii.

11. On the importance of the idea of a written constitution in early American political thought, see Gordon Wood, *The Creation of the American Republic, 1776–1787* (New York: W. W. Norton, 1969), pp. 259–305.

12. Thomas Jefferson, "From the Minutes of the Board of Visitors, University of Virginia, 1822–1825," in *Writings*, p. 479. On constitutional hermeneutics during the period of framing and ratification, see H. Jefferson Powell, "The Original Understanding of Original Intent," *Harvard Law Review* 98 (1985): 885–913.

13. On the significance of "active, civilized, public debate" in the new republic, see Furtwangler, *The Authority of Publius*, esp. pp. 98–111. For a less sanguine view, see Gordon Wood, "The Democratization of Mind in the American Revolution" in Library of Congress Symposia on the American Revolution, *Leadership in the American Revolution* (Washington, D.C., 1974), pp. 62–88.

14. I am indebted here to Ian Hacking, *Why Does Language Matter to Philosophy?* (New York: Cambridge University Press, 1975), pp. 1–56, although my assessment proceeds in a substantially different direction. See also Stephen K. Land, *From Signs to Propositions: The Concept of Form in Eighteenth-Century Semantic Theory* (London: Longman, 1974); Murray Cohen, *Sensible Words: Linguistic Practice in England, 1640–1785* (Baltimore, Md.: Johns Hopkins University Press, 1977); Ernst Cassirer, *The Philosophy of Symbolic Forms*, 3 vols. (New Haven: Yale University Press, 1955), 1:133–139; and Hans Aarsleff, *From Locke to Saussure: Essays on the Study of Language and Intellectual History* (Minneapolis: University of Minnesota Press, 1982). Morton White's *Philosophy, The Federalist, and the Constitution* (New York: Oxford University Press, 1987) does not consider the philosophy of language.

15. Francis Bacon, *The Advancement of Learning*, quoted in Hacking, *Why Does Language Matter*, p. 5; Thomas Hobbes, *Leviathan*, in *The English Language: Essays by English and American Men of Letters, 1490–1839*, ed. W. F. Bolton (Cambridge: Cambridge University Press, 1966), pp. 46, 51; David Hume, *Essays and Treatises on Several Subjects*, 2 vols. (Dublin, 1779), 2:365; *The Port Royal Art of Thinking* (trans., London, 1818), p. 65.

16. "Proper Words in proper Places, makes the true Definition of a Stile." Jonathan Swift, *A Letter to a Young Gentleman Lately Entered into Holy Orders*, in *Works*, ed. Herbert Davis et al. (Oxford: Basil Blackwell, 1963), 9:65.

17. John Locke, *An Essay concerning Human Understanding*, 2 vols., ed.

Alexander Campbell Fraser (New York: Dover Publications, 1959), 2:118–119. Hereafter, *CHU*.

18. On the politics of Locke's critique of language, see John Barrell, *English Literature in History, 1730–1780: An Equal, Wide Survey* (London: Hutchinson, 1983), pp. 113–119; Simpson, *PAE*, pp. 35–36; and Perry Miller, *Errand into the Wilderness* (New York: Harper & Row, 1956), pp. 169–171.

19. John Witherspoon, *Essays upon Important Subjects*, 4 vols. (Edinburgh, 1805), 2:134–135; Francis Hutcheson, *Collected Works of Francis Hutcheson* (facsimile reprint, Hildesheim: Georg Olms Verlagsbuchhandlung, 1969), 4:195.

20. Thomas Reid, *Essays on the Intellectual Powers of Man* (Edinburgh, 1785; facsimile reprint, New York: Garland Publishing, 1971), pp. 9, 10, 21.

21. Witherspoon, *Essays*, 2:137; Hutcheson, *Works*, 6:28; Witherspoon, *Essays*, 2:136; Hutcheson, *Works*, 4:198; Witherspoon, *Essays*, 2:136; Hutcheson, *Works*, 4:198; Hutcheson, *Works*, 6:35.

22. John DeWitt, *Essays of John DeWitt*, in *The Complete Anti-Federalist*, ed. Herbert J. Storing, 7 vols. (Chicago: University of Chicago Press, 1981), 4:21.

23. *Letters of Cato*, in Storing, *Anti-Federalist*, 2:104–105, 113–114, 117.

24. James Madison, *Notes of Debates in the Federal Convention of 1787*, ed. Adrienne Koch (Athens: Ohio University Press, 1966), pp. 34, 36, 653–654.

25. On language and politics in Brackenridge and Brown, see, e.g., Jordan, *Second Stories*, pp. 58–97; Mark Patterson, *Authority, Autonomy, and Representation in American Literature, 1776–1865* (Princeton: Princeton University Press, 1988), pp. 34–78; and (on Brown) Bell, *DAR*, pp. 40–61.

26. Madison, *Letters and Other Writings*, 3:442, 172, 519.

Chapter Five
A "Christian Commonwealth"

1. On the revaluation of Bushnell's thought, see, e.g., William R. Adamson, *Bushnell Rediscovered* (New York: United Church Press, 1966); Frederick Kirschenmann, "Horace Bushnell: Cells or Crustacea?" in *Reinterpretation of American Church History*, ed. Jerald Brauer (Chicago: University of Chicago Press, 1968), pp. 67–90; and Daniel Walker Howe, "The Social Science of Horace Bushnell," *The Journal of American History* 70 (1983): 305–322.

2. Horace Bushnell, *God in Christ* (Hartford, 1849). Hereafter, *GC*. The "Preliminary Dissertation" is found on pp. 1–122. Bushnell defended himself and reiterated his ideas in *Christ in Theology* (Hartford, 1851) and in "Our Gospel a Gift to the Imagination," *Hours at Home* 10 (December 1869): 159–172. Feidelson drew upon *Christ in Theology* as well as *God in Christ*. See Feidelson, *SAL*, pp. 151–157. For other scholarly works that posit the centrality of these writings, see, most recently, James O. Duke, *Horace Bushnell: On the Vitality of Biblical Language* (Chico, Calif.: Scholar's Press, 1984). See also: Philip F. Gura, *The Wisdom of Words*, pp. 51–71; Conrad Cherry, *Nature and Religious Imagination: From Edwards to Bushnell* (Philadelphia: Fortress Press, 1980), pp. 157–190; Donald A. Crosby, *Horace Bushnell's Theory of Language in the Context of Other Nineteenth-Century Philosophies of Language* (The Hague: Mouton, 1975); Lawrence Clinton Foard, "The Copernican Revolution in Theol-

ogy: Studies of the Critical and Romantic Elements in the Theory of Religious Language Proposed by Horace Bushnell" (Ph.D. diss., Temple University, 1970); Kirschenmann, "Horace Bushnell: Cells or Crustacea?"; and Harold A. Durfee, "Language and Religion: Horace Bushnell and Rowland Gibson Hazard," *American Quarterly* 5 (1953): 57–70.

3. On Bushnell's "modernity," see Gura, "Language and Meaning: An American Tradition," *American Literature* 53 (1981): 10–16; Wayne C. Minnick, "Horace Bushnell: Precursor of General Semantics," *ETC.* 5 (1948): 246–251; and Sherman Paul, "Horace Bushnell Reconsidered," *ETC.* 6 (1949): 255–258. In another context, Howe argues that Bushnell "anticipated many ideas developed by great secular social scientists in the next generation, such as Emile Durkheim, Max Weber, and Sigmund Freud." See "The Social Science of Horace Bushnell," p. 306.

4. Barbara Cross places Bushnell's language theory in the broader context of his career but fails to look beyond the "Preliminary Dissertation." See *Horace Bushnell: Minister to a Changing America* (Chicago: University of Chicago Press, 1958), pp. 73–115. One work which traces the development of Bushnell's linguistic speculations in a way that complements mine is David L. Smith, *Symbolism and Growth: The Religious Thought of Horace Bushnell* (Chico, Calif.: Scholar's Press, 1981). For interpretations of the patterns in Bushnell's thought different from mine, see Conrad Cherry, "The Structure of Organic Thinking: Horace Bushnell's Approach to Language, Nature, and Nation," *Journal of the American Academy of Religion* 40 (1972): 3–20; and William Alexander Johnson, *Nature and the Supernatural in the Theology of Horace Bushnell* (Lund: CWK Gleerup, 1963).

5. Mary Bushnell Cheney, *Life and Letters of Horace Bushnell* (New York: Scribners, 1903), pp. 208–209. For biographies of Bushnell, see Cheney, *Life and Letters*, and Cross, *Horace Bushnell.*

6. Bushnell, "American Politics," *The American National Preacher* 14 (1840): 189. Hereafter, *AP.* On the transformation of political rhetoric in the Jacksonian period, see John Patrick Diggins, *The Lost Soul of American Politics: Virtue, Self-Interest, and the Foundations of Liberalism* (New York: Basic Books, 1984), pp. 105–118. On the notorious campaign of 1840, see Glyndon G. Van Deusen, *The Jacksonian Era, 1828–1848* (New York: Harper and Row, 1959), pp. 132–150, and Arthur M. Schlesinger, Jr., *The Age of Jackson* (Boston: Little, Brown, 1945), pp. 283–305.

7. Bushnell, *Politics under the Law of God* (Hartford, 1844), p. 17. Hereafter, *PLG.*

8. *Barbarism the First Danger: A Discourse on the Home Missions* (New York, 1847), p. 32.

9. "The True Wealth or Weal of Nations" (1837), in *Representative Phi Beta Kappa Orations*, ed. Clark Sutherland Northrup et al. (Boston: Houghton Mifflin, 1915), p. 2. Hereafter, *TWW.*

10. G. C. Verplanck, quoted in Perry Miller, *The Life of the Mind in America, from the Revolution to the Civil War* (New York: Harcourt, Brace, Jovanovich, 1965), p. 39. On the churches' reactions to the separation of church and state, see Miller, *Life of the Mind*, pp. 36–72; Robert T. Handy, *A Christian America: Protestant Hopes and Historical Realities* (New York: Oxford University Press,

1971), pp. 27–64; Martin Marty, *Righteous Empire: The Protestant Experience in America* (New York: Harper and Row, 1970), pp. 89–99; and Cushing Strout, *The New Heavens and New Earth* (New York: Harper and Row, 1975), pp. 91–125.

11. Bushnell, *A Discourse on the Slavery Question* (Hartford, 1839), p. 28. Hereafter, *DSQ.*

12. In effect, Bushnell here significantly revises the distinction, widespread among Jacksonian political thinkers, between a democratic "government by opinion" and a tyrannical "government by force." (See Rush Welter, *The Mind of America, 1820–1860* [New York: Columbia University Press, 1975], pp. 253–297.) Tyranny, Bushnell argues, could be a function of opinion too, if language were debased so far as to ignore its relation to truth. A similar critique of political discourse written in reaction to the campaign of 1840 may be found in the writings of another antebellum philosopher of language, Rowland Gibson Hazard. See "The Causes of the Decline of Political Morality," in *Complete Works*, ed. Caroline Hazard (Boston: Houghton, Mifflin, 1889), 4:1–22, and Michael P. Kramer, "Language and Liberty in America, 1830–1860" (Ph.D. diss., Columbia University, 1983), pp. 118–128. It is interesting to compare Bushnell's and Hazard's argument to Michel Foucault, "Truth and Power," in *Power/Knowledge: Selected Interviews and Other Writings 1972–1977*, ed. Colin Gordon (New York: Pantheon, 1980), pp. 109–133. Foucault argues, "It's not a matter of emancipating truth from every system of power . . . but of detaching the power of truth from the forms of hegemony, social, economic, and cultural, within which it operates at the present time" (p. 133). The difference between the two underscores, I think, the essential difference between Bushnell's Romantic discourse and the discourses of modernism and postmodernism.

13. Bushnell, "Unconscious Influence," *The American Pulpit* 2 (1847): 233. Hereafter, *UI*. (For Bushnell's works throughout the text, I have indicated the original publication date and form of publication. My references are often to later editions and forms.) On Bushnell's retreat from politics, see Cross, *Horace Bushnell*, pp. 80 and 73–92. For a reading of this sermon that supports mine, see Smith, *Symbolism and Growth*, pp. 49–57. The ideas developed here are crucial to Bushnell's educational theory. See *Views of Christian Nurture* (Hartford, 1848) and the substantially revised and enlarged *Christian Nurture* (New York, 1861). See Smith, *Symbolism and Growth*, pp. 70–85, and Howe, "The Social Science of Horace Bushnell," pp. 311–317. My point is here to underscore the linguistic nature of Bushnell's social thought and to discover its ideological underpinnings.

14. Cheney, *Life and Letters*, p. 289. According to Cyrus A. Bartol, in preaching "Unconscious Influence," Bushnell "exemplifie[d] his own doctrine." Quoted in Cheney, *Life and Letters*, p. 188.

15. Ibid., p. 288.

16. According to G. P. Mohrmann, "The belief that tones, looks, and gestures were external signs of internal emotions was firmly established by the middle of the eighteenth century" and was one of the central principles of the elocutionary movement spearheaded by Thomas Sheridan and of Commonsense philosophy. See Mohrmann, "Introduction" to Thomas Sheridan, *A Discourse . . .*

on Elocution and the English Language (Los Angeles: Augustan Reprint Society, 1969), p. v. For Sheridan, "there are two kinds of language, necessary to all, who would wish to answer the end of public speaking. The one is, the language of ideas; by which the thoughts which pass in a man's mind are manifested to others; and this language is composed chiefly of words properly ranged, and divided into sentences. The other, is the language of emotions; by which the effects that those thoughts have upon the mind of the speaker, in exciting the passions, affections, and all manner of feelings, are not only made known, but communicated to others; and this language is composed of tones, looks and gestures." See Sheridan, *A Course of Lectures on Elocution* (London, 1762; reprint, New York: Benjamin Blom, 1968), pp. 132–133. Thomas Reid refers to a "*natural language of mankind*": "It appears evident from what hath been said on the subject of language, that there are natural signs, as well as artificial; and particularly, that the thoughts, purposes, and dispositions of the mind have their natural signs in the features of the face, the modulation of the voice, and the motion and attitude of the body: that without a natural knowledge of the connection between these signs, and the things signified by them, language could never have been established among men." See Reid, *An Inquiry into the Human Mind*, ed. Timothy Duggan (Chicago: University of Chicago Press, 1970), p. 65. See also pp. 54–58 and 65–68. Significantly, Bushnell's version opposes not the rational and the passionate or the natural and the artificial but the conscious and the unconscious, the voluntary and the involuntary, and emphasizes their disjunctions, not their connections.

17. On the "speech situation," see Erving Goffman, "The Neglected Situation," in *Language and Social Context: Selected Readings*, ed. Pier Paolo Giglioli (New York: Penguin Books, 1972), pp. 61–66. In *Unconscious Influence*, Bushnell deals only with speech and the speech situation and only tangentially with writing and literature, which, as I will show, he deals with more directly in other works.

18. Bushnell, *The Fathers of New England* (New York, 1850), p. 11. Hereafter, *FNE*.

19. Bushnell had earlier developed his theory of moral history in *A Discourse on the Moral Tendencies and Results of Human History* (New York, 1843), where he argues, "It is then a law . . . of humanity, in all its forms of life and progress, that the physical shall precede the moral." In it, too, he speaks of language in terms that adumbrate the "Preliminary Dissertation": "If we speak of language, this, as every scholar knows, is physical in every term. Words are only the names of external things and objects, as seen by the eye of a child, or of the unreflecting man. Next, the words, which are mere physical terms, pass into use as figures of thought—they become endued with intelligence and a moral power. Sublimed by the penetration of a moral nature, they are wrought up, at length, into the highest forms of literature. The physical world takes a second and higher existence in the empire of thought. Its objects beam out, transfigured with glory, and the body of matter becomes the body of letters. The story of Orpheus is now no more a fiction; for not only do the woods and rocks dance after this one singer, but all physical objects, in heaven and earth, having now found an intellectual as well as a material power, follow after the creative agency of thinking

souls, and pour themselves along, in troops of glory, on the pages of literature" (p. 4).

20. Bushnell, "Prosperity Our Duty," in *The Spirit in Man: Sermons and Selections* (New York: Scribners, 1903), p. 145. Hereafter, *SIM*.

21. Bushnell, "Work and Play," in *Work and Play; or, Literary Varieties* (New York, 1864), p. 1. Hereafter, *WP*.

22. I am concerned in this section only with elements of *God in Christ* that relate to my thesis. For other explications of the work, see above, n. 2.

23. Cheney, *Life and Letters*, p. 209.

24. For Bushnell's view of Locke, see *GC*, pp. 36–37.

25. Bushnell is here, of course, echoing Berkeley and Coleridge, as well as Emerson. See James C. McKusick, *Coleridge's Philosophy of Language* (New Haven: Yale University Press, 1986), pp. 18–32. For Bushnell's relation to Emerson, see Feidelson, *SAL*, and Gura, *WOW*.

26. On the linguistic aspects of the Unitarian-Trinitarian controversy, see Gura, *WOW*, pp. 15–71; and "The Transcendentalists and Language: The Unitarian Exegetical Background," *Studies in the American Renaissance* (1979): 1–16; and Crosby, *Horace Bushnell's Theory of Language*, pp. 179–228.

27. Cheney, *Life and Letters*, pp. 207–208. For the attacks on Bushnell's theory, see Crosby, *Horace Bushnell's Theory of Language*, pp. 229–286.

28. The target of this attack is, of course, Jonathan Edwards's *Freedom of the Will*. See Bushnell, *Nature and the Supernatural* (New York, 1890), pp. 42–58, for a more detailed version of this argument. On the issue of free will in nineteenth-century American philosophical discourse, see Jay Wharton Fay, *American Psychology before William James* (New Brunswick, N.J.: Rutgers University Press, 1939), pp. 50–169; and A. A. Roback, *History of American Psychology* (New York: Library Publishers, 1952), pp. 105–118.

29. See Cross, *Horace Bushnell*, pp. 136–137.

Chapter Six
Beyond Symbolism

1. Feidelson, *SAL*, pp. 10, 13, 10, 15. See also Feidelson's essay, "*The Scarlet Letter*," in *Hawthorne Centenary Essays*, ed. Roy Harvey Pearce (Columbus: Ohio State University Press, 1964), pp. 31–77.

2. Irwin, *AH*, pp. 245; Millicent Bell, "The Obliquity of Signs: *The Scarlet Letter*," *Massachusetts Review* 23 (1982): 9–26, reprint, in *Critical Essays on Hawthorne's The Scarlet Letter*, ed. David B. Kesterson (Boston: G. K. Hall, 1988), pp. 157–169. See also Viola Sachs, "The Gnosis of Hawthorne and Melville: An Interpretation of *The Scarlet Letter* and *Moby Dick*," *American Quarterly* 32 (1980): 123–143; Michael Ragusis, "Family Discourse and Fiction in *The Scarlet Letter*," *ELH* 49 (1982): 863–888; Louise K. Barnett, "Speech and Society in *The Scarlet Letter*," *ESQ* 29 (1983): 16–24; as well as Carton, *RAR*, pp. 191–227, and Michael Davitt Bell, *DAR*, pp. 173–181. Reed Sanderlin, "Hawthorne's *Scarlet Letter*: A Study of the Meaning of Meaning," *Southern Humanities Review* 9 (1975): 145–157; and Gura, *WOW*, pp. 154–156, all recall Feidelson while embodying some of the more recent negativity.

3. David Van Leer, "Hester's Labyrinth: Transcendental Rhetoric in Puritan Boston," in *New Essays on The Scarlet Letter*, ed. Michael Colacurcio (Cambridge: Cambridge University Press, 1985), p. 73; Jonathan Arac, "Reading the Letter," *Diacritics* 9 (1979): 43.

4. Nathaniel Hawthorne, *The Scarlet Letter*, in *The Centenary Edition of the Works of Nathaniel Hawthorne*, ed. Roy Harvey Pearce et al. (Columbus: Ohio State University Press, 1962–), 1:201. Hereafter, *CE*.

5. George Berkeley, *The Principles of Human Knowledge*, in *The Works of George Berkeley, Bishop of Cloyne*, ed. A. A. Luce and T. E. Jessop (London: Thomas Nelson and Sons, 1949), 2:40.

6. On Reid and natural language, see James C. McKusick, *Coleridge's Philosophy of Language* (New Haven: Yale University Press, 1986), pp. 10–12; and above, chap. 5, n. 16. Rousseau's remarks on the "cry of nature" are found in his *Discourse on the Origin of Inequality*, in Jean-Jacques Rousseau, *Basic Political Writings*, ed. and trans. Donald A. Cress (Indianapolis: Hackett Publishing Company, 1987), p. 49. Hereafter, *BPW*.

7. Emerson to Thomas Carlyle, 14 May 1834, in *The Correspondence of Thomas Carlyle and Ralph Waldo Emerson, 1834–1872*, 2 vols. (Boston: Houghton Mifflin, 1883), 1:17.

8. Nathaniel Hawthorne, *Tales and Sketches*, ed. Roy Harvey Pearce (New York: The Library of America, 1982), p. 331. Hereafter, *T&S*.

9. On the economic problems of antebellum authors, see William Charvat, *The Profession of Authorship in America, 1800–1870*, ed. Matthew J. Bruccoli (Columbus: Ohio State University Press, 1968), pp. 282–316.

10. See James A. Berlin, *Writing Instruction in Nineteenth-Century American Colleges* (Carbondale: Southern Illinois University Press, 1984), esp. chaps. 3 and 4.

11. Samuel P. Newman, *A Practical System of Rhetoric*, 10th ed. (New York, 1842), pp. 13, 17. Hereafter, *PSR*. The textbook was first published in Portland, Maine in 1827.

12. All historical readings of "The Minister's Black Veil" inevitably owe much to Michael Colacurcio, *The Province of Piety: Moral History in Hawthorne's Early Tales* (Cambridge: Harvard University Press, 1984), pp. 314–385. The term "surprising conversions" is, of course, from Jonathan Edwards's narrative of the 1735 revival at Northampton, the "Narrative of Surprising Conversions." See Clarence H. Faust and Thomas H. Johnson, eds., *Jonathan Edwards: Representative Selections* (New York: Hill and Wang, 1935; reprint, 1962), pp. 73–84. On preaching during the Awakening, see Harry S. Stout, *The New England Soul: Preaching and Religious Culture in Colonial New England* (New York: Oxford University Press, 1986), pp. 185–255.

13. Charles Chauncy, *Enthusiasm Described and Caution'd Against*, in *The Great Awakening, Documents Illustrating the Crisis and Its Consequences*, ed. Alan Heimert and Perry Miller (Indianapolis: Bobbs-Merrill, 1967), pp. 248–249, 229.

14. Jonathan Edwards, *Thoughts on the Revival*, in Heimert and Miller, *The Great Awakening*, pp. 278, 276. On the sermonics of the Great Awakening, see, for instance, Perry Miller, *Errand into the Wilderness* (New York: Harper and

Row, 1964), pp. 153–183; Stout, *The New England Soul*, pp. 185–211; and Donald Weber, *Rhetoric and Revolution in Revolutionary New England* (New York: Oxford University Press, 1988), esp. pp. 14–46.

15. Edwards, "Sinners in the Hands of an Angry God," in Faust and Johnson, *Jonathan Edwards*, p. 164.

16. *Love Letters of Nathaniel Hawthorne, 1839–1863*, 2 vols. (Chicago: The Society of Dofobs, 1907).

17. One example may be useful here. On 15 March 1840, Hawthorne playfully complains about the late arrival of one of Sophia's letters: "It were desirable that the new Salem postmaster be forthwith ejected, for taking upon himself to withhold the outpourings of thy heart in due season." On that same day, he had written to John O'Sullivan, "That Post-Office would have suited me. . . . When I next see you, I shall have some queer tales to tell about the faith and honor of politicians." See *CE*, 15:419, 420. See also his letter of 8 February 1840 to W. B. Pike (*CE*, 15:407).

18. I do not mean to suggest that Hawthorne was not naturally reticent. Rather, I want to show that he understood his diffidence in surprisingly linguistic terms, and that his "public" style issues from his understanding of how language works.

19. Jean-Jacques Rousseau, *La Nouvelle Héloïse*, trans. and abr. Judith H. McDowell (University Park: Pennsylvania State University Press, 1968), p. 200. We have no explicit record of what Hawthorne may have thought about Rousseau, but we do know that he read extensively in Rousseau's *Oeuvres* during the early years of his putative seclusion (1829–1832) and returned to them in the early summer of 1848, about a year before he was expelled from the Salem Custom-House and began writing *The Scarlet Letter*. See Marion L. Kesserling, *Hawthorne's Reading, 1828–1850: A Transcription and Identification of Titles Recorded in the Charge-Books of the Salem Athenaeum* (New York: The New York Public Library, 1949), p. 60. See also Julian Hawthorne, *Hawthorne Reading: An Essay* (Cleveland: The Rowfant Club, 1902; reprint, The Folcroft Press, 1969), pp. 82–83.

20. Rousseau, *La Nouvelle Héloïse*, p. 17. The entire "Dialogue" may be found in translation in Rousseau, *Eloisa: or a Series of Original Letters*, 4 vols. (London, 1803), 1:ix–xlii.

21. Rousseau, *Essay on the Origin of Languages*, in *On the Origin of Language*, ed. and trans. John H. Moran and Alexander Gode (New York: Frederick Ungar), pp. 21–22, 9.

22. [George Ripley], review of *The Scarlet Letter*, *New York Tribune Supplement*, 1 April 1850, in *Hawthorne: The Critical Heritage*, ed. J. Donald Crowley (London: Routledge & Kegan Paul), pp. 158–159; [Anne W. Abbott], review of *The Scarlet Letter*, *North American Review* 62 (1850), in Crowley, *Hawthorne*, p. 163.

23. For accounts of the Custom-House affair, see Stephen Nissenbaum, "The Firing of Nathaniel Hawthorne," *Essex Institute Historical Collections* 114 (1978): 57–86; William Charvat, "Introduction" to *The Scarlet Letter*, *CE*, 1:xv–xxviii; Hubert J. Hoeltje, "The Writing of *The Scarlet Letter*," *New England Quarterly* 27 (1954): 326–346; and Winfield S. Nevins, "Nathaniel Haw-

thorne's Removal from the Salem Custom House," *Essex Historical Institute Collections* 53 (1917): 97–132.

24. I have found both Jean Starobinski, *Jean-Jacques Rousseau: Transparency and Obstruction*, trans. Arthur Goldhammer (Chicago: University of Chicago Press, 1988), and Paul de Man, *Allegories of Reading: Figural Language in Rousseau, Nietzsche, Rilke, and Proust* (New Haven: Yale University Press, 1979) helpful in formulating the reading of Rousseau that follows.

25. In the *Essay on the Origin of Languages*, Rousseau complicates this linear notion of linguistic development. As his subject here is languages rather than language, he structures the work as a series of discriminations between modes of human communication: gestures and words, speech and writing, primitive and more developed languages, Northern and Southern languages, and (in music) melody and harmony. Whether the differences are determined historically, geographically, or politically, the *Essay* presents a rhetoric of alternatives that parallel the fundamental distinction of the *Discourse* but, had they been included in the *Discourse*, would have seriously weakened its force.

26. John Winthrop, *The History of New England from 1630–1649*, ed. James Savage (Boston, 1853), excerpted in *Puritan Political Ideas, 1588–1794*, ed. Edmund S. Morgan (Indianapolis: Bobbs-Merrill, 1965), pp. 138–140. On Winthrop's political philosophy, see Stanley Gray, "The Political Thought of John Winthrop," *New England Quarterly* 3 (1930): 681–705. See also Loren Baritz, *City on a Hill: A History of Ideas and Myths in America* (New York: John Wiley, 1964), pp. 3–45. Michael Colacurcio comments on the importance of Winthrop's political thought to the romance briefly in "Footsteps of Ann Hutchinson: The Context of *The Scarlet Letter*," *ELH* 39 (1972): 482n, and more fully in "'The Woman's Own Choice': Sex, Metaphor, and the Puritan 'Sources' of *The Scarlet Letter*," in Colacurcio, *New Essays on The Scarlet Letter*, pp. 101–135. It is important to remember that Winthrop's death plays a pivotal role at the center of Hawthorne's narrative, the night of Dimmesdale's vigil on the scaffold in the marketplace (*CE*, 1:147–158).

27. We should remember that the *Discourse on Inequality* can be construed to be, for the Genevan Rousseau, as much a critique of Calvin as it is of Hobbes.

28. Winthrop, "A Model of Christian Charity," in Morgan, *Puritan Political Ideas*, pp. 92, 85. See Rousseau's explanation of the "general will" in relation to the "body politic" (*BPW*, p. 114).

29. Winthrop, *History*, in Morgan, *Puritan Political Ideas*, p. 139.

30. My analysis of the double plot of *The Scarlet Letter* parallels in various ways, and adds a political dimension to, Richard Brodhead's reading of the romance in *Hawthorne, Melville, and the Novel* (Chicago: University of Chicago Press, 1976), pp. 43–68.

Index

Abbot, Anne W., 179
Adams, John, x, 18, 30–31, 111, 119, 120, 210n.9
Adams, John Quincy, 31
Addison, Joseph, 62
Advancement of Learning, The, 125
Aids to Reflection, 16, 138
Alcott, Bronson, 19
Allaback, Steven, 64
American Crisis, The, 45, 46
American Democrat, The, 28
American Dictionary of the English Language, 19, 213n.30
American Hieroglyphics, 7–8
American Instructor, The, 38
American Language, The, 20–21, 23, 25
American Primer, An, 19, 23, 32, 90–91, 92, 94, 103, 106–115, 221n.1, 223n.23
"American Politics," 138–141
American Renaissance, 3–4, 10–11, 13, 19, 27, 90–91, 198–200
American Scholar, The, 198
American Spelling Book, 19. See also *American Instructor, The; Blue-Back Speller; Grammatical Institute of the English Language, A*
"America's Mightiest Inheritance," 94, 96–97, 98–106, 114, 115
Ames, Fisher, 119
Anne (queen of England), 56
Arac, Jonathan, 162
Arcadia, 80, 83
Aristotle, 71
Articles of Confederation, 124
Arvin, Newton, 66
Ash, John, 104

Bacon, Francis, 125, 131
Bailey, Nathan, 104
Barlow, Joel, 18, 24, 39, 40
Baron, Dennis, 24–26, 29, 30, 50, 95
Barrell, John, 212n.21
Beard, Charles, 122
Beattie, James, 53

Belcher, Jonathan, 170
Bell, Michael Davitt, 11, 12–13, 14, 17, 30
Bell, Millicent, 162
Benjamin, Walter, 162
Bercovitch, Sacvan, 208
Berkeley, George, 165
Blair, Hugh, 53, 168
Blue-Back Speller, 35, 95. See also *American Instructor, The; American Spelling Book; Grammatical Institute of the English Language, A*
Brackenridge, Hugh Henry, 27, 52, 135
Bridge, Horatio, 166
Bristed, Charles Astor, x, 24
Brown, Charles Brockden, 12, 13, 135
Brown, Goold, 25
Bryant, William Cullen, 65
Buckminster, Joseph, 39, 40
Bunsen, Christian Charles Josias, 96, 105, 222–223n.18
Bushnell, Horace, x, xii, xiii, 6, 9, 12, 15, 16, 17, 18, 32, 137–161, 166, 178, 179, 191, 192, 198, 199, 200, 228nn.12 and 13, 229–230n.19
Butler, Pierce, 134

Cadmus, 24, 25
Calverton, V. F., 3
Campbell, George, 15, 168
Cardell, William, 24, 136
Carlyle, Thomas, 97
Carton, Evan, 8–9, 13, 17
Cassirer, Ernst, 6, 163
Champollion, Jean François, 7
Chase, Richard, 8, 11
Chauncy, Charles, 170–171
"Circular Letter from the Secretary of the American Academy of Belles Lettres," 24–25
Clinton, Sir Henry, 30
Cobbett, Thomas, 97
Coleridge, Samuel Taylor, xiii, 16, 18, 138, 154, 164, 199, 200
Columbian Alphabet, The, 24

Common Sense, 45, 46
Compendious Dictionary of the English Language, A, 213n.30, 215n.39
Condillac, Etienne Bonnot de, xi, xiii, 7, 49, 50–51, 53, 54–57, 60, 62, 69, 71, 110, 185, 186, 216n.42
Confessions, 93, 182
Constitution of the United States, The, 120, 123, 124, 130, 131–132, 134, 136, 160, 199
Cooper, James Fenimore, x, 8, 12, 18, 21, 23, 24, 27, 28, 29, 50
Copernicus, Nicholas, 59
Cornwallis, Charles, 30
Cotton, John, 195
"Custom-House, The," 178–184. See also *Scarlet Letter, The*

Dahl, Robert A., 122
Danforth, Samuel, 195
Dante Alighieri, 102
Declaration of Independence, The, 26, 121, 160
Defence of Poesy, The, 79–82
"Defence of Poetry," 32, 79–86, 87
De la littérature du Midi de l'Europe, 73
de Man, Paul, 162, 163
Democracy in America, 52
Derrida, Jacques, 163
Descartes, René, 5, 7
Development of American Romance, The, 11, 13
"Devil in Manuscript, The," 167–169, 177
DeWitt, John, 130
Dialogue, A, 46
Dickinson, Emily, 8, 9, 13
Dillard, J. L., 24, 27
Dilworth, Thomas, 38–44, 47–49
"Dilworth's Ghost," 38
Discourse on the Moral Tendencies and Results of History, A, 229–230n.19
Discourse on the Origins and Foundations of Inequality among Men, 185–187, 233nn.25 and 27
Discourse on Political Economy, 190
Dissertation on the Influence of Opinions on Language and of Language on Opinions, A, 58
Dissertations on the English Language, 32, 37, 49–63, 66, 97
Diversions of Purley, The, 61

Douglass, Frederick, ix
Druid, The, 52

Eagleton, Terry, xi
Edwards, Jonathan, 170–171
"Eighteenth Presidency! The," 112–114
Ekirch, Arthur A., 205n.4
Eliot, T. S., 3
Elizabeth I (queen of England), 53, 56
Emerson, Ralph Waldo, ix, xi, 3, 4, 5, 6, 7, 8, 10, 12, 15, 16, 17, 18–19, 27–28, 29, 36, 65, 90, 95, 103, 110–111, 113, 129, 137, 154, 166, 177, 198
Empson, William, 6
English Grammar Adapted to Different Classes of Learners, 25, 95, 96
English Language in America, The, 21–24, 25
Epstein, David, 122
Essay concerning Human Understanding, 126, 128
Essay on the Origin of Human Knowledge, An, 53, 56
Essay on the Origin of Languages, 175, 233n.25
Everett, Edward, 18, 21, 24
Ewing, James, 24

Fathers of New England, The, 145–147. See also "Founders Great in Their Unconsciousness, The"
Federalist, The, xii, 18, 32, 119–136, 138, 168, 199
Feidelson, Charles, xii, 4–7, 8, 9, 14, 15–16, 17, 29, 30, 66, 137, 162–163, 200
Fenning, David, 43
Fish, Stanley, xi
Forester's Letters, The, 46
Foucault, Michel, 228n.12
"Founders Great in Their Unconsciousness, The," 145. See also *Fathers of New England, The*
Franklin, Benjamin, x, 24, 57–58, 106, 134–135
Fuller, Margaret, ix, 177
Furtwangler, Albert, 122

Garrick, David, 59
George III (king of England), 45, 47, 56, 57
Glossology, 15

God in Christ, 16, 17, 32, 137, 138, 141, 153–158, 164. *See also* "Preliminary Dissertation on Language, as Related to Language and Spirit"
Good English, 25
Goodrich, Elizur, 39
Gould, Edward S., 25
Grammar in Familiar Lectures, 25
Grammar and Good Taste, 24
Grammatical Institute of the English Language, A, 35, 37, 38–49, 51, 53, 54, 58, 66, 97, 199. See also *American Instructor, The; American Spelling Book; Blue-Back Speller*
Grimm, Jacob, 96, 98, 99, 104
Gura, Philip, 15–17

Hamilton, Alexander, 32, 119, 120, 121, 124, 131, 132, 135
Hand-book of English Orthography, 96, 98, 99, 100, 101, 103, 104, 105, 223n.23
Harris, James, 61, 71–72, 97
Harrison, Matthew, 25
Hawthorne, Nathaniel, ix, xi, xii, xiii, 3, 4, 6, 8, 9, 12, 13, 16, 17, 18, 32, 64, 90, 145, 162–197, 198, 199, 200, 232nn.17, 18, and 19
Hawthorne, Sophia Peabody, 172–177, 232n.17
Hazard, Rowland Gibson, x, 228n.12
Hegel, Georg Wilhelm Friedrich, 9, 12
Herder, Johann Gottfried von, 7, 110
Hermes, 71–72
Historical Novel, The, 28
Hobbes, Thomas, 125, 155, 184, 185
Hooker, Thomas, 160
Horace, 22
Howard, Leon, 207n.24
Howells, William Dean, 64, 65
Humboldt, Wilhelm von, xiii, 5, 6, 96, 102, 110, 137, 164
Hume, David, 125
Hutcheson, Francis, 128–130, 155, 165
Hutchinson, Anne, 191

"Influence of National Character upon Language: and of Language upon National Character, The," 72
Institutes of English Grammar, 25
Irving, Washington, 12, 13, 52
Irwin, John, 7–8, 9, 17, 28, 162

Jacobs, Harriet, ix
Jakobson, Roman, xi
James, Henry, 8, 64–66, 88
Jay, John, 32, 120, 124, 135
Jefferson, Thomas, x, 18, 50, 94, 108, 119, 120, 121, 124, 160, 192, 210n.9
Johnson, Alexander Bryan, x, 137
Johnson, Samuel, 38, 58, 60, 61, 96, 104
Jones, Howard Mumford, 74
Jones, Sir William, 71, 94, 218n.19
Judd, Sylvester, 19

Kant, Immanuel, 5, 7, 9
Kavanagh, a Tale, 79, 86–88, 99
Kenrick, William, 104
Kirkham, Samuel, 25
Koch, Adrienne, 121–122, 123, 125, 130, 135
Kraitsir, Charles, 15
Krapp, George Philip, 20, 21–24, 25, 26, 27, 30

Laird, Charlton, 24, 207n.23
Langer, Suzanne K., 6
Leatherstocking tales, 28
Leaves of Grass, 19, 90, 91, 93, 94, 199, 221n.7. *See also* "Song of Myself"
Letters of Cato, 131
Life Illustrated, 96, 98, 104
Lincoln, Abraham, 159
Literary History of the United States, 121, 135
"Literary Spirit of our Country, The," 67, 69–70, 80
Literature Considered in Its Relation to Social Institutions, 214n.32
"Little Speech on Liberty," 189, 193
Locke, John, xiii, 5, 7, 18, 50, 61, 121, 125–128, 129, 130, 134, 135, 137, 144, 153, 154, 165, 168, 185, 192, 200
Longfellow, Henry Wadsworth, x, xii, 32, 37, 64–89, 90, 94, 99, 103, 115, 166, 180, 196, 198, 199, 218nn.18, 19, and 22, 220n.42
Love Letters of Nathaniel Hawthorne, 172–177, 178, 179
Lowell, James Russell, 19, 65
Lowth, Robert, 58, 60, 61, 97
Lukács, Georg, 28
Luther, Martin, 102

Madison, James, 18, 32, 119, 120, 121, 122, 124–136, 138, 139, 144, 160, 165, 168, 192, 198, 199
Marckwardt, Albert H., 24
Marsh, George P., 96
Marsh, James, 16, 18
Mather, Cotton, 6, 195
Matthews, Cornelius, 86
Matthiessen, F. O., ix, x, xii, 3–4, 5, 6, 7, 8, 9–11, 12, 13, 16, 17, 18–19, 27, 28, 29, 30, 36, 66, 88, 90–91, 92, 165, 198–200
Melville, Herman, ix, xi, 3, 4, 6, 8, 12, 13, 16, 17, 18, 64, 90, 198
Mencken, H. L., xii, 20–21, 23–24, 25, 26, 27, 30, 95, 208n.1
Michaelis, Johann David, 49, 53, 54, 58–60, 61, 62, 71, 72, 102, 216n.45
Miller, J. Hillis, 203n.3
Miller, Perry, 207–208n.26
"Minister's Black Veil, The," 169–172, 177
Modern Chivalry, 52, 135
Mohrmann, G. P., 228n.16
Montesquieu, Charles de Secondat, baron de, 44, 70, 214n.32
Moody, Joshua, 6
Morris, Gouverneur, 135
Müller, Max, 96, 105
Murray, Lindley, 25, 95, 96, 106, 107, 114

Nature, xi, 17
New Guide to the English Tongue, 38, 40–44, 48
Newman, Edwin, 25
Newman, Samuel P., 166, 168–169, 174
New York Journal, 131
New York Times, 93
Nietzsche, Friedrich Wilhelm, xi
North American Review, 72
Notions of the Americans, 23, 28, 50
Nouvelle Héloïse, La, 174, 190

Oegger, J.G.E., 18
"On the Education of Youth," 215n.38
On Germany, 214n.32
On Language, 25
On the Social Contract, 184, 187, 190
On the Study of Words, 15
Origen, 71
Origin and Growth of the Languages of

Southern Europe and of Their Literature, 72–79, 80, 86
O'Sullivan, John, 232n.17
"Our Native Writers," 66–70, 78, 79, 80, 81, 88
"Our Language and Literature," 94, 96–97, 98, 100, 103, 104, 107
Outlines of Comparative Philology, 96, 99, 102
Outlines of Universal History, Applied to Language and Religion, 96

Paine, Thomas, 38, 40, 44–49, 57, 213n.27
Paradigms Lost, 25
Parker, Theodore, 19
Parrington, V. L., 3, 5, 28
Paulding, James Kirk, 27
Peabody, Elizabeth, x
Peirce, Charles Sanders, xi
Perry, 104
Pickering, John, 24, 108–109, 110
Pickering, Timothy, 39
Pierce, Franklin, 181
Poe, Edgar Allan, xi, 6, 7, 8, 9, 12, 13, 17, 28, 64, 90
Poirier, Richard, 11–12, 30
Politics of American English, 1776–1850, The, 26–29
"Politics under the Law of God," 138–141
Pope, Alexander, 77
Port-Royal Logic, 125
Practical System of Rhetoric, A, 168
"Preliminary Dissertation on Language, as Related to Thought and Spirit," 137, 154, 155, 158. See also *God in Christ*
Priestley, Joseph, 53
Prospects of a National Institution to be Established in the United States, 24
Prosperity Our Duty, 147–150
Publius, 120–121, 122, 123, 124, 132, 134, 135, 153

Quadrion, Francesco, 71
Quest for Nationality, The, 35–37

Rambles among Words, 94, 104, 115, 223n.23
Randolph, Edmund, 134
Raynal, Abbé Guillaume de, 45
Read, Allen Walker, 27, 207n.22

Reed, Sampson, 18
Reid, Thomas, 129, 165, 229n.16
Reverses Needed, 159–161
Rhetoric of American Romance, The, 8
Richards, I. A., xi, 3, 4, 6, 163
Ripley, George, 179
Rise, Progress, and Present Situation of the English Language, 25
Rossiter, Clinton, 121
Rousseau, Jean-Jacques, xiii, 7, 44, 71, 93, 165, 174–176, 182, 184–190, 192, 195, 232n.19, 233n.25

Safire, William, 25
Salmagundi, 31, 52, 200
Scarlet Letter, The, 17, 32, 145, 162–166, 177, 178, 179, 180, 184–197. See also "Custom-House, The"
Schele de Vere, Maximilian, 96, 102
Schlegel, August Wilhelm von, xiii, 18, 71, 75, 88
Schlegel, Friedrich von, 71, 83, 96
Scott, Walter, 28, 68
Second Treatise of Government, The, 127. See also *Two Treatises on Government*
Shakespeare, William, 62, 68, 97, 102
Shelley, Percy Bysshe, 84
Sheridan, Thomas, 59, 104, 228–229n.16
Sidney, Sir Philip, 79–82, 83, 85, 220n.35
Simms, William Gilmore, 8
Simon, John, 25
Simpson, David, 26–29, 30, 31
Sinners in the Hands of an Angry God, 171
Sismondi, J.C.L. Simonde di, 71, 72–76, 77, 79, 88
"Slang in America," 19
Smart, Christopher, 104
"Song of Myself," 92, 93. See also *Leaves of Grass*
Spencer, Benjamin, 35–37, 40, 49
Spiller, Robert, 121
Spirit of Laws, The, 214n.32
Staël, Germaine de, 214n.32
Stewart, Dugald, 15
Stowe, Harriet Beecher, ix
Strictly Speaking, 25
Swift, Jonathan, 125
Swinton, William, 93, 94, 96
Symbolism in American Literature, 4–7

Tennent, Gilbert, 171
Tetard, John Peter, 44

Thoreau, Henry David, ix, xi, 3, 4, 6, 15, 16, 17, 18, 90
Thornton, William, x, 24, 25
Tocqueville, Alexis de, 10, 50–53, 54, 55, 57, 63, 69, 78, 94, 103, 108, 166, 179, 213–214n.32, 215n.34
Todorov, Tzvetan, x
Tompkins, Jane, 64
Tooke, John Horne, 49, 53, 54, 61–63, 71
Traubel, Horace, 90–91
Trench, Richard, 15
Trilling, Lionel, 8, 11
Two Treatises on Government, 128. See also *Second Treatise of Government*

"Unconscious Influence," 141–145, 147, 150, 153

Van Leer, David, 162
Vico, Giovanni Battista, xi

Wagenknecht, 64
Walden, 15
Walker, John, 104
Washington, George, 121
Webster, Noah, x, xii, 18, 19, 20–21, 22–23, 24, 26, 27, 29, 30, 32, 35–63, 66, 68, 69, 70, 71, 88, 90, 94, 95, 96, 97, 103, 104, 106, 107, 108–109, 111, 114, 115, 120, 136, 198, 199, 200, 210–211n.13, 213nn.27 and 30, 215nn.38, 39, and 40, 216nn.42 and 45, 223n.27
Whitefield, George, 171
Whiter, Walter, 15
Whitman, Walt, ix, xi, xii, 3, 4, 6, 7, 10, 17, 18, 19, 23, 24, 28, 30, 32, 36, 37, 65, 90–115, 179, 198, 199, 200, 221nn.5 and 7
Whittier, John Greenleaf, 65
Wieland, 135
Willard, Samuel, 6
Wills, Garry, 122
Winthrop, John, 6, 188–190, 191, 193, 194, 195, 233n.26
Wisdom of Words, The, 15, 17
Witherspoon, John, 24, 52, 108, 120, 128–130, 131, 155, 165
Worcester, Joseph, 18, 96, 104, 106
Wordsworth, William, 70, 85, 97
Work and Play, 150–153, 154, 179
World Elsewhere, A, 11